Senator Joseph McCarthy and the American Labor Movement

SENATOR JOSEPH McCARTHY
and the American Labor Movement

David M. Oshinsky

University of Missouri Press, 1976

Part of Chapter 8 appeared as "Wisconsin Labor and the
Campaign of 1952" in *Wisconsin Magazine of History* 56:2 (Winter
1972–1973):9–18. Part of Chapter 6 was included in "Labor's
Cold War: The CIO and the Communists" in *The Specter: Original
Essays on American Anti-Communism and the Origins of McCarthyism*
(New York: Franklin-Watts, 1974).

Library of Congress Cataloging in Publication Data

Oshinsky, David M   1944–
    Senator Joseph McCarthy and the American labor movement.

    Bibliography: p.
    Includes index.
    1. McCarthy, Joseph Raymond, 1908–1957. 2. Trade-
unions—United States—Political activity—History.
I. Title.
E748.M143083   322'.2'0924   75–23426
ISBN 0–8262–0188–1

For My Parents

Preface

Many of my friends and colleagues gave willingly of their time and expertise during the preparation of this manuscript. Gerd Korman and Vernon Jensen of Cornell University helped me to formulate and to begin researching the project. Leonard Levy of the Claremont Graduate School; John Roche of the Fletcher School of Diplomacy, Tufts University; Morton Keller and Marvin Meyers of Brandeis University; and David Thelen of the University of Missouri, all provided much valuable information and encouragement. Several colleagues at Rutgers University, including Rudolph Bell, Gerald Grob, and Larry Cohen, supplied scholarly assistance, as did James Medoff of Harvard University. I am most grateful to Shirley Meinkoth, who typed and retyped parts of the manuscript with patience and skill.

I wish also to acknowledge the Crown Foundation and the Rutgers University Research Council for providing ample grant money for research, travel, and typing expenses.

Finally, I would like to thank Katherine Olstein of Tufts University and Tyrone DaNucci for more reasons than I could possibly enumerate.

D.M.O.
New Brunswick, New Jersey
July, 1975

Contents

Chapter 1

The Road to Portage

I

The election of Joseph R. McCarthy to the United States Senate in 1946 was one of the most bewildering chapters in modern political history. A brash, unprincipled Democrat-turned-Republican, young Judge McCarthy won his party's senatorial primary by defeating not only a family legend but also the Republican progressivism that had become its legacy. Early political polls predicted a landslide victory for Robert M. LaFollette, Jr., and the feeling most prevalent in Wisconsin was that "not even a reincarnation of Abraham Lincoln could make any inroads against the powerful LaFollette name."[1] Yet, by narrowly defeating the incumbent, McCarthy overcame both name and tradition. Stunned by their own miscalculations, political pundits hunted for a scapegoat, and the LaFollette debacle was soon placed squarely at the feet of labor; organized labor had turned its back on an old friend.[2]

In his political postmortem of the Wisconsin primary, Morris Rubin, editor of *Progressive*, spoke for many embittered LaFollette supporters when he noted that "large segments of organized labor buried the knife in one of the best friends they ever had."[3] While state unionists were quick to disagree, a superficial analysis of the primary tended to substantiate Rubin's hypothesis. First, the senator had attained national recognition over the past twenty years as an avid union supporter. As a member of the Committee on Labor and Public Welfare, he distinguished himself by unmasking many of the brutal and unlawful techniques employed by management to obstruct the process of unionization in its establishments. It was LaFollette who pressed for congressional investigations into labor disturbances in the New Jersey textile factories and the Pennsylvania anthracite

1. Jack Anderson and Ronald May, *McCarthy: The Man, the Senator, the 'Ism'* (Boston: Beacon Press, 1952), p. 72.
2. See, William Evjue in the *Madison Capital-Times*, August 15, 1946; Lawrence Eklund in the *Milwaukee Journal*, August 15, 1946; James Reston in the *New York Times*, August 15, 1946.
3. Morris Rubin, "The First Column," *Progressive* 10 (August 26, 1946): 1.

coal fields, and it was his subcommittee that revealed the actual scope of lawlessness authorized by many of the nation's blue-ribbon industries to deal with labor problems. During World War II, the senator lobbied consistently for the extension of the collective bargaining principle throughout the defense industries, for greater labor participation in decisions relating to national defense, and for the defeat of all legislative proposals designed to weaken labor's civil rights. And, at war's end, LaFollette composed a major article for *Progressive* in which he condemned the Smith-Connally Act "for putting unions in a strait jacket," while chastizing the large corporations, including General Motors, for using their substantial tax rebates "to finance a last-ditch fight against labor."[4]

Second, a look at the voting statistics seemed to indicate that labor did "bury the knife" in LaFollette. In the 1940 general election, he carried the lakeshore counties of Milwaukee, Kenosha, and Racine, all labor strongholds, by overwhelming margins. In the 1946 primary, however, he came into these counties with victory in hand only to be defeated by the very votes that once perpetuated his political career.[5]

The theory that organized labor deserted LaFollette is based primarily on two factors: Communist domination of the Wisconsin State Industrial Union Council (CIO) and the increasing interest of the state's non-Communist labor leaders in the Democratic party. According to the standard analysis of the primary, "the Communists and Democrats were out for LaFollette's hide; and the blast explosion of their negativism blew Joe McCarthy right into the United States Senate."[6] In order to assess the validity of this theory, these two factors must be carefully considered. The following three chapters describe the growth of both the Communist and Democratic organizations in Wisconsin, with particular emphasis added to their distinctive relationships with the state labor movement. Other considerations, including the demise and final destruction of the Progressive party in Wisconsin and the actual amounts of time, money, and effort ex-

---

4. For a history of the LaFollette Subcommittee, see, Jerold Auerbach, *Labor and Liberty: The LaFollette Subcommittee and the New Deal* (Indianapolis: Bobbs-Merrill, 1966). LaFollette's views on labor's participation in the defense buildup are expressed in a pamphlet published by the Workers' Defense League, *Labor, Defense and Democracy*, 1941. The senator's statement on postwar labor problems is found in *Progressive* 10 (February 11, 1946): 1.

5. Election statistics are found in Chapter 3, pp. 43–48.

6. Anderson and May, *McCarthy*, p. 85.

pended by the major political candidates are also analyzed. Only a careful study of all of these factors and the interaction of each with the other could possibly lead to a thoughtful understanding of the events that made the 1946 primary so controversial and so tragic.

II

Like many of its midwestern neighbors, Wisconsin grew to political maturity as a one-party state. While experiencing a moderate share of anti-Monopolist, Greenback, and Populist unrest in agrarian areas and an occasional upsurge of Democratic and Socialist sentiment along the industrial lakeshore, it remained firmly rooted to the Republican tradition. However, the absence of an effective opposition party often presented GOP leaders with more problems than it solved. They quickly discovered that such a conglomeration of vocations, religions, moral persuasions, and ethnic backgrounds under one political umbrella could hardly avoid the pitfalls of bitter factional strife.[7]

For much of the twentieth century, the conflict within state Republican ranks centered around two diametrically opposed groups: Progressives and conservatives (or Stalwarts). Despite the fact that multiple candidacies and plurality victories often marked local GOP primary elections, the ideological alternatives resulting from this bifactionalism were clearly defined and understood.[8] Indeed, the battle for organizational supremacy between the Progressive and Stalwart forces was so fiercely contested that the primary campaigns usually outdrew the general elections. "Wisconsin voters concentrated on the Republican primary," wrote one analyst, "in the same manner, if not in the same degree, as have Southern voters in the Democratic primary."[9]

Led by the ubiquitous LaFollette family, Progressives attracted a diverse political following. On the one side were urban immigrants, university professors, poor farmers, and reform-minded liberals who supported constructive programs to alleviate industrial abuses; on

7. Stuart Rice, *Farmers and Workers in American Politics* (New York: Columbia University Press, 1924), pp. 156–59. Fred Haynes, *Third Party Movements Since the Civil War* (Iowa City: State Historical Society of Iowa Press, 1916), pp. 55–60.

8. Leon Epstein, *Politics in Wisconsin* (Madison: University of Wisconsin Press, 1958), pp. 39–41.

9. Ibid., p. 38.

the other were many conservative German–Americans who remembered "Battling Bob" LaFollette's intense opposition to American involvement in World War I.[10] From 1901 until 1946, at least one member of this political dynasty sat in the Wisconsin executive mansion or in the United States Senate. As dedicated and innovative public servants, they waged a well-publicized, politically rewarding struggle against the privileged interests by implementing a series of reforms designed to lessen corporate domination and corruption of popular institutions.[11] "Few families in American public life," noted one biographer, "have rivaled the LaFollettes of Wisconsin in intellectual brilliance, uncompromising integrity and in success at the voting booth. And few families have experienced so much travail."[12]

When the Great Depression came to Wisconsin in 1929, Progressives captured the statehouse by promising swift governmental relief. With true family spirit, Governor Philip LaFollette introduced a recovery program that included the nation's first unemployment compensation law, a state-financed public works project, and a steeply graduated personal income tax. Among the other reforms the governor could not coax through the legislature were those advocating public ownership of natural resources, severe restrictions on the centralized control of credit and banking, and the development of a strong farmers' cooperative movement.[13]

This alleged socialist trend so enraged the conservative opposition that it initiated a massive propaganda campaign among state GOP voters to restore "Americanism in Government." The Stalwarts contended that the statehouse and the University of Wisconsin were infested with Communists, Socialists, American Civil Liberties Union members, and Jews who, like parasites, were "sucking at the blood of industries they did not create."[14] Their theme never varied: "Throw

10. Michael Rogin, *The Intellectuals and McCarthy* (Cambridge: M.I.T. Press, 1967), pp. 59–103. Karl Meyer, "The Politics of Loyalty, from LaFollette to McCarthy in Wisconsin, 1918–1952," Ph.D. dissertation, Princeton University, 1956, pp. 1–24.

11. Edward Doan, *The LaFollettes and the Wisconsin Idea* (New York: Rinehart, 1947), pp. 36–176. Eric Goldman, *Rendezvous With Destiny* (New York: Knopf, 1952), pp. 130–32. Meyer "The Politics of Loyalty," pp. 1–24.

12. Donald Young, ed., *Adventure in Politics: The Memoirs of Philip LaFollette* (New York: Holt, Rinehart and Winston, 1970), p. vii.

13. Meyer, "The Politics of Loyalty," pp. 74–127. *The Progressive* 3 (January 23, 1932) : 1.

14. John Chapple, quoted in Meyer, "The Politics of Loyalty," p. 82. Two pamphlets preserved at the Wisconsin State Historical Society are also of special interest: *The Socialist Trend in Wisconsin*, 1932, and *LaFollette Socialism*, n.d.

the Bolsheviks Out of Office." In the 1932 primary, the Republican electorate—with German–Americans responding once more to appeals for economic and ideological conservatism—did just that, as Stalwart candidates defeated their Progressive opponents for every major office on the GOP ballot.[15]

Before the Stalwarts could savor their impressive victory, however, they were overwhelmed in the November election by a Democratic organization whose political impotence was taken for granted. This latter party, while traditionally devoid of any constructive program for economic or social reform, had aligned itself with Franklin Roosevelt's candidacy to attract Wisconsin's financially distressed population as well as its demoralized Progressive voting bloc. The strategy worked well. With Roosevelt capturing 67 per cent of the state's popular vote (as opposed to his national total of only 59 per cent), the Democrats found themselves in control of the legislature, the governor's office, and a seat in the United States Senate. It seemed as if two-party politics had finally arrived in Wisconsin.[16]

The LaFollette brothers perceived at once the dangers of remaining Republicans during this period. Not only were they now the leaders of a minority faction within the minority party, but they realized that the recent Democratic landslide had been fashioned by voters who had previously supported Progressive Republican candidates. As Philip LaFollette recalled, "the resurgence of the Democratic party in the 1932 primary was a controlling factor in the defeat of most of our Progressive candidates. The primary had once again proved the bitter lesson that when the Progressive vote, which was both Democratic and Republican, was divided, the Progressives went down to defeat."[17]

With their personal success the paramount consideration, the LaFollettes took their large Progressive following and bolted the party; after all, one observer wrote, "it was not the place for a family accustomed to winning office."[18] In forming the Progressive party of Wisconsin, the brothers ensured their political futures by initiating a strong working alliance with the national Democratic Administration. It was the LaFollettes, not the Wisconsin Democrats, who supported New Deal domestic programs, endorsed Roosevelt's political campaigns, and distributed Democratic patronage throughout the

15. Meyer, "The Politics of Loyalty," pp. 74–127.
16. Epstein, *Politics in Wisconsin*, pp. 39–50.
17. Young, *Adventure in Politics*, p. 207.
18. Epstein, *Politics in Wisconsin*, p. 41. For Philip LaFollette's admissions of political expediency, see, Young, *Adventure in Politics*, pp. 207–8.

state. In short, "Wisconsin Progressives were the state's true New Dealers . . . providing the . . . voter with a real political alternative to the Republican party."[19]

Furthermore, with Progressives in a position to compete successfully for Wisconsin's pro-Roosevelt vote, they were able to enlarge their former base of support to include the state's growing legion of trade union members who might normally have filtered into the Democratic column. By 1936, the blue-collar communities of Milwaukee, Racine, and Kenosha were solidly in the Progressive camp.[20] Relegated once again to an unwanted minor-party status, state Democrats returned quickly to their familiar conservative ways.[21]

Although most Progressives were reasonably satisfied with President Roosevelt's Administration, the severe economic recession of 1937 presented Philip LaFollette with a chance to forward his national political ambitions. The aggressive young governor claimed that the economic downswing was characteristic of both the New Deal's inability to solve critical domestic problems and its callous disregard for the poor and unemployed.[22] His own personal remedy was announced on April 28, 1938, when, flanked by steel-helmeted national guardsmen and a red, white, and blue cross and circle (resembling, some thought, a circumcised swastika), he launched the National Progressive Party of America. "Make no mistake, this is not a third party," LaFollette told a crowd of 3,500 supporters in Madison. "As certain as the sun rises, we are launching the party of our time."

Despite the fervent emotionalism of most delegates, this new organization never had a chance for success. In the first place, its heavy reliance upon banners, flags, and massed guardsmen reminded too

19. Richard Haney, "A History of the Democratic Party in Wisconsin Since World War II," Ph.D. dissertation, University of Wisconsin, 1970, p. 13.
20. Rogin, *The Intellectuals and McCarthy*, pp. 72–80.
21. The LaFollettes, of course, also had the option of taking their Progressive following into the state Democratic party. President Roosevelt actually desired this arrangement, but neither the LaFollettes nor the state Democrats thought much of the idea. Wrote Epstein: "Old Democrats were now office holders and they coupled a conservative antipathy for Progressivism to an understandable desire to keep the LaFollettes from taking over the jobs which the Democrats had so recently won. And the LaFollettes knew that the Democratic label, whatever its value in the early 1930's, was traditionally disrespectable in Wisconsin and might well be so again" (Epstein, *Politics in Wisconsin*, p. 41). Ironically, as Rogin indicates, the Progressive party of the 1930s was the precursor of the modern Wisconsin Democratic party. Rogin, *The Intellectuals and McCarthy*, p. 75.
22. Young, *Adventure in Politics*, p. 347.

many Americans of the fascist mentality then sweeping the world.[23] More significantly, in contrast to his earlier political and administrative ingenuity, LaFollette relied on pompous rhetoric that was noticeably devoid of any program to alleviate the very social ills he described. "The National Progressives had no real issue—monopoly, tariff, free silver, big business, railroads, none of the great rallying points for the discontented," wrote Russel Nye. "Nor did they have a leader of the stature of the elder LaFollette or Theodore Roosevelt, who was great enough to override issues."[24] Disaster struck later in the year when, after abortive attempts to organize party chapters in Iowa and California, Philip LaFollette was easily defeated in his bid for reelection as governor of Wisconsin.

Senator Robert LaFollette, Jr., had been wary of his brother's third-party movement from the beginning. On a practical level, he knew it would divide state Progressives into two warring camps; on a personal one, he feared the loss of President Roosevelt's valuable political endorsement. However, while scrupulously avoiding any direct contact with the Madison convention, the senator still endorsed the new party for reasons of personal loyalty. As one prominent Progressive recalled, "Bob always followed Phil."[25]

After the movement failed, the senator attempted to regroup his forces and lead them back into the New Deal coalition. But, as before, this tenuous alignment proved to be of short duration. When President Roosevelt took a more active role in foreign affairs and national defense during the late 1930s, he seriously offended LaFollette's isolationist mentality. The senator was forced to repudiate the Administration, thereby losing both his cherished endorsement and the support of many Wisconsin voters who agreed with the President's war policy.[26] When world peace was finally restored the Progressive

23. Ibid., pp. 252–55. William Leuchtenburg, *Franklin D. Roosevelt and the New Deal, 1932–1940* (New York: Harper and Row, 1963), pp. 283–84.

24. Russel Nye, *Midwestern Progressive Politics, 1870–1958* (East Lansing: Michigan State University Press, 1959), p. 341.

25. Thomas Amlie to Howard McMurray, October 10, 1947, Thomas Amlie Papers, Wisconsin State Historical Society.

26. Samuel Lubell, *The Future of American Politics* (New York: Harper, 1952), pp. 144–45. Rogin, *The Intellectuals and McCarthy*, p. 79. Because of "Old Bob" LaFollette's opposition to American involvement in World War I, he had picked up the support of Wisconsin's conservative German–American constituency. However, Progressives steadily lost this support over the next fifteen years because of their reform-minded domestic programs. In 1934, for example, the German–Americans remained Stalwarts rather than switch to the new state Progressive party. Yet, by 1940, when the U.S. was on the verge of entering another European war, Wisconsin's German–Americans realigned

party was in shambles, its once-powerful creator fighting for his political life. In an effort to decide the future of his organization, LaFollette called upon Progressives to select delegates to a statewide convention at Portage. The response was less than enthusiastic. "The most puzzling thing about Progressives, wherever they may be headed," wrote political columnist Fred Sheasby, "is their striking indifference about organizing their forces. . . . From any point of view they might well be organizing to stick to their own wobbly party or to switch to some other party."[27]

*   *   *

The alleged indifference of many Wisconsin Progressives was in marked contrast to the lively interest displayed by the state's Republican and Democratic leaders. These pragmatic individuals realized that with the end of progressivism as an effective third-party force, LaFollette had no alternative but to choose one of their organizations to perpetuate his political career. With this thought in mind, they did everything possible to inform the senator of the unique reception awaiting him within their respective ranks. Indeed, while Democrats encouraged LaFollette to join them in the formation of a new liberal coalition, their Republican counterparts were badly divided on the issue. The Stalwart majority viewed his possible re-entry with utter contempt; the less powerful moderate faction was willing to accept him in order to restore a more equitable balance to the highly conservative Republican organization.[28]

The Republican reaction was certainly not unexpected. When Senator LaFollette departed from the state GOP in 1934 he left it in the hands of his Stalwart adversaries; in his twelve-year absence, the party had become the focal point of anti-New Deal sentiment in Wisconsin. The most influential factor in the Republican reconstruc-

---

themselves with the Progressives for reasons relating solely to foreign policy. On the other hand, much of the state's urban blue-collar constituency, which had turned to the Progressive party in increasing numbers during the 1930s, began to desert the party in 1940 for its isolationist outlook. In sum, the Progressives had two different constituencies—one that was attracted by its isolationism but disliked its domestic liberalism, and one that supported its domestic liberalism but was alienated by its isolationism.

27. *Milwaukee Journal*, February 24, 1946.

28. Roger Johnson, *Robert M. LaFollette, Jr. and the Decline of the Progressive Party in Wisconsin* (Madison: Wisconsin State Historical Society Press, 1964), p. 124.

tion was the formation of a Voluntary Republican Committee, which was composed primarily of wealthy state industrialists. Aside from its great financial resources, the VRC's voluntary status gave it a decided advantage over the regular Republican and Democratic organizations. Its campaign expenditures were not subject to the Wisconsin Corrupt Practices Act, and it could endorse candidates in the local primary elections while the regular organizations had to follow a policy of strict neutrality. By 1946, the VRC controlled most of the finances and patronage within the state GOP.[29]

Even when Senator LaFollette and his supporters were safely domiciled in their own organization, Stalwart leaders remained suspicious of a possible Progressive attempt to reenter their ranks. Their worst fears were realized in 1944 when moderate Republican Governor Walter E. Goodland, sensing the apparent weakness and confusion in Progressive circles, invited the senator to return to the GOP. "They used to be Republicans," he claimed, "and that's where they belong today."[30] The governor's cordial invitation was bitterly criticized by most prominent Stalwart leaders, including VRC Chairman Thomas Coleman.

In an effort to prevent such a maneuver, the Stalwarts rammed a bill through the Wisconsin legislature making it impossible for Progressives to run candidates in the 1946 elections on any ticket but their own. However, this well-publicized "fence-me-in" proposal was vetoed by Goodland, who feared Coleman's dogmatic conservatism far more than LaFollette's alleged opportunism. The Stalwarts were particularly embittered by the governor's action, since he had promised repeatedly to let the bill become law. By late 1945, the conservative-moderate debate over LaFollette's candidacy had reopened the GOP's long-standing ideological feud.[31]

The moderate Republican forces, although a distinct minority, used Goodland's veto as evidence of LaFollette's great grass-roots support among state GOP voters. The Milwaukee Third Ward Republican Club endorsed a resolution "welcoming the Progressive party back into the Republican ranks," while Walter Melchoir, secretary of the Outagamie County Republican party, claimed that the Coleman-led VRC was formed "merely to keep the Republican party out of the control of the voters." His organization supported a La-Follette–Goodland coalition to unseat Coleman.[32] The moderates

29. Ibid., p. 127.
30. Doan, *The LaFollettes and the Wisconsin Idea*, p. 190.
31. John Steinke, "The Rise of McCarthyism," M.A. thesis, University of Wisconsin, 1960, pp. 29–45.
32. *Madison Capital-Times*, November 30, 1945; December 14, 1945.

also received the overwhelming endorsements of national Republican leaders—from Wayne Morse to Robert Taft—who realized the potential value of LaFollette's support in upcoming elections. Taft, in fact, circulated a letter among state Republicans endorsing LaFollette for the GOP senatorial nomination.

This "moderate" revolt, coupled with the defeat of the election proposal, forced Thomas Coleman to prepare his forces for a possible Progressive onslaught. The major task before him was to convince fellow Republicans of the importance of uniting behind a single candidate—no mean task in an organization filled with ambitious politicians. Coleman was adamant on this point, however, for he feared that "a split among Republicans in the primary may put candidates from another party into ours."[33] One journalist put it more succinctly: "If LaFollette should run in the Republican primary and the Republicans produced one strong candidate against him, LaFollette would be in hot water, but he would look more like a winner if opposed by more than one candidate."[34] After enjoying twelve years of relative tranquility, Coleman was taking no chances.

The VRC heeded the warning of its chairman and voted overwhelmingly to endorse a single slate of candidates. Moreover, in an effort to discourage Progressives from entering the Republican primary, the committee resolved to support only those individuals "honestly in favor of the Republican platform and its political principles . . . believing that honesty of political principles is more important than the success or defeat of candidates."[35] This resolution was not meant to be an idle gesture; several Republican county chairmen actually appointed committees to determine which candidates were "loyal Republicans" and which were "Progressive turned Republican."[36] In sum, the Stalwarts had clearly warned LaFollette that an attempt by Progressives to enter the GOP primary would not go unchallenged.

* * *

Like the Republicans, the state Democratic party underwent a major political transformation before World War II. When, in the late 1930s, the Progressive coalition came apart under the combined

33. Thomas Coleman, *Janesville* (Wis.) *Daily Gazette*, December 12, 1945.
34. Fred Sheasby, *Milwaukee Journal*, February 10, 1946.
35. *Madison Capital-Times*, January 5, 1946.
36. Ibid., April 11, 1946.

strain of Philip LaFollette's abortive national third-party movement and President Roosevelt's increased international involvement, many urban liberals, labor leaders, and rank-and-file union members began joining the Democratic organization in large numbers. Their choice was made almost by default; the Progressive party remained isolationist, the Socialist party was weak and ineffective, and the Republican party was dominated by conservatives. As the *Kenosha Labor* noted: "There is hope in the Democratic party because of the great many liberals joining its ranks. What the other parties have to offer hardly requires discussion in a labor paper."[37]

Most of the electoral support for the revamped Democratic party was centered in the lakeshore counties of Kenosha, Racine, and Milwaukee. Indeed, this heavily industrialized, predominantly blue-collar area was virtually a state within a state. Unlike the rest of Wisconsin, where the pattern of "decentralized urbanization," with city populations ranging from 10,000 to 50,000, was the rule, the combined population of these three metropolitan districts totaled almost one million. The labor force here, comprising approximately 60 per cent of the state's total union membership, differed substantially from its urban counterpart in the rest of Wisconsin.[38] It was far more industrial in nature, working primarily in massive factory complexes like Allis-Chalmers, J. I. Case, American Motors, and the Milwaukee breweries. It also contained a higher percentage of foreign-born and first-generation Americans, the great bulk of whom were Catholics of German, Polish, and East European extraction.[39] These factors indigenous to the lakeshore counties proved to be highly significant—a heavy concentration of industry facilitating the process of effective political action by union leaders, and the unique

37. *Kenosha Labor,* March 8, 1946.
38. For figures on union membership, see, Douglas Knudson, "The Extent of Unionism in Wisconsin," M.A. thesis, University of Wisconsin, 1964.
39. For the number of workers employed in different categories in Milwaukee, Racine, Kenosha, and the rest of Wisconsin, see, U.S., Bureau of the Census, *Seventeenth Census of the United States: 1950. Characteristics of the Population,* Part 49, Wisconsin, pp. 49–63. In Milwaukee the industries employing the greatest number of workers were motor vehicles, food products, primary and fabricated metals, and the construction industry. In Racine, heavy machinery, primary and fabricated metals, and motor vehicles headed the list. In Kenosha, the dominant industries were motor vehicles, furniture and lumber products, and primary metals. As noted in the text, these lakeshore counties had large Catholic populations, especially in the working-class districts. See, U.S., Department of Commerce, *Religious Bodies* (1936): 555, 584, 646, 846; National Council of the Churches of Christ in the U.S.A., *Churches and Church Membership in the United States,* Series C, 18, Wisconsin. For further ethnic data relating to Milwaukee see Chapter 8, pp. 140.

ethnic and vocational composition of the labor force increasing its affinity for a national Democratic Administration that expressed keen interest in both the growth of industrial unionism and the rise of minority group aspirations.

Table 1. Percentage of Employed Males in Leading Occupations

Occupation	Statewide	Milwaukee County	Kenosha County	Racine County
Professional, technical	6.3	9.1	4.9	6.6
Farmers, etc.	21.2	.5	6.2	6.6
Proprietors	9.2	10.6	8.7	10.0
Clerical	5.4	8.5	5.8	6.5
Sales	5.5	7.0	4.5	5.4
Service workers	4.8	5.7	4.9	5.1
Craftsmen	18.1	24.3	22.2	24.6
Operatives	20.9	25.7	35.4	26.7
Laborers	6.8	7.2	6.2	7.2
Unreported	1.8	1.4	1.2	1.3
	100.0	100.0	100.0	100.0

SOURCE: U.S., Bureau of the Census, *Census of the Population: 1950. Characteristics of the Population*, Vol. 2, pt. 49, Wisconsin, p. 61.

In spite of the new strength enjoyed by the Democratic party among Wisconsin's urban, working-class voters, most unionists continued to support Senator LaFollette's candidacy on the Progressive ticket. It was the labor vote in 1940, cast overwhelmingly for Roosevelt and LaFollette, that kept the senator in office.[40] Throughout the war, however, as the Progressive party continued its painful political demise, Wisconsin labor leaders tried many times to convince LaFollette to take his supporters into the Democratic ranks. By 1946,

40. Senator LaFollette had long been a popular figure to Wisconsin workers. In 1934, the senator swept every labor ward in Milwaukee, where brother Phil and the rest of the Progressive ticket had been overwhelmed by the Democratic candidates. LaFollette also won the labor vote in the industrial suburbs of Cudahy and South Milwaukee as well as in Racine, Kenosha, and Madison. This situation was repeated in 1940, leading one to surmise that the senator's impressive totals in these labor areas were related more to his personal popularity and political record than to his party affiliation.

the gentle art of persuasion was abandoned in favor of more threatening tactics. The senator was warned publicly that if he attempted either to keep his third-party movement alive or to reaffiliate with the Republicans he would risk the loss of future labor support.

The unions also used their political influence in the lakeshore counties to select delegates to the Portage convention who were partial to alignment with the Democratic party. In Kenosha, the local AFL and non-Communist CIO organizations worked together to secure a clean sweep for the Democrats. Unionists in Racine obtained similar results. "All twelve delegates selected to attend the Portage Convention, March 12," wrote the *Racine Labor*, "are members of the Racine Political Action Committee, an independent local organization composed of AFL-CIO unionists and unattached liberals."[41] In fact, this organization was far from independent; one of its officials admitted in private correspondence that "the PAC here has worked very closely with the Democratic party in Racine and has been able to receive funds from that source."[42] The strength of this labor-Democrat alliance along the lakeshore was displayed by the fact that Racine Mayor Francis E. Wendt, a popular Progressive who favored reaffiliation with the Republican party, was defeated as a delegate.

State Democratic leaders also encouraged LaFollette to join their ranks. As practical politicians, they realized that all hope for a unified liberal party in Wisconsin would be shattered if the senator decided in favor of the Republicans. Therefore, Robert Tehan, Democratic state chairman, offered a resolution "welcoming into the Democratic ranks . . . all citizens who subscribe with us to liberal, forward-looking principles, and particularly former members of the Progressive party," while former U.S. Congressman Howard J. McMurray personally guaranteed LaFollette that he would encounter no opposition in the Democratic senatorial primary.[43] Local Democratic committees also extended open invitations to Progressives to join them "in supporting liberal candidates for every office from U.S. Senator to Coroner."[44] On the national level, Democratic pressure was equally intense. Robert Hannegan, national party chairman, spoke privately with LaFollette in an effort to persuade him to accept the senatorial nomination. Henry Wallace, a very popular figure

41. *Racine Labor*, March 8, 1946.
42. Harold Thompson to Albert Schumacher, September 20, 1946, Papers of the United Automobile Workers, Local 95, Janesville, Wis., Wisconsin State Historical Society.
43. *Madison Capital-Times*, February 12, 1946. Steinke, "The Rise of McCarthyism," p. 31.
44. *Madison Capital-Times*, November 11, 1945.

within Progressive circles, issued a public statement calling upon the senator "to come to the party of Roosevelt rather than the party of Hoover."[45]

III

Even after considering the growing strength of the Democratic party in urban Wisconsin, most Progressives still favored the Republican organization. Although wary of Stalwart control, they knew that the Grand Old Party offered them then exactly what it could not in 1934, the greater chance for victory. While an impatient nation watched President Truman attempt to solve the staggering problems engendered by postwar reconversion, 1946 seemed to all observers a Republican year, especially in Wisconsin where the Democratic party had not yet reached maturity. "I, for one, won't pretend that the desire of Progressives to rejoin the Republican party is anything but opportunistic," wrote LaFollette supporter Aldric Revell in the *Madison Capital-Times*. "Progressives know that the GOP is the only ticket on which they can get elected. . . . LaFollette can't afford to suffer from ideological squeamishness now."[46]

After six hours of open and bitter debate at Portage, the convention called upon Bob LaFollette to make his position known. The senator began by demeaning both the national and state Democratic organizations. Truman's Fair Deal Administration, he noted, was "stalled on dead center," unable to act with purpose or to deal effectively with urgent national problems; the state party, although attracting some "able, sincere liberals" to its ranks in recent years, was still dominated by machine-oriented reactionaries.[47] Furthermore, the state organization had a disturbing history of losing elections. "Only once in fifty years have the Democrats succeeded to power here," LaFollette said, "and a party which can succeed only once in half a century doesn't offer much opportunity to translate progressive principles into law."

The only alternative, then, was the Republican party. LaFollette claimed to have no illusions about the reactionary elements within that organization, both on the state and national level, but pledged to continue his battle for progressivism from within the GOP. Wisconsin, he added, was a Republican state and one that could easily

45. Ibid., March 14, 1946.
46. Ibid., February 28, 1946.
47. The full text of Senator LaFollette's Portage address is found in ibid., March 18, 1946.

reacquire its reputation for good government with Progressives in control of the majority party. "I am convinced," the senator concluded, "that the Republican party offers us the best opportunity for the advancement of progressive principles."

The convention overwhelmingly endorsed LaFollette's views; 284 delegates voted to return to the Republican party, 77 sought to retain the third party, and only 51 Progressives cast ballots in favor of the Democrats. Even so, the split was far more pronounced than the final tally indicated. Every one of the four labor leaders and three returning war veterans who spoke at Portage favored the Democratic party. Furthermore, many influential Progressives, including *Capital-Times* Editor William Evjue and former U.S. Congressman Thomas Amlie, were conspicuously absent. They, and others like them, refused to acquiesce in a decision that was "too much LaFollette and too little Progressive." Although Evjue finally gave the senator his public endorsement, Amlie did not. "When Bob LaFollette asserts that the Republican party can be liberalized, he is making a claim that is at complete variance with any reasonable interpretation of the facts," the ex-legislator asserted. "Progressives in Wisconsin have no valid choice but to back some good liberals who will make the race for the senate on the Democratic ticket."[48] The battle had begun.

48. Ibid., April 25, 1946. Wrote Evjue in the lead *Capital-Times* editorial of March 18, 1946: "The action at Portage yesterday was decided by the feeling that . . . LaFollette couldn't be re-elected . . . on the Progressive ticket. Here again, a personal consideration, affecting one of the LaFollettes, is made the paramount consideration in charting the future . . . of the Progressive movement. The *Capital-Times* . . . will vigorously support LaFollette's candidacy . . . but with the feeling that there must be something higher and bigger, no matter how big the individual may be, on which to build the future of a militant people's movement than the personal interests of one man."

Chapter 2

Labor's Political Response

I

Although Senator LaFollette realized that his choice of the Republican party would bring intense Stalwart opposition, he seemed relatively unconcerned about the hostile reactions of his former labor supporters. Their admonitions about joining the Democratic party regardless of the Portage decision were not taken seriously; instead LaFollette listened to the comforting words of a few political analysts and close friends who told him that most union leaders would eventually fall into line. Moreover, LaFollette himself was convinced that he could carry the working-class vote with or without labor's official endorsement.[1]

Still, organized labor's response to the Portage decision, which ranged from lukewarm support to anger and dismay, was cause for some anxiety. The state AFL, for example, was badly fragmented by the decision. In the first category was a small minority of federationists, representing several of the conservative, craft-oriented construction unions, whose ambiguous feelings towards the Democratic party were far outweighed by memories of LaFollette's consistent devotion to the cause of labor. One of the few expressions of labor's concern for the senator in the days following the Progressive convention occurred when a group of twenty-nine prominent AFL state leaders, led by William Cooper, president of the Building Service Employees; William Nagorsne, secretary of the Wisconsin Federation of Labor; and Frank Ranney, secretary of the Milwaukee Federated Trades Council, formed the Milwaukee AFL Committee for the Re-Election of Robert M. LaFollette. How miserably these unionists failed in their attempt to gather labor support for the senator was demonstrated when only four political contributions, totaling $175, were received during the organization's existence (of which two, totaling $125, came from Cooper and Nagorsne). In all, the committee held two small luncheons and then disbanded.[2] However, a

---

1. Interview with Loren Norman, April 5, 1971; interview with Miles McMillin, April 3, 1971; both interviews by the author. See also the statement of Dane County Progressive leader John Lawton in the *Madison Capital-Times*, March 3, 1946.
2. Secretary of State of Wisconsin, *Political Contributions to the 1946*

few other AFL officials still expressed the belief that labor would somehow rally to LaFollette's side. "I think the workers will vote solidly for Bob," claimed Milwaukee-based AFL general counsel Joseph Padway. "Some, it is true, differ with him on his war record, but LaFollette has had a twenty-year record of pro-labor activity and that's what will count at the showdown." And to prove his point, Padway contributed $500 to LaFollette's campaign.[3]

A few other AFL officials attempted to support LaFollette without either aligning with the Republicans or alienating the Democrats. At times, their methods were so indirect that his name went unmentioned. A case in point was the editorial board of the *Madison Union Labor News*, which, while refraining from a public endorsement of the senator, decided to separate his campaign from those of other Republican candidates. "There are some very fine candidates on *both* the Democratic and Republican tickets," it claimed, "but there is one type of candidate we wouldn't consider; namely regular Republicans, especially those endorsed by the conservative branch of that party, and smiled on by the NAM [National Association of Manufacturers]."[4] The journal also recorded a few of LaFollette's liberal accomplishments and dutifully printed the endorsements of national AFL leaders like William Green.[5] From a practical standpoint, however, this self-imposed timidity was of little help in drumming up real rank-and-file support.

Most state federationists fell instinctively into a neutral posture. As newly recruited Democrats, they openly condemned LaFollette's reentry into the Republican party; yet, as individuals they could not in good conscience endorse someone else. Milwaukee's AFL journal exemplified this neutrality when, despite the urgings of Padway, Cooper, and others, it asked its subscribers to vote in the primary but refused to endorse a candidate for senator. The newspaper simply stated: "Primary election day is August 13, this year. It is a day of importance to every citizen. . . . Voters should see to it that elections do not go by default. Voting is a great privilege—and should be utilized as such."[6] However, some labor spokesmen were more to the point. Peter Schoeman, president of the powerful Milwaukee Building and Construction Trades Council, echoed the latter sentiment

---

Primary Elections, Folder 4396 (AFL Committee for the Re-Election of Senator LaFollette), September, 1946, Wisconsin State Historical Society.

3. *Milwaukee Journal*, August 10, 1946.

4. Italics mine. *Madison Union Labor News*, August, 1946.

5. For the views of national labor leaders towards LaFollette's candidacy, see, this chapter, pp. 33–35.

6. *Milwaukee AFL Labor Press*, July 25, 1946.

when he wrote, "I do not believe that labor should endorse anyone in a Wisconsin primary."[7]

Finally, there were some AFL leaders who attempted to use the Progressive dissolution to good advantage. In April, 1946, Editor Evjue received an invitation from five prominent federationists to help organize a new political party. "With the demise of the Progressive party," the letter stated, "it seems to a group of laboring men that now is the time to found an American Labor Party—one that will not be dominated by AFL or CIO . . . but shall represent every man and woman who earn their living by the toil of hand or brain."[8] The Madison journalist was not interested in their scheme, although he did offer some advice. Any political action labor took, he responded, should be directed primarily at "kicking the old fogies and reactionaries out of the top thrones of the AFL."[9] Taking a cue from Evjue's stinging rebuttal, these officials soon discarded their opportunistic plans.

II

The state's CIO leadership, which was bitterly divided into pro-Communist and anti-Communist factions, viewed the Portage pro-

7. *Milwaukee Journal*, July 5, 1946. Ironically the peculiarities inherent in Wisconsin's primary law, which was a law written by Robert LaFollette, Sr., did much to ensure this neutrality. In many other states these labor leaders easily might have enacted a compromise. For example, they could have endorsed LaFollette for senator and then switched over to support Democrats for every other office on the ballot. In Wisconsin this was not possible. Although the voters were free to enter the Republican or Democratic primaries, regardless of previous party affiliation, they were forbidden to split their ballots by supporting candidates from both parties. Therefore, a Democrat wishing to enter the Republican primary would have been forced to endorse Republican candidates for every other elected position. Few labor leaders or liberals were willing to go this far. As the Socialist party of Wisconsin noted in a letter to the *Capital-Times* (June 10, 1946): "A grave blow will be dealt to all forward-looking legislation if labor and cooperators rush into the Republican primary to support one or two favorite candidates. . . . They will necessarily put into office a hundred reactionaries for the single candidate."

8. *Madison Capital-Times*, April 25, 1946.

9. Ibid. Editor Evjue was one of the AFL's greatest critics. As an old Progressive, he believed the federation was far too conservative, especially in relation to its stand against the public ownership of railroads and utilities and its belief in exclusive, craft-oriented unions. For example, when reviewing Saul Alinsky's *Reveille for Radicals*, Evjue wrote: "It is rather too much to hope for that the fat and lazy labor leaders at the AFL Labor Temple would ever read a book that so penetratingly appraises the present labor movement" (*Capital-Times*, February 14, 1946).

ceedings with grave apprehension. The anti-Communists already were committed firmly to the Democratic party and pictured LaFollette's return to the GOP as the Waterloo for liberal unity in Wisconsin. In fact, these leaders had been wary of the senator since his refusal to support Roosevelt's candidacy in 1944 but decided to defer final judgment until LaFollette's official announcement at the Progressive convention. When the Portage delegates chose the party of Robert Taft and Thomas Coleman the latent hostilities of these industrial unionists fell squarely upon the convention and the men who had so successfully manipulated it for their own political ends. "It was a gathering of old men," fumed the *Kenosha Labor*. "They talked about Old Bob, dead now twenty years. . . . They had nothing to say about Franklin Roosevelt. . . . They booed Henry Wallace."[10] A week later, the Racine Political Action Committee passed a resolution, as did its counterparts in Kenosha and Sheboygan, that sealed LaFollette's tragic political fate. "We are not interested in the prospects of selfish office-holders who would resort to any expediency in order to gain office," it read. "We therefore decide to support liberal candidates in the forthcoming election on the Democratic ticket."[11]

Senator LaFollette's only real support among non-Communist state CIO officials came from Dane County. Here, the local Industrial Union Council issued a formal statement calling upon all Wisconsin unionists to remember the senator's unexcelled record on matters pertaining to the welfare of common people and then to vote accordingly.[12] This isolated endorsement was quite understandable, since Dane County was the center of Progressive strength in Wisconsin, and the president of the local IUC (and author of the resolution) was Aldric Revell, a longtime friend and supporter of Senator Bob LaFollette. Overall, the majority of non-Communist CIO leaders in Wisconsin had placed their allegiance to the Democratic party far above any moral commitment to perpetuate LaFollette's political career.

III

Less than a month after the Portage convention, a conclave of Democratic unionists, urban liberals, and state party regulars chose

10. *Kenosha Labor*, March 25, 1946.
11. *Racine Labor*, March 22, 1946.
12. Minutes of the Dane County Industrial Union Council, April 3, 1946, Dane County Industrial Union Council Papers, Wisconsin State Historical Society.

Howard J. McMurray to be the Democratic candidate for U.S. senator. As a former New Deal legislator and a strong supporter of organized labor, McMurray was well received along the industrial lakeshore.[13] Here was a man, claimed the labor journals, with impeccable credentials; a man who could fill the vacuum left by LaFollette's pragmatic departure. Plans were quickly prepared for a vigorous campaign in the labor strongholds. Many Wisconsin unionists had discovered the new workingman's hero.[14]

In order to capitalize fully on McMurray's benevolent image, LaFollette had to be discredited both as a liberal and as a friend of organized labor. McMurray, therefore, set out to inform the voters about their senator's "calculated subversion" of the liberal forces in Wisconsin. He claimed the betrayal began in 1944 when LaFollette refused to support Franklin Roosevelt for reelection. The president, it seemed, never forgot this desertion. Indeed, he allegedly told McMurray: "Howard, I've made many mistakes in office and one of my worst ones was in Wisconsin. But we'll correct that in 1946."[15] With the enormous prestige of a fallen leader behind him, McMurray hoped aloud that "the voters of Wisconsin would do what the president told me he wanted done." The Democratic candidate must have also hoped that the voters of Wisconsin had short memories, since two months earlier he had personally asked LaFollette to run for senator on the Democratic ticket.[16]

McMurray was also aware of labor's fear that LaFollette had lost his crusading spirit. The *Racine Labor*, for example, conceded that while the senator was still a liberal, he seemed to be "voting right on bills just for the record in recent years, but putting up no battle to get them through."[17] In an effort to demonstrate just how this change

---

13. At the time of the 1946 primary election campaign, McMurray was a professor of political science at the University of Wisconsin.

14. *Racine Labor*, July 12, 1946; August 9, 1946. *Kenosha Labor*, July 18, 1946; August 8, 1946.

15. Howard McMurray, *Madison Capital-Times*, August 6, 1946.

16. According to McMurray's own recollection: "I visited with Senator LaFollette early in 1946 in an attempt to get him to become the Democratic candidate for the United States Senate. . . . I promised [him] that he could have the Democratic nomination without any serious opposition whatsoever. . . . I promised him that I would stay out of the race and that I would campaign for him both in the primary and in the general election." McMurray did state, however, that if LaFollette decided to run as a Republican he would vigorously oppose him. See, Roger Johnson, *The Decline of the Progressive Party in Wisconsin* (Madison: Wisconsin State Historical Society Press, 1964), p. 110.

17. *Racine Labor*, June 12, 1946.

came about, McMurray produced a letter that Senator Robert A. Taft had circulated among Wisconsin Republicans in behalf of LaFollette's candidacy. In it, the Ohio legislator stated that LaFollette was actually closer to his own brand of conservatism than he was to the liberalism of Republicans like Wayne Morse. When the letter was made public, McMurray campaigned throughout the state asking a single rhetorical question: If LaFollette were as liberal as everyone supposed, why was a monolithic reactionary like Taft supporting his candidacy? The answer, he noted, was quite simple. In return for Taft's endorsement, LaFollette would come out strongly in favor of the Ohioan's bid for the Republican presidential nomination in 1948.[18]

McMurray's charge produced such a furor that both state and national labor leaders demanded an explanation:

> Bob LaFollette did not repudiate Taft's letter. Does this mean that LaFollette, too, expects to start his next term of office in Taft's corner . . . if he is re-elected this fall? Some time has passed since Taft adopted LaFollette and forecast his future plans. LaFollette has said nothing. If Taft is wrong, let LaFollette tell us so, immediately and emphatically. We're listening, senator.[19]

Although LaFollette never bothered to issue a rebuttal, the name of Robert A. Taft remained conspicuously absent from the rest of his campaign.[20]

While McMurray's bitter attacks enraged some former Progressives, others were certain that they would work to LaFollette's advantage. "I know a little about politics," wrote one columnist, "and if McMurray goes around the state attacking LaFollette, he'll wind up so far behind the eight ball politically, it will take him three days travel on the Twentieth Century Limited to get to where he can knock his head against it."[21] McMurray, however, was unimpressed. He knew well that the success of his campaign depended on how many disenchanted liberals he could win away from LaFollette. A short

---

18. One McMurray advertisement, printed in the *Milwaukee Journal* of August 11, 1946, read: "LaFollette poses as a liberal—yet Senator Taft, Arch-Reactionary, endorses him. LaFollette Betrayed the Progressives. LaFollette Betrayed President Roosevelt. LaFollette Will Betray the Republicans."

19. *International Teamster*, June, 1946, p. 15.

20. When, for example, an advertisement in the *Milwaukee Journal* of August 4, 1946 ("A Senator To Be Proud Of") carried the endorsements of many U.S. senators, Taft's name was not among them.

21. Aldric Revell, quoted in the *Madison Capital-Times*, June 6, 1946.

while later, when discussing the senator's position on foreign policy, he claimed that "Nazi and Fascist newspapers approved and reprinted many of Senator LaFollette's views."[22]

McMurray's political efforts were centered primarily in the lakeshore counties of Milwaukee, Kenosha, and Racine, where organized labor used every available resource to promote his candidacy. From an editorial standpoint, the labor press pictured him as an able, energetic New Dealer of the Roosevelt mold; LaFollette, on the other hand, was viewed as a tormented individual who had forsaken his principles for personal political gain. According to the *Racine Labor*: "Senator LaFollette must be a lonely man these days. We can just picture him lying awake at night, tossing in his scorching bed, wondering how he ever came to be in there with so many reactionaries."[23] These journals also called upon the rank and file to vote for McMurray, even though he was running unopposed in the Democratic primary. Their reasoning was that first, if LaFollette won his primary race he would surely defeat McMurray in the general election, thereby winning over a large liberal constituency to the Republican party; and second, if McMurray were to have any chance for success in November he would have to impress these same unattached liberals with his increased voter appeal. As the *Kenosha Labor* warned: "We must be deeply concerned about the turnout of voters at the polls and about support for the liberal Democratic ticket. . . . A strong Democratic vote in the primary will encourage liberals in November."[24]

From an organizational standpoint, union leaders along the lakeshore were just beginning to realize the political potential of the blue-collar vote. During the primary campaign, a series of United Voter Clubs were formed to register union members and to inform them of the importance of voting in the Democratic primary. In some areas —most notably Milwaukee and Kenosha—the more sophisticated Political Action Committees compiled an indexing system for all CIO members on a ward-by-ward basis to inquire about voter registration and, wherever possible, political affiliation. The results exceeded even the most optimistic expectations. In Kenosha, for example, more citizens were registered to vote in the 1946 primary than in any past municipal election; in Racine and Milwaukee, Demo-

22. Ibid., August 7, 1946. McMurray's attacks on LaFollette's isolationism were carried extensively in the labor press. See, *Kenosha Labor*, July 18, 1946; July 25, 1946. *Racine Labor*, July 12, 1946; August 16, 1946. *Wisconsin CIO News*, June 7, 1946; July 19, 1946.
23. *Racine Labor*, July 12, 1946.
24. *Kenosha Labor*, July 30, 1946.

cratic candidates led torchlight parades and addressed packed gatherings as a result of massive labor publicity drives. Clearly, McMurray was on the move.[25]

IV

Certainly the most controversial aspect of the 1946 senatorial primary campaign was the role played in LaFollette's defeat by a group of Communist labor leaders. As the years passed and McCarthy gained international attention for his anti-Red crusade, the theory that this man was brought to power by the very forces he allegedly despised became prominent in liberal circles. Much of the work on this subject has taken careful note of Milwaukee's "notorious trade union Bolsheviks."[26] Indeed, Senator LaFollette himself believed that his desertion by labor in the primary was a deliberate move by the Communists to defeat him because of his firm stand against the

25. *Wisconsin CIO News*, July 26, 1946. *Kenosha Labor*, July 25, 1946; August 8, 1946. *Racine Labor*, August 1, 1946.
26. Some of those convinced of the major role played by the CIO Communists in the Milwaukee area are: Max Kampelman, *The Communist Party vs. the CIO* (New York: Praeger, 1957), pp. 42–44; Philip Taft, *Organized Labor in American History* (New York: Harper and Row, 1964), pp. 611–12; James Rorty and Moshe Dechter, *McCarthy and the Communists* (Boston: Beacon Press, 1954), p. 150; Walter Uphoff, *Kohler on Strike* (Boston: Beacon Press, 1966), pp. 402–3; Fred Cook, *The Nightmare Decade* (New York: Random House, 1971), pp. 102–4; Donald Young, editor of Philip LaFollette's memoirs, *Adventure in Politics*, took a more moderate position when he wrote: "The role played by the Wisconsin Communists in the primary is still in dispute. . . . Though few in number, they dominated the Wisconsin CIO and used the CIO newspaper to denounce LaFollette, one of the best friends labor ever had. . . . McCarthy's victory with Communist support was to prove ironic indeed." Donald Young, *Adventure in Politics* (New York: Holt, Rinehart and Winston, 1970), p. 278. Only Richard Rovere has taken issue with this analysis. He has noted: "The facts will not sustain the theory that McCarthy owed his nomination to votes controlled by Communists in Milwaukee. There is no evidence that the Communists instructed their following to enter the Republican primaries or gave McCarthy any assistance beyond their generalized attacks on LaFollette." Richard Rovere, *Senator Joe McCarthy* (Cleveland: World Publishing Co., 1960), p. 104. However, Rovere admits that the bulk of his information on this subject comes from a single doctoral dissertation (Karl Meyer, "The Politics of Loyalty, from LaFollette to McCarthy in Wisconsin 1918–1952," Ph.D. dissertation, Princeton University, 1956), which, Rovere claimed, thoroughly canvassed the available material. In fact, Meyer's analysis is little more than a sketchy three-page summary, most of which is taken directly from Anderson and May. Meyer simply used their research and came to a different conclusion.

Soviet Union after World War II.[27] In view of the events surrounding the Portage convention, this one-dimensional analysis seemed totally inaccurate; yet to fully appreciate its significance one must, so to speak, begin at the beginning.

Until the Great Depression, the only notable feature of communism in Wisconsin was its classic impotence, but the ensuing economic disorder fostered a climate that proved highly favorable to the spread of radical ideologies. The Communist trade unionists seized upon this unexpected opportunity, abandoning their unsuccessful attempts at dual unionism in favor of "boring from within" existing labor organizations. In the spring of 1935, Eugene Dennis, newly appointed district organizer for the Communist party in Wisconsin, issued a call to arms.

> We Communists must redouble and extend our day to day work in the trade unions and factories. We must intensify and broaden our efforts to become the most active builders and defenders of trade unions. We must work in the trade union field to overcome the strong remnants of opposition and energetically transform the existing rank-and-file movements. Party recruiting and building, above all in the key shops, must be tackled with real Bolshevik enthusiasm and persistence to establish the base of our Party more solidly in the auto, metal, machine and transportation industries.[28]

The very next year, Dennis and his followers infiltrated the federal labor union established by the AFL at the huge Allis-Chalmers plant in West Allis, Wisconsin. When the union left the AFL to join, as Local 248, the United Automobile Workers, a bitter struggle ensued between Communist and non-Communist leaders for control of the organization. Years later, Dennis recalled that although the right wing of the local tried to resist, the well-organized Communists "used violence, short strikes and coercion, to which the company, through its policy of neutrality in internal union affairs, acquiesced, in order to eliminate opposition within the union." By 1938, the Communists gained complete control of the local, thus becoming the exclusive bargaining agent for much of the Allis-Chalmers work force.

Local 248 quickly gained the confidence and respect of its membership. Its leaders—Communist party members Harold Christoffel, Linus Lindberg, and Mel Heinritz—succeeded not only in improving the wage scales and working conditions at Allis-Chalmers, but also

27. See Marquis Child's column in the *Washington Post*, August 19, 1946.
28. Quoted in Thomas Gavett, *The Development of the Labor Movement in Milwaukee* (Madison: University of Wisconsin Press, 1965), p. 177.

in educating the workers about the need for a strong trade union movement. "It is doubtful if any local union ever put greater energies into its educational endeavors," wrote one labor historian. "As a new, struggling union, Local 248 published its own newspaper, hired a full time educational director, set up its own library, ran an extensive set of classes, drama programs, town halls, ladies auxiliary meetings, as well as meetings for the unemployed."[29] These programs convinced most unionists that the local was working diligently to protect its interests.

By virtue of their superb organizational expertise, the Milwaukee Communists gained a strong foothold in the Wisconsin State Industrial Union Council and took over control of its publicity organ, the *Wisconsin CIO News*. Quite understandably, a pro-Soviet editorial policy soon characterized the journal; such headlines as "UE Repudiates Red-Baiting by Overwhelming Vote" and "Fur and Leather Workers Convention Beacon of Progress" became commonplace, as were diatribes against those who criticized Henry Wallace during his Russian friendship crusade.[30] "We are not fooled by the words about the 'menace of Communism' any more than we were fooled by Adolph Hitler's words about a 'crusade against Bolshevism,' " wrote Local 248 Secretary-Treasurer Lindberg in a postwar editorial. "We have learned through bitter experience that a cry for a renewal of the 'anti-Communist axis' can only mean what Hitler's talk meant—a world war in which common people die and the corporations wax richer."[31]

29. Robert Ozanne, "The Effects of Communist Leadership on American Trade Unions," Ph.D. dissertation, University of Wisconsin, 1954, p. 277.

30. *Wisconsin CIO News*, September 13, 1946; June 7, 1946. Both the United Electrical Workers (UE) and the Fur and Leather Workers were expelled from the CIO in 1949–1950 for their alleged Communist activities.

31. Linus Lindberg to Harry S. Truman, March 7, 1946, Milwaukee County Industrial Union Council Papers, Wisconsin State Historical Society. The Wisconsin Communists also backed up their rhetoric with action. When, for example, the Soviet Union and Nazi Germany signed their nonaggression pact in 1939, Local 248 followed the lead of the Communist party by bitterly attacking America's defense mobilization program. Labeling participating industrial concerns, including Allis-Chalmers, "reactionary war-makers," the local began a series of work slowdowns to hamper production. These minor harassments, coupled with a series of legitimate union grievances, led directly to a strike that shut down the plant for seventy-six days. Only the combined pressures of an aroused public opinion and the Defense Mediation Board brought about a settlement. Yet, the local continued to employ disruptive techniques until June 22, 1941—the fateful day on which Germany attacked the Soviet Union. Local 248 then reversed its policy and initiated a campaign to defeat the "fascist enemy" through increased production. See, especially, Donald Schwartz, "The 1941 Strike at Allis-Chalmers," M.A. thesis, Univer-

Since the Communists were particularly sensitive to criticism of the Soviet Union and made it their policy to denounce those individuals and organizations responsible for it, Senator LaFollette soon became the prime target of the *Wisconsin CIO News*. On May 31, 1945, before the United States Senate, "Young Bob" delivered his major foreign policy address, entitled "America Must Raise A Standard."[32] While concluding that the U.S. had to deliver massive economic aid to war-torn European countries or face the prospect of Communist takeovers, LaFollette dealt at length with alleged Soviet violations of the Atlantic Charter and Yalta agreements. However, the most crucial point in his speech concerned the reconciliation of Russian aims with those of the United Nations. While speaking on this particular subject, LaFollette was interrupted by Senator William Fulbright of Arkansas, then, as now, deeply committed to internationalism. Fulbright wanted to know if "it were not essential to have Russia in this organization?" LaFollette declared that he believed Russia's membership to be highly desirable but only if she abided by the rules and were treated as an equal rather than someone for whom concessions would always have to be made. "I am as anxious as is any man to have Russia in this organization," he retorted, "and I think she will come in; but I think that up to and through Yalta, there has been too much of an attitude of believing that we had to pay a price to get her in and that we voluntarily offered too big a price. . . . She seems to have no faith in the efficacy of the organization which is being created."

The *Wisconsin CIO News* lost little time informing its 75,000 readers about the "reactionary attitudes" of their senior senator. On June 11, 1945, under the headline "Blast LaFollette Plea For Tolerance Towards Nazi Germany, Fascist Leaders," the newspaper, in direct reference to the senator's stand on the United Nations, claimed that he was disagreeing "not with details or parts, but with the whole plan for peace and security."[33] It also stated that LaFollette's appeal for "tolerance not vengeance" in dealing with conquered Germany was proof of his inherent sympathy for Fascist leaders. The obvious insinuation here was that because of his large German–American constituency in Wisconsin, LaFollette was unwilling to have America prosecute the captured Nazi leaders. In actuality, the senator had

---

sity of Wisconsin, 1943; Ozanne, "The Effects of Communist Leadership on American Trade Unions," pp. 217–21.

32. For the text of LaFollette's speech, see, U.S., Congress, *Congressional Record*, 79th Cong., 1st sess., 1945, 91, pt. 4:5322. This speech is particularly interesting because it is a major departure from the senator's long-standing isolationist position.

33. *Wisconsin CIO News*, June 11, 1945.

stated clearly during his speech that he was determined to see "all Nazi and Fascist criminals brought to trial."[34] Not only did the Communist journal ignore this part of the text, but Local 248's edition of the *Wisconsin CIO News* noted that more than a thousand postcards were received from Milwaukee unionists protesting LaFollette's pro-Fascist, anti-Soviet attitude.[35]

The attempt to label LaFollette "reactionary" in international affairs was certainly nothing new. As a lifelong isolationist, the senator had heard this charge leveled against him many times before; it was common knowledge that his reputation as a spokesman for the liberal and progressive forces in America was based exclusively on domestic matters. Yet, by using the techniques of slander and guilt by association, the Communists linked LaFollette with the extreme right-wing elements in the United States. Indeed, they insinuated that the unwanted and highly embarrassing endorsements of the senator's campaign by native Fascists like Gerald L.K. Smith and Joseph Kamp were proof of his inherent antidemocratic philosophy. Articles like "LaFollette Shields Role of Reactionary" and "Pro-Fascist Group Supports Bob" appeared with such regularity that Democratic senatorial candidate Howard McMurray picked up the cue and used it to his own advantage.[36]

At one point, the Communists attempted to portray LaFollette as an antilabor legislator. When, in 1946, the senator voted with other liberals to defeat a minimum wage bill containing an undesirable farm parity rider, he was censured by the *Wisconsin CIO News* for "favoring the reduction of a minimum wage and other restrictive labor legislation."[37] In this case, the charge backfired because it provoked spirited rebuttals from several non-Communist labor sources. Nathan Cowan, CIO national legislative representative, wrote openly to LaFollette that his vote on this issue "was fully in consonance with the position of the CIO . . . and in line with your own good record on legislation affecting labor's rights, civil liberties, and the social welfare of the people."[38] Furthermore, CIO Vice-President John Brophy sent a personal note to Linus Lindberg calling the attack "completely unjustified" and demanding that the Milwaukee IUC "communicate its apologies promptly to the senator."[39] Even the *Milwaukee AFL*

34. U.S., Congress, *Congressional Record*, 79th Cong., 1st sess., 1945, 91, pt. 4:5330.
35. *Wisconsin CIO News* (Local 248 Edition), June 11, 1945.
36. Ibid., June 25, 1945; July 2, 1945.
37. Ibid., March 1, 1946.
38. *Madison Capital-Times*, April 10, 1946.
39. John Brophy to Linus Lindberg, April 12, 1946, Milwaukee County Industrial Union Council Papers, Wisconsin State Historical Society.

Labor Press came to the senator's aid, claiming that he had "long been on the side of the laboring man . . . and to say that he betrayed labor by voting against a bill containing an obnoxious rider . . . is nonsense."[40] Ironically, this particular defense of LaFollette's record came on March 14, 1946, a few days before the controversial Portage convention; it seems very doubtful that such a statement would have been forthcoming if the Communist charge had occurred a week later.

On the other hand, Wisconsin Communists were aware that La-Follette's Republican opponent, Judge Joseph McCarthy, took a more ambiguous position toward the Soviet Union. For virulent anti-Communists, he related a sordid tale of "American appeasement in foreign affairs." "We retreated mentally and morally in Austria, in Poland, in Manchuria, in the Balkans, and today in Iran," he told a gathering of Young Republicans in Eau Claire. "And there is no reason to believe that tomorrow we shall not do the same thing in Norway, Sweden and Turkey, which apparently are next on the agenda." For Soviet sympathizers, McCarthy offered a different line. "I do not subscribe to the theory that a war with Russia is inevitable," he noted in Milwaukee. "I believe we can and will avoid it. . . . Stalin's proposal for world disarmament is a great thing and he must be given credit for being sincere about it."[41] Sensing the political opportunism that permeated McCarthy's campaign, as opposed to LaFollette's dedicated anti-Communist stand, CIO leaders viewed him as the lesser of two evils.

*   *   *

Using these facts, analysts of the 1946 senatorial campaign drew their conclusions about the deleterious effects of the Communist publicity barrage. As noted earlier, most believed the damage done to LaFollette's candidacy was extensive, possibly irreparable. A few, however, did take note of several mitigating factors.[42] In the first place, the Communists were not alone in attacking LaFollette's early

40. *Milwaukee AFL Labor Press*, March 14, 1946.
41. *Madison Capital-Times*, April 10, 1946. Jack Anderson and Ronald May, *McCarthy: The Man, the Senator, the 'Ism'* (Boston: Beacon Press, 1952), p. 104.
42. Rovere, *Senator Joe McCarthy*, pp. 103–4. Richard Haney, "A History of the Democratic Party in Wisconsin Since World War II," Ph.D. dissertation, University of Wisconsin, 1970, pp. 40–47. John Steinke, "The Rise of McCarthyism," M.A. thesis, University of Wisconsin, 1960, pp. 84–89.

postwar foreign policy statements. Following his hard-line speech against the Soviet Union, for example, the senator was subjected to much criticism. The liberal *Milwaukee Journal* commented that "if Senator LaFollette's purpose is to sabotage the work being done at San Francisco and enthrone the isolationism which became so tragic a failure after the First World War, he could have hardly done better than in his speech in the Senate," while the conservative *Wisconsin State Journal* stated:

> LaFollette is done with Russia. He charges them with almost every crime in the book. . . . We too are suspicious of Russia and rightly so. But certainly we have not always played fair with Russia. She cannot begin to understand our vacillating policies, our lack of certainty. . . . Probably, the major reasons in Russia's sometime lone wolf role are . . . performances like Senator LaFollette's which still draw alarming applause. . . . Truly enough the major people who have learned the cost of war are not so lightly to tear at the chances for peace.[43]

Ironically, it was not until several months later, when the Cold War became an established political reality, that LaFollette's inflexible anti-Soviet position was readily accepted in America. By that time, however, the alleged damage to the senator's candidacy had already been accomplished.

Second, it has been noted that the Communists never actually endorsed a senatorial candidate in the 1946 Wisconsin primary. Their major concern, in fact, was not LaFollette but rather a local politician named Edmund Bobrowicz who, as an official of the Communist-dominated International Brotherhood of Fur and Leather Workers, was trying to unseat a conservative Democratic representative from Milwaukee's Fourth Congressional District.[44] The Communists, therefore, tried their best to get CIO members to vote in the Democratic primary for Bobrowicz. In line with this policy, they alternately condemned and ignored LaFollette's candidacy in an effort to keep the rank and file from entering the Republican primary in the senator's behalf.[45] But at no time did the Communists throw their support

43. *Milwaukee Journal*, June 3, 1945. *Wisconsin State Journal*, June 4, 1945.
44. *Wisconsin CIO News*, June 7, 1946; June 21, 1946; July 19, 1946; July 26, 1946; August 2, 1946; August 9, 1946.
45. The volume of the publicity used by the Wisconsin Communists against LaFollette in 1946 has been greatly exaggerated. Indeed, during the last three months of the primary campaign, the *Wisconsin CIO News* made only two references to LaFollette—both derogatory. See, *Wisconsin CIO News*, July 19, 1946; June 14, 1946.

to Howard McMurray or any other senatorial candidate. Aside from Bobrowicz's campaign, they remained officially neutral.

Oddly enough, not one analysis of the 1946 primary has attempted to study the Communist involvement in light of such momentous post-World War II changes as the Cold War, the new and vigorous anti-Soviet propaganda campaign by many government officials and newspapers, and the obvious change of attitude by U.S. citizenry toward the Soviet Union and its sympathizers. By applying prewar standards to events that occurred in 1946, these researchers assumed that the once secure relationship between the leaders of Local 248 and the rank and file had not been greatly altered by Cold War anxieties. In fact, this was not the case. The brief postwar history of the Christoffel–Lindberg–Heinritz administration was marked by bitterness, confusion, and the final dissolution of all Communist authority.

Shortly after the Portage convention, Local 248 called for a strike against Allis-Chalmers. According to the union, the major issues were wages, union security, and changes in the grievance machinery. There was some feeling, however, that the walkout was called by the Communists to overwhelm, with a strong show of solidarity, an increasing number of right-wing insurgents within the union. On April 29, 1946, the local voted to strike by 8,091 to 251.[46]

As the strike dragged on with no settlement in sight, the leadership of Local 248 slipped in popularity. Both Allis-Chalmers and the local press (particularly the *Milwaukee Sentinel*) initiated a massive propaganda drive to persuade the workers that the strike was a Communist-inspired plot to disrupt American industry. This telling campaign coincided with a grass-roots movement by anti-Communists in the Milwaukee IUC to "oust the Reds." While these right-wing unionists supported the strike and condemned company officials for trying to break the union, they also worked to "democratize" the union from within. Petitions were circulated by local CIO leaders stating that "No Nazi, Communist, or Ku Klux Klan member shall be allowed to hold office in the Milwaukee County Industrial Union

46. Both sides in the dispute—Allis-Chalmers and Local 248—were looking for a showdown. Prior to the strike, the company had made clear its refusal to bargain in good faith with Communists by unilaterally restricting the privileges of union shop stewards to investigate grievances on company time and by refusing to consider a maintenance of membership clause which had been inserted into the previous contract by the War Labor Board in 1943. Local 248, on the other hand, had been purposely abusing the grievance procedures in the hope of provoking the company into an antiunion stance, thereby winning the sympathy of apathetic or dissident members. See, Ozanne, "The Effects of Communist Leadership on American Trade Unions," pp. 213–20. Gavett, *The Development of the Labor Movement in Milwaukee*, pp. 190–96.

Council."[47] Union members took the floor at local meetings to challenge election returns, demand free access to financial records, and encourage the rejection of all directives that seemed to ignore the prevailing majority opinion. In many instances, letters, telegrams, and resolutions were sent to both the United Automobile Workers in Detroit and the CIO national office in Washington demanding immediate action against "Milwaukee's labor dictatorship." One such letter, written by the wife of a local union leader to CIO President Philip Murray, expressed these sentiments well:

> In the spring of this year (1946), the members of Local #1344, Milwaukee, have seen fit to bar Communists from getting control. . . . Since that time, the Communists have embarked upon a deliberate campaign to ruin Local #1344. I appeal to you as President of the CIO . . . to take proper steps to stop the ruination of a very prosperous Steel local . . . which will not permit itself to become a tool for foreign ideologies. . . . You have many locals here which are looking to you for fair, honest cooperation in making the CIO the outstanding guide for all working people.[48]

This campaign soon took its toll. In October, and again in December, 1946, the Milwaukee IUC rejected the slate of Communist-sponsored candidates. Within the next year, the entire work force was back at Allis-Chalmers with a new anti-Communist union hierarchy but no contract.

47. Minutes of the Milwaukee County Industrial Union Council, September 18, 1946, Milwaukee County Industrial Union Council Papers, Wisconsin State Historical Society. To make matters worse for the leadership of Local 248, the local anti-Communist effort was actively supported by powerful national UAW leaders (led by Walter Reuther) who were attempting to purge the "Reds" and their alleged supporters from positions of power at the national level. See, for example, Irving Howe and B.J. Widick, *The UAW and Walter Reuther* (New York: Random House, 1949), pp. 165–66; James Prickett, "Communism and Factionalism in the Union Automobile Workers, 1939–1947," *Science and Society* 32 (Summer 1968): 272–73.

48. Mae Baum to Philip Murray, October 27, 1946, Wisconsin State Industrial Union Council Papers, Wisconsin State Historical Society. Nor was this sentiment indigenous only to the industrial lakeshore. The president of the Dane County Industrial Union Council stated that although he and many other unionists had fallen prey to the "character assassinations of the Milwaukee Communists," his council would continue to encourage the "decent majority" of CIO members in their quest for "trade union democracy." At one point the Dane County IUC seriously considered withdrawing from the state body, but decided that "the whole organization should not be condemned because 5% of it was objectionable and that we should get rid of these undesirables by the regular voting process." Minutes of the Dane County Industrial Union Council, October 1, 1946, Dane County Industrial Union Council Papers, Wisconsin State Historical Society.

This hostile criticism of the entrenched Communist leadership obviously affected the credibility of a publication like the *Wisconsin CIO News*. It seems unlikely that many CIO members were noticeably influenced by its diatribes against LaFollette for his anti-Soviet position. At this very time, for example, a comprehensive analysis on the subject of newspaper credibility was completed in Boston among Catholic members of the United Electrical Workers, a popular union whose newspaper and organizational structure were dominated by Communists.[49] The researchers discovered that less than 15 per cent of these workers believed that their union was telling the truth in matters relating to foreign policy, the Soviet Union, or alleged critics and supporters of American policy concerning the Soviet Union. Actually, these workers found the *UE News* to be far less believable than either the Boston daily newspapers or the journal published by the local archdiocese. Considering now that the industrial work force along the Wisconsin lakeshore was composed predominantly of Catholics of German, Polish, Czech, and Italian descent, it can be hypothesized that they found the *Wisconsin CIO News* to be equally unbelievable. This theory is further enhanced by the fact that many Milwaukee area locals were consistently at odds with the pro-Russian attitude of their CIO labor journal. A resolution sponsored by Local 1114 of the United Steelworkers of America was demonstrative of this feeling.

> Whereas, the facts have established that the *Wisconsin CIO News* has gone far afield in the matter of foreign "isms" in its attempt to inoculate the rank-and-file with ideologies that are un-American and which are contrary to the desires of the vast majority of CIO members. . . . Resolved, the Milwaukee and Wisconsin State Centrals should give full and complete statement of the future editorial policy of the *Wisconsin CIO News* not directly related to the betterment and ideals of American labor.[50]

These vigorous dissents, coupled with the fact that CIO unionists in Kenosha, Racine, Madison, and other cities were Democrats, not Bolsheviks, indicate that while the Milwaukee Communists controlled much of the organizational machinery of the state CIO they did not control the minds or votes of many CIO members during the 1946 campaign. And, in relation to some of the other factors re-

---

49. Martin Krieseberg, "Public Opinion in Soviet-American Relations," Ph.D. dissertation, Harvard University, 1947, Appendix 111.

50. Resolution of Local 1114, United Steelworkers of America, Milwaukee County Industrial Union Council Papers, Wisconsin State Historical Society.

sponsible for LaFollette's defeat—including the Progressive dissolution and labor's choice of the Democratic party—their role seemed almost insignificant. As Thomas Amlie so well put it: "I do not think the Communists should be blamed for Bob's defeat. Labor made up its mind . . . long before . . . that they must fight their battles in the Democratic party. It was stressed to Bob . . . that labor would not go into the Republican primaries and that he would be fighting in an arena where his friends would not be able to help him."[51]

V

Because of the marked contrast between Robert LaFollette, Jr., as an ally of labor on the national level, and a cohort of reactionaries within his own state, there were often differences of opinion among national and state union leaders over his candidacy. On the one hand, most national unionists felt that the senator's past record merited labor's appreciation and support; on the other, they were wary of alienating state and local union leaders by forcing an unwanted candidate upon them. Within the AFL, which had a long tradition of local autonomy in political affairs, the national policy toward LaFollette's candidacy was one of "informal persuasion."[52] In an attempt to bolster the senator's image among state workers, AFL President William Green wrote an open letter "heartily endorsing the candidacy of Robert LaFollette for nomination and reelection to the United States Senate," while Wisconsin-based federationists like Joseph Padway encouraged local officials to work for the senator.[53] However, no real pressure was exerted upon state AFL leaders. In fact, Wisconsin federation President George Haberman recalled years later that the national office did little more than suggest that the senator's candidacy be given close consideration.[54]

For national CIO leaders, the problem was far more serious. In the first place, the newly formed CIO-PAC was working closely with the national Democratic Administration and could not easily endorse a Republican candidate.[55] More important, however, was the matter of LaFollette's anti-Soviet posture. Since Communists occupied

51. Thomas Amlie to Howard McMurray, October 10, 1947, Thomas Amlie Papers, Wisconsin State Historical Society.

52. Interview with George Haberman, September 30, 1969.

53. *Racine Labor*, March 8, 1946.

54. Interview with Haberman.

55. J. David Greenstone, *Labor in American Politics* (New York: Knopf, 1969), pp. 49–58.

prominent positions on both the CIO Executive Board and the Political Action Committee, any attempt to support the senator would have met stiff resistance. Therefore, in an attempt to preserve internal harmony, the CIO ignored LaFollette's campaign altogether. Although Nathan Cowan did write an open letter defending the senator's position on several critical labor issues, this single piece of correspondence was the sum total of CIO participation in the primary election. When, in the spring of 1946, the organization's Political Action Committee endorsed more than thirty legislators for various state and national offices, LaFollette's name was absent. Furthermore, an article in the *CIO News* of June 26, 1946, covering the "main primary tests . . . in the midwest" made no mention of the Wisconsin senatorial race.[56] In fact, this intensely political labor paper did not volunteer one printed line of support for the senator.

Even more noticeable was the lack of interest displayed by the CIO's powerful United Automobile Workers. Because LaFollette had vigorously supported that union in its most recent strike with General Motors to the point of donating money and speaking time at UAW rallies, political observers were certain that the Reuther brothers would come to Wisconsin to stump for the senator.[57] Actually Victor Reuther did fly to Kenosha, Racine, and Milwaukee during the campaign, but his primary purpose was to raise the morale of striking UAW workers, not to endorse LaFollette's candidacy. And, as was the case with the *CIO News*, the UAW's highly partisan newspaper made no mention of the senator's candidacy. In this instance, too, the UAW's indifferent attitude was based on pragmatic grounds. Because Wisconsin's two large automobile locals—248 in West Allis and 72 in Racine—were then engaged in bitter strikes against Allis-Chalmers and J. I. Case, the national office was in no mood to increase their displeasure over a partisan political matter.

The only national labor organizations to come to LaFollette's aid were the railroad brotherhoods. They believed that his major role in deliberations leading to passage of the Railway Labor Act, the Wagner Act, the Fair Labor Standards Act, and other prounion legislation far outweighed local political considerations. "The senator is running on the Republican ticket this year and it is generally conceded his real fight will be in the primary election," noted one memorandum from the national office of the International Brotherhood of Railway and Steamship Clerks to all state representatives. "His defeat would be a great loss to Wisconsin. . . . He has a 100% Railroad

56. *New York Times*, May 10, 1946. *CIO News*, June 26, 1946.
57. *Madison Capital-Times*, June 26, 1946.

Labor voting record and has consistently championed the cause of the common people."[58]

To aid LaFollette, railroad volunteers were sent throughout the state to "talk up" the senator and to distribute a "Special LaFollette Edition" along with their national newspaper, *Labor*. These brotherhoods were one of the few sources who realized how close the primary election might be. "As we said in the beginning, we know you will back Bob," claimed the lead editorial, "but just voting may not be enough. . . . See that members of your families and your friends go to the polls. Don't permit LaFollette's enemies to rob him of the prize because his friends were 'asleep at the switch.' "[59] Yet even this eleventh-hour attempt to help LaFollette revealed how dramatically labor had deserted him, for while this "Special Edition" contained the endorsements of journalists, state and federal bureaucrats, veterans' groups, and prominent politicians, only one Wisconsin labor representative, Joseph Padway, was quoted as being for LaFollette. As far as most of organized labor was concerned, "Young Bob" was on his own.

58. Circular 29, July 23, 1946, Papers of the Brotherhood of Railway and Steamship Clerks, Marinette, Wis., Wisconsin State Historical Society.

59. *Labor* ("Special LaFollette Edition"), July 27, 1946. The railroad brotherhoods had also given strong support to "Young Bob's" father, Senator Robert M. LaFollette, Sr. Indeed, when the elder LaFollette ran for president in 1924, the railroad brotherhoods' official publication, *Labor*, issued a special "Victory Edition" of 2.5 million copies in his behalf. See, Belle LaFollette and Fola LaFollette, *Robert M. LaFollette*, Vol. 2 (New York: Macmillan, 1953), p. 1118.

Chapter 3

The Senatorial Campaign

I

Senator LaFollette's decision to reenter the Republican party came as no surprise to Stalwart leaders. As noted earlier, they had anticipated such a development and were well prepared for the upcoming primary campaign. Yet, in spite of their massive war chest, keen organizational expertise, and alleged unanimity of purpose, Republicans still lacked one vital commodity: a truly exceptional candidate capable of defeating Robert LaFollette. Although the state GOP was filled with prominent businessmen and influential politicians, it needed an exciting figure who could continue the conservative resurgence while appealing to a substantial percentage of the state's independent voting bloc. Republican leaders realized that they had to locate such an individual if they were to repel LaFollette's latest challenge.

In their search for the proper candidate, GOP strategists found one prospect almost impossible to overlook—a young circuit court judge from Outagamie County named Joe McCarthy. The affable Irishman was a political dynamo, crisscrossing the state in an old sedan, trying his best to impress Republican leaders with his popularity if not his aggressiveness. Within a month's time, McCarthy had visited seventy-one local GOP meetings, given hundreds of speeches, and discouraged all competition for the senatorial nomination by threatening in one instance to publicize a rival's recent marital problems and in another to highlight a candidate's civilian status during the past war.[1] At times, the judge campaigned so intensively that some observers feared he was pushing too hard. "For a while it appeared he was making some headway," wrote one unimpressed reporter, "but he has over-campaigned and has run smack-dab into the law of diminishing returns."[2]

McCarthy refused to change tactics, and his whirlwind campaign soon brought the desired result: the Republican senatorial endorsement. After some deliberation, the state convention at Oshkosh decided that a forceful campaigner might prove more successful against

1. Jack Anderson and Ronald May, *McCarthy: The Man, the Senator, the 'Ism'* (Boston: Beacon Press, 1952), pp. 78–91.
2. Aldric Revell, *Madison Capital-Times*, April 25, 1946.

LaFollette than some better-known body with less ambition. But most delegates were disappointed with the choice. In fact, while they applauded politely when McCarthy accepted the endorsement, no attempt was made to give him the traditional standing ovation.[3]

Most political observers were puzzled by the selection. "Coleman is too intelligent to believe that McCarthy . . . can carry the party to victory this fall," wrote one. "Boiled down to minimum essentials, the Republican Convention laid an egg."[4] Another commented:

> After the Progressive Convention at Portage . . . the political speculators were spending double time on LaFollette's chances to go back to the Senate. There was [*sic*] some grounds . . . to feel that Bob faced an up-hill fight. It was pointed out that in the face of an early primary he would go into that fight with a badly shattered political organization; that much of his traditional vote had gone over to the Democratic column; that he would face opposition from an Old Guard candidate with the concerted strength of the Voluntary Committee behind him, plus the considerable funds it is ready to throw into the race. . . . But since the Oshkosh Convention, there has been a vast change. It is still too early to make final judgment, but there is no gainsaying that Bob's re-election is no longer an important point of political speculation.[5]

The powerful *Milwaukee Journal* reacted by demanding McCarthy's immediate withdrawal from the race. A judge, it claimed, was forbidden by the state constitution from campaigning for any political office during his term as an elected judicial official.[6] Even John Wyngaard, a pro-McCarthy journalist for the *Waukesha Daily Freeman*, was forced to admit that his candidate "took the endorsement literally by default because the convention found no one of any consequence willing to take on the job of opposing Senator LaFollette."[7] Opposition to the endorsement mounted so quickly that political writers picked up (or possibly initiated) rumors of a top-level Republican meeting to reconsider the senatorial nominee.[8]

At Coleman's insistence, the Republican party decided not only to stand by McCarthy but to make every possible resource available to him, including a public relations firm, a professional campaign staff, and an enormous capital outlay. The VRC raised well over $100,000 during the first half of 1946, with the greatest single share going to the senatorial candidate. According to official campaign

3. Ibid., May 12, 1946.
4. Aldric Revell, ibid., May 7, 1946.
5. Miles McMillin, ibid., June 2, 1946.
6. *Milwaukee Journal*, May 15, 1946.
7. *Waukesha Daily Freeman*, May 9, 1946.
8. *Madison Capital-Times*, May 16, 1946.

records, the committee funneled $30,000 through U. Van Susteren, McCarthy's personal secretary, and an equal amount through the various "McCarthy For Senator" clubs. On the other hand, Senator LaFollette's backers spent a grand total of $13,000.[9]

Candidate McCarthy appeared unruffled by the turmoil around him. Promising a "very rough but clean fight," he enthusiastically began the campaign that would lead him to Washington. The young judge first bombarded LaFollette with a series of sharp allegations, charging him with living on a plush Virginia plantation, with drawing "fat rations" on the home front "while fifteen million Americans were fighting the war," and with using his legislative masterpiece, the Congressional Reorganization Act, to raise the salaries of congressmen. More serious, however, was McCarthy's contention that the senator had been a war profiteer. LaFollette had purchased a radio station in Milwaukee in 1942 that made a substantial profit, and McCarthy implied that the senator had used his extensive political influence to obtain special privileges from the Federal Communications Commission. "Something has to be done," McCarthy proclaimed indignantly, "to prevent you or any other senator from doing what you did during the war, namely make huge profits from dealing with a federal agency which exists by virtue of your vote."[10] Soon, a series of advertisements blanketed the state. "How Did LaFollette Get That Money?" they asked. "Is There No Regulation of LaFollette's Profits?"[11]

9. Secretary of State of Wisconsin, *Political Contributions of the 1946 Primary Elections*, Folder 2062 (Voluntary Republican Committee); Folder 4480 (Joseph R. McCarthy for U.S. Senate, State Citizens Club). For LaFollette: Folder 4364 (Milwaukee County LaFollette for Senator Club); Folder 1897 (Personal Campaign Committee of Robert LaFollette, Jr.). The LaFollette family contributed well over half of the $13,000 used by the incumbent.

10. Anderson and May, *McCarthy*, p. 103.

11. Analysts of the 1946 campaign have written extensively of the damage caused by this "rash accusation." See, Karl Meyer, "The Politics of Loyalty, from LaFollette to McCarthy in Wisconsin, 1918–1952," Ph.D. dissertation, Princeton University, 1956, pp. 134–35; Richard Rovere, *Senator Joe McCarthy* (Cleveland, World Publishing Co., 1960), pp. 102–3; Anderson and May, *McCarthy*, pp. 101–5. However, in their attempts to dismiss this allegation as simply a factor of partisan politics, they failed to note that some liberals and former Progressives were equally concerned about the senator's foray into the capitalist arena. Wrote Thomas Amlie: "Bob had no right or business with that ownership of WEMP. Coleman was right. Bob and his friends made almost $200,000 a year on that station. No man can get involved in that way and still be with the common people. . . . Small wonder that Bob felt he had to save his seat. . . . He was taking counsel with his friends in WEMP who felt that their slice of the monopoly depended on Bob keeping his seat in the Senate." Thomas Amlie to Howard McMurray, October 10,

McCarthy then shifted his attack to the incumbent's alleged favoritism toward organized labor. At a gathering in LaCrosse he told his supporters that "people should know how LaFollette has catered to labor and how he has damaged . . . other groups—the farmer, industry, business, and the mis-referred-to white collar worker. . . . If you have a man go to the Senate he should represent all the people."[12] Several weeks later, in Oshkosh, McCarthy accused the senator of encouraging union violence through his refusal to vote for legislation designed to penalize strikers and his failure to condemn the "radical eastern labor bosses."[13] And in Appleton, the young candidate not only repeated these charges but concluded that LaFollette would rather destroy the nation than curb the abuses of organized labor.[14]

Not surprisingly, McCarthy's own campaign rhetoric on labor-management problems centered primarily on the importance of controlling union abuses. In an interview with the vehemently anti-LaFollette *Wisconsin State Journal* the candidate outlined his four-point program for labor.

1—All unions should be required by law to account to the membership for all money received and spent.

2—Labor unions should be prohibited from making political contributions, just as corporations are barred.

3—There should be teeth in the law to prevent wildcat and jurisdictional strikes.

4—When a contract is approved between management and labor, both sides should be absolutely bound to the contract and the party guilty of a breach held liable for damages.[15]

State labor leaders were appalled by the interview. "McCarthy didn't even preface his remarks with the usual 'I believe in unions but,' " wrote the *Racine Labor*, "which the anti-labor skates usually pull when they have their knives whetted for us."[16] A short while later, the candidate further enraged unionists by coming out against the closed shop and in favor of the abolition of the Office of Price Administration.

As the campaign drew to a close, however, and McCarthy, with characteristic perception, saw the cool reception afforded LaFollette

1947, Thomas Amlie Papers, Wisconsin State Historical Society. Furthermore, LaFollette made no attempt to deny this charge.

12. *LaCrosse Tribune*, June 13, 1946.
13. *Oshkosh Daily Northwestern*, August 1, 1946.
14. *Appleton Post-Crescent*, June 18, 1946.
15. *Wisconsin State Journal*, April 26, 1946.
16. *Racine Labor*, July 26, 1946.

along the industrial lakeshore, he began to moderate his entire approach to labor problems, especially in relation to the many postwar strikes then sweeping the nation. In a statewide address on August 7, the judge reversed his earlier position by placing the responsibility for the "vast majority of strikes [on] a few hard-headed, short-sighted men in industry who have not yet learned that labor unions are as much a part of the American way of life as industry itself, and a few short-sighted labor bosses. . . . I do not blame labor for strikes and stoppages. . . . The vast majority of workingmen are hurt infinitely more by work stoppages than any other group."[17] McCarthy also became a frequent visitor at the factory gate. In Beloit, for example, after two campaign aides informed him that the Republican party there was closely associated with white collarism, he donned a pair of overalls and visited several industrial concerns, making friends with the workers by talking of the days when he too worked in a foundry.[18] Two days before the primary, the candidate placed a series of advertisements in major urban journals claiming that he, as well as two of his brothers, had been directly associated with labor unions.[19]

Furthermore, like Howard McMurray, McCarthy shifted his attack away from LaFollette's alleged favoritism towards labor and suddenly condemned him for his "anti-union position."[20] He claimed that while the senator had been an errand boy for a few bureaucratic New Dealers, he had actually betrayed the majority of working people by voting against their interests on several crucial proposals. In an attempt to document this charge, McCarthy noted LaFollette's lack of support for the Case bill (then before Congress), which contained a minor provision protecting the wages of men on strike. "It would be one of the best things ever done for labor," he stated.[21] McCarthy failed to mention that the bill was roundly condemned by every liberal legislator for its reliance upon the labor injunction, its prohibitions on picketing and political action, and its negation of large segments of the Wagner Act. As the *CIO News* wrote: "The Case bill is an open declaration of war on organized labor and the democratic rights of the people. The one-sided anti-labor character of this act is particularly outrageous at a time when big corporations encourage the current showdowns by the conspiracy to reject collective bargaining, defy the government, and profit from low wages

17. *Milwaukee Journal*, August 8, 1946.
18. Anderson and May, *McCarthy*, pp. 88–89.
19. *Milwaukee Journal*, August 11, 1946.
20. *Madison Capital-Times*, August 3, 1946.
21. *Milwaukee Journal*, June 21, 1946.

and high profits."²² McCarthy was well aware of labor's antipathy for the Case bill because almost every national union official in America had spoken out against it; but he correctly figured that organized labor would not come to LaFollette's defense over this or any other charge leveled against him.

Throughout the campaign, McCarthy exhibited the traits he would later use so effectively on the national level: cunning, aggressiveness, and a reliance upon poorly documented though highly sensational material. As the candidate of Thomas Coleman and the state's conservative Republican interests, the young judge overcame his greatest weakness—political anonymity—with a massive publicity buildup and an incredibly strenuous campaign schedule. And, as primary day approached, Joseph McCarthy was issuing optimistic predictions of victory.

II

In retrospect, after considering the many factors working against Robert M. LaFollette, Jr., in the 1946 primary contest—the Progressive dissolution, organized labor's massive desertion, the CIO Communist crusade, and Joe McCarthy's aggressive, well-financed campaign—there was every reason to assume he faced an uphill battle. Yet, the senator seemed totally oblivious to these dire circumstances. He came to Wisconsin only ten days before the election and, quite obviously, had neglected his political fence-mending. Some observers believed that the senator could not bear to return to his home state; possibly the very thought of it bored him. Richard Rovere, in his analysis of the primary, has written perceptively of LaFollette's problem of "losing sight of the grass roots."

> It is unsettling to think that in a free election in what has often been spoken of as one of the most politically civilized communities . . . Bob LaFollette, Jr. should be defeated by a scapegrace whose campaign slogan was "Congress Needs a Tail-Gunner." Yet, there is something about the U.S. Senate . . . that makes tragedies of this sort every few years. The Senate offers great scope to men of intellect and imagination. They come to it as ambassadors from rather meager sovereignties, and before long they are likely to find themselves dealing with affairs of the entire nation and the great world beyond. . . . They are very likely to alienate and become alienated from provincial politicians upon whose favor they are dependent. The more time they devote to seeking just

22. *CIO News*, February 4, 1946.

solutions to national and international problems, the less time they have for dipping into the pork barrel for the people back home. . . . In time, someone, not necessarily a McCarthy, but in all likelihood a man of limited perspectives, is bound to come along and point out to the people that their senator has been neglecting them and their interests and has become too involved in the life of Washington and other capitals to represent the humble folk who elected him.[23]

Wisconsin labor leaders were acutely aware of this change in La-Follette. As the senator became more engrossed in the problems of foreign affairs and congressional reorganization, his interest in state matters declined. George Haberman told of several instances in which a plea for action on some matter from the Wisconsin Federation of Labor would be answered by a simple form letter. "Here we were, an organization with more than a hundred thousand members," claimed Haberman, "and all we ever got from LaFollette was a stock reply from one of his secretaries."[24] George Hall, then a member of the state federation's Executive Board, had similar recollections. "I was in LaCrosse in 1946," he recounted, "and although state labor leaders still knew the meaning of the LaFollette name, there had been a real cooling off. His crusading spirit was gone."[25]

Many LaFollette supporters have contended that the senator's failure to campaign in the primary was due not to apathy on his part, but rather to a sincere dedication to the congressional tasks at hand. LaFollette at this time was busily engaged in the formulation of a bill to reorganize Congress, a bill that in the words of Milton Mayer, writing in *Progressive*, was so important as to be "democracy's answer to the totalitarian cry of parliamentary inefficiency." Mayor continued: "It had been Bob LaFollette's baby for years. Nobody cared about it; certainly not you; certainly not I; certainly not his constituents. The important thing you and I said was to come home and get re-elected. But Bob LaFollette was performing the purest kind of public service. He got his bill through and he lost his job."[26]

While there is a thread of validity to this contention, it seems clear from LaFollette's past political dealings that he would have returned home if he believed his political future were in jeopardy. Actually, the senator's supporters viewed McCarthy's campaign as something of a joke. "I have yet to hear a single one of the scores with whom I talked say that McCarthy has a ghost of a chance," wrote a confident

23. Rovere, *Senator Joe McCarthy*, p. 100.
24. Interview by the author with George Haberman, September 30, 1969.
25. Interview by the author with George Hall, September 29, 1969.
26. Milton Mayer, "The People Lose," *Progressive* 10 (August 26, 1946): 5.

Aldric Revell. "The invariable reply, translated for family consumption is: 'Hell, nobody can beat LaFollette this year.' "[27] Even LaFollette's wife, Eleanor, noted that few people thought the race would even be close. In her column, published weekly in *Progressive*, she stated: "For months before the election, people on every side assured me as they did others, 'There's nothing to it; no one can beat Bob.' "[28] More than likely, the senator was lulled into a false sense of security by those who had always taken LaFollette victories for granted, and it was this unwarranted optimism that made Young Bob consider traditional Progressive stumping unnecessary against such meager opposition.[29]

III

The final primary tabulations showed Joseph McCarthy with 207,935 votes, Robert LaFollette, Jr., with 202,539, and Howard McMurray, who ran unopposed, with 62,361. An analysis of Racine, Kenosha, and Milwaukee counties revealed clearly LaFollette's dreadful showing in the labor areas that once provided him with his overwhelming majorities. In the 1934 senatorial race, the senator swept almost every working-class district along the lakeshore. Six years later, the same result salvaged a victory; he actually ran behind his Republican opponent, Fred Clausen, in the rest of the state. In 1946, however, the situation was completely reversed. La-Follette came into these counties with a slim lead and proceeded to lose every one of them—and the election.

Furthermore, a study of the predominantly working-class wards in Milwaukee, centered in the state's Fourth Congressional District, emphasized just how much support the Democrats had acquired between 1940 and 1946.[30] In 1940, LaFollette received 49.4 per cent of

27. *Madison Capital-Times*, August 3, 1946.

28. Eleanor LaFollette, "A Room of our Own," *Progressive* 10 (August 26, 1946) : 5. See, also, Donald Young, *Adventure in Politics* (New York: Holt, Rinehart and Winston, 1970), pp. 276–77; John Steinke, "The Rise of McCarthyism," M.A. thesis, 1960, pp. 25–26.

29. Interview by the author with Miles McMillin, April 3, 1971.

30. It is, of course, somewhat risky to compare primary election results with general election results. The turnouts in the primaries are usually much lower than in general elections and those who do vote in the primaries tend to feel more strongly about the candidates or the issues for which they stand. Moreover, as noted earlier, Wisconsin has long had a "cross-over" primary which allows voters to enter either the Republican or Democratic primary, regardless of previous party affiliation. Still and all, a comparison of the La-Follette vote in the 1940 general election with his 1946 Republican primary

Table 2. Wisconsin Election Statistics, 1940–1946, by Percentage

1940 General Election				
For senator:	Finnegan (Dem.)	LaFollette (Prog.)	Clausen (Rep.)	*Total vote*
Kenosha	16.5	48.6	34.9	28,600
Milwaukee	17.3	49.4	33.3	338,899
Racine	14.2	46.6	39.2	41,070
	16.9	49.1	34.0	408,469
State total:	13.2	45.3	41.5	1,335,989

1946 General Primary				
For senator:	McMurray (Dem.)	LaFollette (Rep.)	McCarthy (Rep.)	*Total vote*
Kenosha	36.7	30.9	32.4	11,030
Milwaukee	26.8	32.3	40.9	118,867
Racine	26.8	32.2	41.0	13,569
	27.5	32.2	40.3	143,466
State total:	13.2	42.8	44.0	472,872

SOURCE: Wisconsin Legislative Reference Bureau, *Wisconsin Blue Book*, 1942, p. 377; 1948, p. 432.

the total county vote and 58.4 per cent of the votes cast in the sample labor wards, as opposed to the respective figures of 17.3 per cent and 24 per cent for his Democratic opponent, James Finnegan. By the 1946 primary, however, the senator was able to capture only 32.3 per cent of the county vote and a dismal 26.5 per cent of the ballots cast in these working-class wards, while Howard McMurray gained 26.8 per cent of the county total and a very impressive 44.1 per cent in these labor districts. And, although the voter turnout in these labor areas was very low, statistics showed that a greater percentage of registered voters went to the polls in these wards (34,163 of 80,675, or 42.4 per cent) than in the city as a whole (107,950 of 272,074, or 39.7 per cent).[31]

---

total clearly demonstrates that the senator's loss of support along the industrial lakeshore was due not to voter apathy but rather to the failure of his old working-class supporters to cross over in this single election and vote Republican in order to perpetuate his political career. Instead, unlike 1940, large numbers of them supported the Democratic senatorial candidate and remained in the Democratic primary to vote for him even though he ran unopposed. Those in the labor wards who did enter the Republican primary gave McCarthy a disproportionately high percentage of their votes.

31. The south side of Milwaukee, comprising, among others, wards 5, 6,

Table 3. Election Statistics in Milwaukee Labor Wards 1940–1946, by Percentage

For senator:	1940 General Election			
	Finnegan (Dem.)	LaFollette (Prog.)	Clausen (Rep.)	Total vote
Ward 5	18.9	60.2	20.9	9,329
6	22.0	57.3	20.7	8,272
8	26.0	54.2	19.8	8,428
10	15.2	66.0	18.8	8,597
12	28.9	57.4	13.7	7,236
14	33.8	54.8	11.4	8,942
	24.0	58.4	17.6	50,804

For senator:	1946 General Primary			
	McMurray (Dem.)	LaFollette (Rep.)	McCarthy (Rep.)	Total vote
Ward 5	31.0	37.9	31.1	2,873
6	27.5	35.9	36.6	2,621
8	45.2	22.3	32.5	3,213
10	36.8	33.2	30.0	2,410
12	53.9	20.9	25.2	2,616
14	63.2	14.0	22.8	3,709
	44.1	26.5	29.4	17,442

SOURCE: *Milwaukee Journal*, November 6, 1940; *Nineteenth Biennial Report of the Board of Election Commissioners*, Milwaukee, 1947, p. 58.

8, 10, 12, and 14, offers a prime example of a working-class population of southeastern and central European descent. Approximately 25,400 of the 36,000 employed male workers in these wards (or 71 per cent) hold blue-collar jobs (craftsman-foreman, factory operative, common laborer). The city average for blue-collar workers in the total labor force is 59.7 per cent, while the state average is only 45.8 per cent. From an ethnic standpoint, 41 per cent of the foreign born in these wards come from Poland (as opposed to the city average of 17 per cent); 34 per cent are from Hungary, Austria, Czechoslovakia, Yugoslavia, and Russia (as opposed to the city average of 28 per cent); and 16 per cent come from Germany (as opposed to the city average of 29 per cent). Moreover, these wards have maintained their ethnic compositions over time (1910–1950) far more rigidly than other areas of Milwaukee. See especially, U. S., Bureau of the Census, *Census of the Population: 1950. Milwaukee County Population Tracts*; Bayrd Still, *Milwaukee: The History of a City* (Madison: State Historical Society of Wisconsin, 1948), pp. 452–55; Richard Davis, "Milwaukee: Our Lady Thrift," in Robert Allen, *Our Fair City*, 1974, p. 202.

McMurray's fine showing was further enhanced by the fact that while the Democrats had few primary contests of sufficient interest to draw voters, their Republican adversaries were enjoying several exciting races. Not many political analysts accepted labor's claim that thousands of unionists would bother to support a candidate who was running unopposed. Yet, the impressive turnout along the lakeshore made believers out of LaFollette's most enthusiastic supporters. "At the Progressive convention at Portage," wrote *Capital-Times* political correspondent Miles McMillin, "labor spokesmen made a strong plea for Progressives to go into the Democratic party. They not only stuck to their guns but proved they could deliver the votes."[32]

However, McMurray was far less successful in labor areas where the Democratic party was still politically ineffective, and where local union leaders were not yet thoroughly committed to that organization. For example, in Madison, long a LaFollette stronghold, the workers remained rooted firmly to their Progressive tradition.

Table 4. Election Statistics in Madison Labor Wards, 1940–1946, by Percentage

	1940 General Election			
For senator:	Finnegan (Dem.)	LaFollette (Prog.)	Clausen (Rep.)	*Total vote*
Ward 6	4.6	67.9	27.5	1,174
9	5.5	80.5	14.0	1,187
17	3.7	83.5	12.8	1,218
18	4.7	74.4	20.9	2,034
	4.6	75.6	19.8	6,153

	1946 General Primary			
For senator:	McMurray (Dem.)	LaFollette (Rep.)	McCarthy (Rep.)	*Total vote*
Ward 6	4.7	62.8	32.5	913
9	6.2	74.7	19.1	530
17	3.6	74.3	22.1	618
18	3.8	68.2	28.0	1,247
	4.4	68.9	26.7	3,308

SOURCE: *Madison Capital-Times*, November 6, 1940; August 18, 1946.

32. *Madison Capital-Times*, August 18, 1946.

Yet, while LaFollette captured 68.9 per cent of the vote in Madison's predominantly working-class wards (as opposed to his astounding total of 75.6 per cent in 1940), the *Capital-Times* tried to pin the senator's defeat on labor by pointing to the low voter turnout here.[33] In reality, the percentage in these wards of registered voters who cast ballots was not significantly below the city average (44.7 per cent as opposed to 45.4 per cent). Unfortunately, the scarcity of voters was due mainly to LaFollette's lackluster campaign. In 1940, hundreds of thousands of Wisconsin voters had flocked to the polls to support both Roosevelt and LaFollette. In 1946, however, there was no great national election to stimulate voter interest. That task was LaFollette's—and in that task he failed miserably.

After considering the labor vote in Milwaukee, where the Democratic party was on the rise, and in Madison, which had a long-standing Progressive tradition, it is at once useful and interesting to focus on a working-class district in a typical Republican area. Janesville, a community of 25,000 situated in conservative Rock County and the home of one of the state's largest automobile assembly plants, provides an excellent example. In this small city, where the Democratic party was all but nonexistent, where political action by the local UAW-CIO had hardly begun, and where the only newspaper (the *Janesville Daily Gazette*) was rabidly Republican, the working-class vote had been traditionally split between Progressive Republican and Stalwart Republican candidates. In 1940, for example, LaFollette received 52.5 per cent of the votes in Janesville's labor wards (as opposed to his city total of only 38 per cent), while Clausen trailed with 35.3 per cent (and a city total of 51 per cent), and Finnegan had 12.2 per cent (and a city total of 11 per cent). By 1946, little change had occurred in Janesville. The workers stayed primarily with LaFollette (54.3 per cent of the working-class vote and a city total of 45 per cent), although McCarthy made some small gains in these wards (38.7 per cent of the working-class vote and a city total of 54 per cent). However, as was the case in Madison, the lack of official labor support for McMurray and the weakness of the Democratic organization made it impossible for him to make any inroads among Janesville's unionists. McMurray's labor support in the 1946 primary, therefore, was limited almost exclusively to the lakeshore counties of Milwaukee, Racine, and Kenosha, where the political influence of the labor unions was coupled with the growing power of the Democratic party.

33. Ibid., August 15, 1946.

Table 5. Election Statistics in Janesville Labor Wards, 1940–1946, by Percentage

1940 General Election

For senator:	Finnegan (Dem.)	LaFollette (Prog.)	Clausen (Rep.)	Total vote
Ward 7	11.2	53.6	35.2	779
8	14.9	48.3	36.8	720
9	12.2	54.1	33.7	584
10	14.2	47.9	37.9	562
11	10.8	57.4	31.8	666
12	10.2	52.4	37.4	638
	12.2	52.5	35.3	3,949

1946 General Primary

For senator:	McMurray (Dem.)	LaFollette (Rep.)	McCarthy (Rep.)	Total vote
Ward 7	6.6	62.9	30.5	197
8	6.7	51.7	41.6	267
9	7.3	50.5	42.2	220
10	7.7	53.8	38.5	182
11	6.6	58.8	34.6	182
12	7.1	48.8	44.1	170
	7.0	54.3	38.7	1,218

SOURCE: *Janesville Daily Gazette*, November 6, 1940; August 15, 1946. Mimeographed material from Walter M. Lindemann, County Clerk for Rock County, Wis.

IV

Who, then, bears the responsibility for LaFollette's defeat? This question could best be answered by stating that a multiplicity of factors caused the senator's downfall, with no single factor standing out above the rest. In retrospect, it seems that if the devil himself had charted LaFollette's political course in 1946 he could not have damaged the senator any more than the senator damaged himself. By choosing to reenter the Republican ranks, LaFollette alienated much of his liberal support, labor included. And by choosing the Grand Old Party rather than adding additional strength to counterbalance that which he lost, he gave conservative Republicans, who wanted no part of his progressivism, additional incentive to vote against him. Yet he still might have won the election had not his sincere dedication to congressional matters, coupled with the outlandish political predictions of those blinded by the magnetism of the LaFollette name, kept him from the political battlefield.

Labor's role in the primary has been exaggerated by those who, in the wake of one of the most bewildering and illogical elections in history, expected it to perform with textbook predictability. Would not LaFollette have won, they asked, with the support of Wisconsin's labor community? Yes, he might well have won had this been the case. But had he come home to refute the slanderous Communist charges or made a single conciliatory gesture in the direction of those labor leaders who were heartsick over his choice of the Republican party, he might well have won anyway. In sum, had he played the role of candidate only half as well as he did that of statesman, there probably would have been no one to blame.

Chapter 4

The Senatorial Election

I

The reaction of organized labor in Wisconsin to Senator LaFollette's defeat followed a familiar pattern. In Madison, where union support for the senator had been less than adequate, the local journal was dismayed to discover that "the public's apathy is what caused LaFollette's demise." All was not lost, however, since a large liberal and labor vote could now be directed towards the candidacy of Howard McMurray. "We have in the past elected a whole state administration on the Progressive ticket," claimed the *Madison Union Labor News*. "We see no reason to believe that Progressive Democrats can't be elected too."[1] Unionists in Milwaukee ignored the primary result as they had ignored the primary, although political action was quickly initiated in McMurray's behalf. Ironically, some four years later when McCarthy was deeply involved in his anti-Communist crusade, the *Milwaukee AFL Labor Press* condemned Wisconsin voters for their lack of interest in the 1946 primary elections: "Too often some people have taken the attitude that their vote doesn't make any difference. Had people turned out in 1946, in the primary, we would not have been burdened with the . . . red-baiting McCarthy, who won the Republican nomination by less than 5,000 votes—or little more than one vote per precinct in the state."[2]

Only in Kenosha and Racine counties, where Democratic unionists had worked openly for McMurray, did the labor journals record their true feelings. Under the banner headline, "What Price Expediency—LaFollette's Defeat," the *Kenosha Labor* editorialized:

> Some there will be who will point to Bob's labor record and will speak of labor's deserting him. Bob's labor record . . . was unquestionably excellent. But there was more involved in the campaign than his record on labor legislation. . . . There was also . . . his desertion of President Roosevelt in 1944 and his unsatisfactory record on foreign policy issues, which workers also consider important. And there was involved his joining the Republican party. . . . No, labor did not desert Bob. It was the other way around—Bob deserted labor.[3]

1. *Madison Union Labor News*, September, 1946.
2. *Milwaukee AFL Labor Press*, August 31, 1950.
3. *Kenosha Labor*, August 15, 1946.

The *Racine Labor* put it more simply. LaFollette's defeat, it claimed, "helped separate sheep from goats." Liberals were now all in one column.[4]

Following the primary, most of organized labor lined up squarely behind the Democratic candidates. The state AFL and CIO, for example, formed a United Labor Committee to maximize their editorial and financial resources. Democratic labor leaders were joined even by the Milwaukee Communists in lauding the liberal leanings of McMurray while condemning McCarthy's "phony" conservatism. "Howard McMurray, the Democratic candidate for United States Senator," the *Kenosha Labor* exhorted, "is qualified in every way that McCarthy is not—in character, in knowledge, in experience in government, and in his sympathies for the people." Certainly, a man of his stature deserved victory over a "judge-politician" with "a willingness to kowtow to the most Tory elements in the Republican party."[5]

There were some notable defections, however, especially among former LaFollette supporters who resented McMurray's aggressive primary campaign against their candidate. The more perceptive state unionists tried to neutralize this ill feeling, as in Racine where the Political Action Committee elected a LaFollette Republican to lead the local McMurray senatorial campaign.[6] But the bitterness prevailed. A few days before the November election, the Wisconsin Legislative Board of the Brotherhood of Locomotive Firemen and Engineers broke its official silence by stating publicly that "Howard J. McMurray's . . . careless handling of the facts [during the primary campaign] does not qualify him as a candidate for the important office of United States Senator." Although the union refused to endorse Judge McCarthy, it urged railroad workers "to remember the primary campaign [and] to vote accordingly."[7]

LaFollette's defeat also split his loyal Progressive following. Although a minority vowed to continue his struggle to liberalize the Republican party from within, a much larger segment gravitated instinctively toward the Democratic organization. They realized that with no leader of major stature to forward their programs, there was no hope for a realistic dialogue with the Coleman-led Stalwart majority. The only alternative was to enter the same political party they had rejected so decisively in Portage for reasons of expediency.[8]

4. *Racine Labor*, August 16, 1946.
5. *Kenosha Labor*, October 31, 1946.
6. *Racine Labor*, September 20, 1946.
7. *Milwaukee Journal*, November 3, 1946.
8. Leon Epstein, *Politics in Wisconsin* (Madison: University of Wisconsin Press, 1958), pp. 45–52. Many Progressives, however, were so angry at Mc-

As might be expected, the Progressive realignment altered the political strategy of candidate McCarthy. With most of the liberal community, including organized labor, now solidly in the opposing camp, he saw little need to continue his moderate stand on many controversial issues. The judge knew well that his indirect union support in the primary had been simply a function of anti-LaFollette sentiment, and he carefully began the process of making inroads into the state's various conservative factions, especially on the issues of militant industrial unionism and subversion in government.[9]

II

As historians have long noted, the 1946 general elections were greatly influenced by the onset of the Cold War. Many Republican candidates for state and national office freely attacked their Democratic opponents for advocating "New Deal socialism," encouraging domestic radicalism, and failing to deal effectively with Soviet aggression in Eastern Europe. GOP National Chairman B. Carrol Reece set the tone by claiming that "Democratic party policy, as enunciated by its officially chosen spokesmen . . . bears a definite made-in-Moscow label. That is why I believe I am justified in saying that from a long-range viewpoint the choice which confronts Americans this year is between Communism and Republicanism."[10]

Most GOP candidates fell quickly into line. Senatorial hopeful

---

Murray for his attacks upon LaFollette that they did not enter the Democratic party until after McMurray had been defeated by McCarthy in the 1946 senatorial election. As Glen Roberts, a Progressive leader, noted before the 1946 election: "Most Progressives are very bitter at McMurray for his attacks on Bob. Whatever they feel about McCarthy, they will always remember that it was McMurray who knifed Bob in the back." Richard Haney, "A History of the Democratic Party in Wisconsin since World War II," Ph.D. dissertation, University of Wisconsin, 1970, p. 25.

9. Most studies of McCarthy's career have noted his "discovery" of the Communist issue in 1950. See, Richard Rovere, *Senator Joe McCarthy* (Cleveland: World Publishing Co., 1960), pp. 119–20; Eric Goldman, *The Crucial Decade* (New York: Knopf, 1956), pp. 134–35; Earl Latham, *The Communist Controversy in Washington* (Cambridge: Harvard University Press, 1966), pp. 268–84. Recent evidence, however, suggests that McCarthy used the Communist issue often and effectively before 1950. See, Michael O'Brien, "McCarthy and McCarthyism," in Robert Griffith and Athan Theoharis, *The Specter* (New York: Franklin-Watts, 1974), pp. 224–40; Les Adler, "McCarthyism: The Advent and the Decline," *Continuum* 7 (Autumn 1968): 404–10.

10. U.S., Congress, *Congressional Record*, 79th Cong., 2d sess., 1946, 92, pt. 11:A3441.

James Kem of Missouri based his campaign on the issue of subversion in government; President Truman, he claimed, was "soft on Communism."[11] In Wisconsin, Republican congressional candidates Charles Kersten ("Put Kersten in Congress and Keep Communism Out") and Alvin O'Konski ran almost exclusively on their promises to rid the federal bureaucracy of "Communists," "New Dealers," and "Communist New Dealers."[12] In Nebraska, Senator Hugh Butler told his supporters that "if the New Deal is still in control of Congress after the election, it will owe that control to the Communist Party in this country."[13] Perhaps GOP stalwart Kenneth Wherry made the point most clearly: "The coming campaign is not just another election. It is a crusade."[14]

To make matters worse, the deterioration of U.S.–Soviet relations offered conservative Republicans and other antiunion forces an opportunity to condemn organized labor for "coddling Communists" and "stirring up trouble" in order to weaken America's position in the world. The Hearst-owned *San Antonio Light* declared that the rash of postwar strikes was part of "a clear and distinct revolutionary pattern . . . timed to serve Russia's political interests," while Charles Wilson, president of General Motors, noted that the two great problems facing America were "Russia abroad" and "labor at home."[15] Some Republicans also did everything possible to inform the voters about their plans to fight "labor Communists." "A Vote for Richard Nixon is a Vote Against the Communist Dominated PAC," read the campaign slogan of one California congressional candidate. In Wisconsin, O'Konski told rural audiences that his strong stand against Bolsheviks and other labor trouble makers had led Joe Stalin to send "a CIO-PAC fieldman to purge me."[16]

Oddly enough, few historians have attempted to study McCarthy's political behavior during the 1946 senatorial election campaign. By simply assuming that he stumbled upon the Communist issue in 1950, they have all but ignored his earlier Red-baiting episodes. This is a mistake, for the evidence suggests that even by the rather vigorous

11. Ronald Johnson, "The Communist Issue in Missouri, 1946–1956," Ph.D. dissertation, University of Missouri, 1973, pp. 9–10.
12. *Milwaukee Journal*, October 24, 1946. *Superior Evening Telegram*, November 4, 1946.
13. Justus Paul, "The Political Career of Senator Hugh Butler," Ph.D. dissertation, University of Nebraska, 1966, p. 249.
14. H.A. Dalstrom, "Kenneth S. Wherry," Ph.D. dissertation, University of Nebraska, 1965, p. 591.
15. Quoted in Les Adler, "The Red Image: American Attitudes Toward Communism in the Cold War," Ph.D. dissertation, University of California, Berkeley, 1970, p. 74.
16. *Superior Evening Telegram*, November 4, 1946.

mudslinging standards of 1946 the Wisconsinite took a back seat to no politician in his exploitation of voter anxiety over the spread of communism.

McCarthy began his campaign with a visit to the Chicago office of right-wing newspaper publisher Robert McCormick. Although he claimed that the discussion carried no political significance, Wisconsin unionists were prepared for the worst. "McCarthy has been down to Chicago for a chat with McCormick, who says the Democratic party is controlled by the Reds," noted the *Racine Labor*. "Is McCarthy to be his stooge?"[17] A few days later, a group known as American Action Incorporated, with the stated purpose of defeating radicals and Communists for Congress, moved into Wisconsin to mastermind the political defeats of Howard McMurray and U.S. congressional candidates Andrew Biemiller and Edmund Bobrowicz. The group was headed by Lansing Hoyt, a former state chairman of the America First Committee, and financed by McCormick and several notorious antilabor industrialists, including Robert E. Wood of Sears, Roebuck; Lammot duPont of E.I. DuPont deNemours; and Ernest T. Weir of Weirton Steel.[18] In a moment of rare candor, one AAI official admitted that although his organization was interested in ferreting out Communists from the federal government, its primary purpose was to force Congress to crack down on militant industrial unionism. "So long as there is a Democratic majority in both houses," he related, "the national CIO-PAC will dominate congressional policies. Therefore, a Republican majority is a necessity in this emergency."[19]

At first, McCarthy denied any affiliation with American Action Incorporated, claiming that if it were part of the old America First Committee he did not want its support. But as the campaign progressed, a series of bizarre events led him to modify his position. The issue first came into focus when Fred Blau, chairman of the Wisconsin Communist party, wrote an open letter to the *Daily Worker* endorsing Howard McMurray's candidacy.[20] Ironically, it went virtually unnoticed until several weeks later when Socialist leader Norman Thomas told an audience in Milwaukee that McMurray's failure to repudiate the *Daily Worker*'s endorsement seemed understandable in light of his recent attacks upon Senator LaFollette's anti-Soviet position. "Does McMurray intend to accept the 'fellow traveler' label

17. *Racine Labor*, October 11, 1946.
18. John Spivak, *The 'Save the Country' Racket* (New York: Specter, 1948), p. 51.
19. Ibid., pp. 45–50. *Milwaukee Journal*, October 7, 1946.
20. *Daily Worker*, August 21, 1946.

the *Daily Worker* pinned on him," Thomas asked bitterly, "or was he just hard up for an issue, knowing the excellence of LaFollette's domestic record when he attacked foreign policy?"[21] Before long, the issue became a *cause célèbre* in Wisconsin's predominantly Republican press. Identical editorials appeared in the *Green Bay Press-Gazette* and the *Appleton Post-Crescent*:

> Mr. McMurray has been silent thus far [about the Blau endorsement] yet there are many sincere Democrats in this state who are doubtless troubled by the company some of the Wisconsin New Dealers have been keeping. Does Mr. McMurray repudiate the Communists who have infiltrated into the New Deal political machine in this state? Or does he crave political success so deeply that he would accept any support disregarding its origin and sinister purpose? Mr. Thomas has issued a serious challenge.[22]

McCarthy went a step further by insinuating that the *Daily Worker*'s endorsement of McMurray was proof of his opponent's disloyalty. Furthermore, he no longer saw any political advantage in disavowing his formal connections with American Action Incorporated. At an open forum in Milwaukee, the judge, after some heckling by McMurray supporters, retorted that "if American Action Incorporated is organized to help fight Communism as they say then I welcome their help in defeating Communists and those who are Communistically inclined like Howard McMurray."[23] This inflammatory remark —so very similar to those he would employ four years later—brought McMurray instantly to his feet.

McMurray. I have never had a responsible citizen—I say responsible citizen—challenge my loyalty to America before. I am sure my friends and my students in my political science courses of past years will not challenge my loyalty. This statement is a little below the belt. I'll leave the answer to the voters.

McCarthy. I said that for the benefit of Howard McMurray. But I also want to ask him, does he not welcome the endorsement of the *Daily Worker*, which referred to him in a recent issue as a "fellow traveler" according to quotations in the *Appleton Post-Crescent* and the *Green Bay Press Gazette*?

McMurray. I welcome that question. I have not seen the reported statement in the *Daily Worker*, nor comments of those two reaction-

21. *Milwaukee Journal*, August 26, 1946.
22. *Green Bay Press-Gazette*, September 6, 1946. *Appleton Post-Crescent*, September 6, 1946.
23. *Milwaukee Journal*, October 17, 1946.

ary newspapers in Appleton and Green Bay. I certainly repudiate that paper [*Daily Worker*] and their whole tribe.[24]

With the issue now squarely before the public, McCarthy decided to make the most of it. The first step was an AAI-financed announcement distributed to Wisconsin newspapers, which read:

> Some candidates for high office running as Democrats have been repudiated because they have been proven to have Communist backgrounds and Communist ways of thinking. Others have been touched with suspicion but the proof is lacking. Joseph R. McCarthy is 100 percent American in thought and deed. . . . This is America. . . . Let's have Americans in government.[25]

As the campaign progressed, McCarthy continued to hammer away at the alleged disloyalty of the opposition party and its candidates. During a speech in Appleton, he told his followers that the Democratic party was controlled by men "with foreign inclinations, yes, foreign obligations. I, too, have responsibilities," he concluded, "but mine are to the people of this country."[26] McCarthy soon reiterated the point by graphically informing a gathering at Janesville that America had been "victimized by a seditious serpent which has us wrapped up in its conniving constrictions until we stand in a perilous position. All Democrats are not Communists. . . . But enough are voting the Communist way to make their presence in Congress a serious threat to . . . our nation."[27] Like O'Konski, he too claimed that the Kremlin leaders in Moscow had personally singled him out for defeat in 1946. One reporter following the campaign wrote disgustedly that "this phony business Judge McCarthy is pulling . . . is an excellent clinical study of how Red Scares are manufactured."[28]

McCarthy also used every opportunity to show that his opponent's alleged affinity for subversive ideas was an outgrowth of his intellectual arrogance and his contempt for the common people. When, for example, he asked McMurray in open debate why so many Democrats supported Henry Wallace's policy of "turning Eastern Europe over to Soviet domination," McMurray replied that Wallace had no intention of abandoning Europe and would come to Madison that very week to discuss his ideas "in words the people of Wisconsin

24. Ibid., October 17, 1946.
25. Ibid., October 24, 1946.
26. *Appleton Post-Crescent*, October 25, 1946.
27. *Janesville Daily Gazette*, October 30, 1946.
28. Miles McMillin, quoted in the *Madison Capital-Times*, October 27, 1946.

can understand." McCarthy took immediate offense at this statement, claiming that the people did not have to be "talked down to." A rather embarrassed McMurray was forced to explain that Wallace was simply coming to "clarify his views," and that the Democratic party certainly respected the intelligence of the Wisconsin electorate.[29]

Even more convincing was McCarthy's performance before a predominantly rural crowd near Eau Claire. He was in the midst of a speech condemning the Democratic Administration for attempting to "Communize and Sovietize the farmers of Wisconsin" through the use of "bureaucratic experts" when a woman from the audience (who was probably a McCarthy campaign worker with a prepared question) interrupted him in midsentence to ask what educational qualifications or political experience he had to compare with those of his opponent. To a rousing ovation, McCarthy replied proudly: "I'm just a farm boy, not a professor."[30] A week later, advertisements appeared in rural newspapers throughout the state proclaiming: "We need practical farmborn men in Washington. There are too many professors there now."

As expected, McCarthy's charges of subversion and disloyalty were widely publicized by the state's Republican press. These newspapers' strategy was simply to bury McMurray under a sordid pile of allegations and innuendos. The *Green Bay Press-Gazette* claimed that the Democratic nominee was "in favor of the enemies of our country. When Judge McCarthy faced the Japs on Guadalcanal," it continued, "he became accustomed to men like McMurray, but it should be said that even the wily Japs had some courage."[31] An editorial appearing in the *Waukesha Daily Freeman* opined that McCarthy's victory would serve the forces of democracy, not totalitarianism, while the *Oshkosh Daily Northwestern* warned its readers not to vote for a man endorsed by the Communists.[32] Similar editorials appeared in the *Wisconsin State Journal*, the *Milwaukee Sentinel*, and the *Janesville Gazette*.[33] Worst of all, perhaps, was the behavior of the *Appleton Post-Crescent*, which called McMurray "a noisy, blatant, unbearably egoistic gentleman upon whom the American editor of the *Moscow Pravda* slobbered," and repeatedly

29. John Steinke, "The Rise of McCarthyism," M.A. thesis, University of Wisconsin, 1960, p. 155.
30. *Milwaukee Journal*, October 23, 1946.
31. *Green Bay Press-Gazette*, November 2, 1946.
32. *Waukesha Daily Freeman*, November 4, 1946. *Oshkosh Daily Northwestern*, October 29, 1946.
33. *Wisconsin State Journal*, November 2, 1946. *Milwaukee Sentinel*, November 1, 1946. *Janesville Daily Gazette*, October 30, 1946.

dared him to repudiate the *Daily Worker* long after the candidate had done so.[34] The message, of course, was quite clear: McCarthy was the man who would combat, not condone, New Deal subversion.

* * *

At the outset of his senatorial campaign, McCarthy employed a relatively moderate posture in relation to labor-management problems. As was the case in the latter stages of his primary battle against LaFollette, the judge continued to admonish the "hard-headed extremists" of both sides for the continued growth of postwar industrial discord. Cooperation was possible, he claimed, where sane, responsible thinking prevailed.[35] McCarthy also issued an occasional position paper on labor in which he advanced the principles of good faith in collective bargaining, impartial mediation, and cooling-off periods before strikes, or cited instances of harmonious industrial relations, as in Wisconsin's Fox River Valley where the paper mills were "shining examples of what sensible managerial leadership and high class unions could do for the benefit of the workingman."[36] Indeed, the candidate appeared to be so neutral in matters pertaining to labor and management that the *Kenosha Labor* believed he was "purposely making a diligent effort to appear to be all things to all people."[37]

However, as the more explosive issue of communism in America pervaded his thoughts, McCarthy had neither the time nor the inclination to formulate a comprehensive labor plank. He therefore used the same four-point program for unions that had served him so well throughout the primary campaign, and whenever and wherever asked about labor-management problems the candidate fell back instinctively upon his trusty rhetoric. In one instance, this reliance upon mindless recall proved quite unsettling. At a question and answer session in Madison, McCarthy quickly rattled off the first three points but then began to stutter. He simply could not remember the fourth point. When someone in the audience called out, "compulsory arbitration," McCarthy thanked him and began discussing that subject. Unfortunately, the crowd was well versed on the judge's program for labor and knew that compulsory arbitration had never been on the list. As the laughter mounted, McCarthy stopped his discourse and

34. *Appleton Post-Crescent*, November 2, 1946.
35. Ibid., October 2, 1946.
36. Ibid.
37. *Kenosha Labor*, September 26, 1946.

returned to his seat on the platform—slightly embarrassed but possibly relieved to discover that the voters were as tired of listening to his redundant statements as he was of giving them.[38]

The mood soon turned uglier. As McCarthy worked to impress the state's traditional Republican majority, his remarks became far more forceful. He began by altering his earlier claims about the "few hard-headed extremists" who were "causing the vast majority of strikes." The root of most labor-management problems, he charged, could now be traced to a labor-New Deal coalition that had "played along with the Communists who know that their theories will grow best in an economy of industrial discord and strikes."[39] Not surprisingly, the best way to deal with this problem was to "get tough," to show the "radical Eastern labor bosses" that America would not tolerate their abusive and unwarranted actions. On the state level, too, McCarthy hammered away at the Democratic party's affinity for trade union militants by alleging that his opponent, Howard McMurray, was "little more than a megaphone . . . being used by the Communist-dominated Political Action Committee in Milwaukee" to foster dangerous class hatreds.[40] This campaign soon took its toll; by election day many Wisconsinites seemed to believe that a vote for McMurray was an endorsement of radical New Dealism, eastern bossism, and militant industrial unionism.[41]

*   *   *

The election results were a foregone conclusion. By identifying himself closely with Republican interests and issues in a predominantly Republican state, McCarthy carried seventy of seventy-three counties and won by a margin of almost two to one. His political career had taken him (opportunistically if not ideologically) from the New Dealism of his early days in Shawano clear across the political spectrum to the regular Republicanism of Thomas Coleman and the VRC. McCarthy went to the Senate as basically an antilabor, anti-New Deal conservative—a position he was to maintain until his death a decade later.

38. *Madison Capital-Times*, October 17, 1946.
39. *Wisconsin State Journal*, October 20, 1946.
40. *Milwaukee Journal*, October 24, 1946.
41. *Madison Capital-Times*, November 1, 1946.

Chapter 5

Wisconsin's Junior Senator

I

Within a period of four months, the meteoric political rise of Joseph McCarthy had taken him from an obscure county judgeship to the United States Senate. Yet, aside from his seemingly personable nature, Wisconsinites knew little about their newest elected official. His campaigns against LaFollette and McMurray, rather than centering on the crucial issues of the day, had been negatively oriented to their personal and political deficiencies. Therefore, in an effort to acquaint his readers with the McCarthy philosophy, Lawrence Eklund of the *Milwaukee Journal* interviewed the new senator at length. "In talking with McCarthy," he wrote, "one gets the impression that he will make a record as a liberal Republican, and he will be closer to the Republicans of the type of former Governor Harold Stassen and Senators Wayne Morse of Oregon and Joseph Ball of Minnesota than he will be to Senator Robert A. Taft of Ohio, the apparent conservative choice for president in 1948." To which McCarthy replied confidently: "I feel that all of the new and younger men in Congress will serve as a nucleus for a really forward-looking Republican party —one geared to 1948 and 1952 and 1956 rather than the 1920's."[1]

In falling prey to the senator's rhetoric, Eklund surprisingly overlooked the most obvious barometer for future McCarthy action: the nature of his political support. In the Republican primary, and later in the senatorial election, McCarthy had been billed as a conservative, as an anti-New Dealer, and, most important, as an antidote to Wisconsin's long-standing Progressive tradition. As the candidate of Tom Coleman, McCarthy was, in the words of one journalist, "financed and engineered . . . by a consortium of Wisconsin businessmen . . . who were fed up with the suspected Socialist leanings of Robert M. LaFollette, Jr."[2] To have expected the new senator to follow the liberal Republican line was to overlook completely the significant developments of the 1946 elections.

In actuality, Joseph McCarthy gave unwavering support to the conservative wing of the Republican party throughout his career in

1. *Milwaukee Journal*, November 20, 1946.
2. Charles J.V. Murphy, "McCarthy and the Businessman," *Fortune* 49 (April 1954): 156.

the United States Senate. His dedicated work in behalf of the business lobbies, his inconsistent though traceable antilabor outlook, and his conservative voting record offer ample proof of his conservative persuasion. In this chapter, McCarthy's early career in the Senate— the three years before he allegedly discovered Communists in the State Department—will be covered, with particular emphasis placed on the factors just mentioned. It is imperative to begin with these early years because they provide a foundation for the McCarthy philosophy, which became so distorted in the hectic years that followed.

II

Joseph McCarthy entered the United States Senate during the period known as "reconversion." Americans, tired of a wartime economy with its multiplicity of restrictions and chronic shortages of consumer goods, yearned for a return to normal conditions. Unfortunately, there seemed to be conflicting viewpoints on how to best bring this about. Organized labor saw the need for a reconversion with modified supervision, which meant the rigid enforcement of price controls and the scrapping of wage controls. Industry, on the other hand, desired the retention of wage controls and the elimination of price controls. It soon became clear that this dichotomy between industry and labor was reaching alarming proportions. Many businessmen, remembering the strong antilabor sentiment that gripped America after World War I, envisioned a golden opportunity to severely weaken their labor opponents.[3] Similarly, the unions, faced with rising prices, lower real wages, and growing unemployment, felt the need for immediate action before their bargaining powers were destroyed.[4]

The country was soon plagued by a wave of strikes. In the year's

3. See, National Association of Manufacturers, *Freedom From Victory: A Program Adopted by the War and Reconversion Committee of American Industry*, New York, 1944; Eric Goldman, *The Crucial Decade* (New York: Knopf, 1956), pp. 16–45; Philip Taft, *Organized Labor in American History* (New York: Harper and Row, 1964), pp. 563–78.

4. Unfortunately for organized labor, President Truman decided to lift price controls before he abolished wage controls. As the Bureau of Labor Standards noted, this policy led to a drastic drop of 16.3 per cent in the average real wage of production workers. In an open letter to Truman, Walter Reuther stated that "because prices continue their inflationary climb and . . . price controls are virtually nonexistant . . . we urge you to abolish immediately the National Wage Stabilization Board and that you strip other government officials of any wartime authority they might have to veto wage increases." *New York Times*, October 26, 1946.

time after Japan's capitulation, 4.9 million workers were involved in 4,630 work stoppages totaling 119.8 million worker's days of labor.[5] The following year was even worse; within a six-month period the major industries of America—steel, coal, auto, and transportation—were shut down. As one strike would end only to be followed by two more, there was a noticeable increase in antilabor sentiment. It was the second mine walkout in four months, however, that added a touch of hysteria to an already aggravated situation.

After accepting the Lewis-Krug agreement of May 29, 1946, which ended a forty-day mine strike, John L. Lewis, president of the United Mine Workers, suddenly called for another strike. The agreement, he claimed, had been violated by the government.[6] As Lewis led his miners from the pits for the second time, public resentment, already aflame over labor strife and the painfully slow course of reconversion, was heaped upon the entire movement. "If this government has not the power to outlaw strikes of this character," the usually prolabor Senator Scott Lucas of Illinois steamed, "then this government has not the power of self-preservation." Lucas then proposed a congressional investigation of all labor organizations to determine whether any union leaders "wielded autocratic power."[7]

Joseph McCarthy arrived in Washington at the height of the furor and immediately called a press conference to air his views on the strike. Since he had not as yet been sworn into office, his presumptuous nature attracted several curious reporters. McCarthy stated:

5. "Work Stoppages Caused by Labor-Management Disputes in 1945," *Monthly Labor Review* 62 (April 1946): 718–35.

6. On May 29, 1946, Lewis signed a contract with the government (acting in conjunction with the mine operators). The new agreement (Lewis-Krug agreement) gave the union an across-the-board wage increase of $.185 per hour, a welfare and retirement fund financed by a nickel-a-ton royalty on all coal mined, and a guarantee by the mine operators of mandatory compliance with the Federal Mine Safety Code. The union hailed the contract as a smashing victory, while the mine operators were "amazed that what we feared had happened, despite the appeal to Secretary Krug to face the possibilities raised by such sweeping concessions to the union." But the operators promised to honor the contract. Suddenly, Julius Krug, the man who had negotiated the contract for the mine owners, was accused by Lewis of making unilateral changes in the agreement. Lewis claimed that miners who had changed or quit their jobs were frozen out of many benefits and that the owners were computing the nickel-a-ton royalties on the basis of railroad weight rather than tipple weight (which is the weight before coal is washed and dusted). Krug denied any breach of contract and warned Lewis that the government would deal severely with a wildcat strike. Nevertheless, Lewis stated that his union considered the contract dead, and the miners walked off their jobs. See, Saul Alinsky, *John L. Lewis: An Unauthorized Biography* (New York: Vintage Books, 1949), pp. 325–45.

7. *New York Times*, December 10, 1946.

I believe that the President should use his powers to immediately draft John L. Lewis into the armed forces. Lewis should be directed to mine coal. If he does not he should be court martialed. We should go straight down the line. If subordinates of Lewis fail to order the men back to work they should be court martialed. All this talk that you can't put 400,000 miners in jail is a lot of stuff. They won't go to jail. They'll mine coal first.[8]

The senator's proposal was not a novel one. In fact, he borrowed the idea from President Truman, who had used similar threats to end the railway strike only seven months earlier. "As part of this temporary legislation," Truman had then stated, "I request the Congress immediately to authorize the President to draft into the armed forces of the United States all workers who are on strike against their government."[9] The stale quality of McCarthy's idea was adequately reflected by the amount of publicity it received. Although the story was picked up by the *New York Times*, it created little commotion. The *United Mine Workers' Journal*, devoting full issues to strike coverage, pro and con, overlooked the McCarthy proposal completely, as did the entire labor press. Ironically, the only other notable mention Wisconsin's senator-elect received was from the *Army and Navy Bulletin*, an unofficial service publication, which criticized him for turning "a noble calling" into a vast penal institution. "Compulsory enrollment," it continued, "was a punitive measure which reflects discredit upon its author."[10]

McCarthy's failure to become a central figure in the coal strike may well have irked him even more than the criticism he received, for as one national magazine was later to note, "he had a horror of senators who quietly tended their fences and got safely re-elected term after term."[11] McCarthy was a man who thrived on controversy and the publicity that inevitably arose from it. However, in attempting to upstage John L. Lewis, long an American symbol of defiance and nonconformism, the freshman senator was in over his head.

*   *   *

As labor strife continued to hinder reconversion efforts, there developed strong public opinion for legislation designed to curb the abuses of unionism. A Gallup Poll conducted in December of 1946

8. Ibid., December 6, 1946.
9. Ibid., May 25, 1946.
10. Ibid., December 7, 1946.
11. "Weighed in the Balance," *Time* 58 (October 22, 1951): 23.

on the question, "Should Congress in this coming legislative session pass new laws to control labor unions?" indicated 66 per cent affirmative, 22 per cent negative, and 12 per cent undecided.[12] Furthermore, with anti-New Deal Republicans controlling both houses of Congress, it seemed clear that such legislation would not be long in coming.

In the first two months of 1947, more than sixty bills and amendments dealing with national labor policy were proposed in Congress. One such bill, S. 327, was forwarded by Joseph McCarthy.[13] The McCarthy proposal was divided into three parts. First, it approved of a maintenance of membership clause in a labor contract if there were a suitable escape clause.

> Nothing contained in this section shall preclude an employer from making an agreement with a labor organization to require employees who are members of such labor organizations to maintain such membership as a condition to the continuation of their employment, if under the terms of such agreement employees who are members of such labor organizations are afforded a reasonable time to withdraw from such membership.

Second, the bill approved of a union shop if two-thirds of the employees desired such an arrangement.

> It shall be an unfair labor practice for an employer—to hire or continue in his employ, within a collective bargaining unit, an employee who is not a member of such organization, or who has not become a member of such organization within sixty days following the day on which he became employed within such unit, if two-thirds of the employees within such unit have voted in an election to exclude from employment within such unit, persons who are not members of such labor organizations.

Third, the proposal prevented an employer from discriminating against any person who had been expelled from the union for any reason except nonpayment of dues.

> It shall be an unfair labor practice for an employer——to discriminate in regard to hiring, tenure, or conditions of employment, against any person for any reason except nonpayment of an initiation fee or other fee assessed against all members of a labor organization.

12. R. Alton Lee, *Truman and Taft-Hartley* (Lexington: University Press of Kentucky, 1966), p. 52.
13. John Fitch, "The New Congress and the Unions," *Survey-Graphic* 36 (April 1947): 231. *S. 327*, 80th Cong., 1st sess. (June 24, 1947).

Although Senator McCarthy's proposal was virtually ignored by the national labor press, it was afforded a critical review in Wisconsin journals. Labor analysts there viewed the bill with contempt; to their thinking it was simply another measure by the Coleman forces to weaken effective trade unionism. It was noted in a lead article entitled, "McCarthy—Is His Name Joe or Charlie," in the *Madison Union Labor News* that the first two points of McCarthy's proposal were acceptable with minor modifications. Point three, however, was the one that really mattered. Its effect "would be to take the power to discipline members away from the unions and place scabs under the protection of the boss. . . . Under McCarthy's bill, a man could connive with the boss to work for less than the union scale or to undermine conditions in some way, and the union would be helpless to discipline such a traitor." The McCarthy proposal was seen as "an entering wedge for conniving employers and scab-hearted workers to break the union."[14]

This harsh reaction seemed way out of proportion to the dangers in Senator McCarthy's proposal. In fact, considering the desire of both Congress and the American people to pass legislation controlling many aspects of unionism, McCarthy's stood out as one of the proposals least offensive to the labor movement. Of the twelve other bills and amendments before Congress dealing with the closed shop or union shop, ten either prohibited such contracts (with fines for such violations averaging $5,000), or made them unfair labor practices.[15] As for the other two, one bill offered by Senator Wayne Morse, the Oregon Republican, made it an unfair labor practice for unions to strike in order to obtain the closed shop; the other, sponsored by Republican Senator Irving Ives of New York, stated that an employer was not committing an unfair labor practice by refusing to bargain over the closed shop issue.[16]

Furthermore, a comparison of Senator McCarthy's proposal with the Taft-Hartley bill, which was enacted four months later, reemphasized its benign quality. Besides outlawing the closed shop, the Taft-Hartley bill allowed the individual states to enact "right to work" laws that prohibited compulsory membership in a union shop. It also enumerated a series of unfair labor practices and other restrictive clauses ranging from the filing of financial reports and non-Communist affidavits by union officers to strict controls on political contributions. In the case of S. 327, at least, the reaction of Wisconsin labor leaders was based less on the merits of McCarthy's proposal

---

14. *Madison Union Labor News*, February, 1947.
15. Fitch, "The New Congress and the Unions," p. 232.
16. Ibid.

than on the credentials of those persons supporting the junior senator. As early as 1947, McCarthy was viewed as a legislative puppet (as was evident from the headline, "McCarthy—Is His Name Joe or Charlie") whose strings were manipulated by Thomas Coleman and the state's conservative business interests.[17]

*   *   *

While McCarthy's proposal was certainly not in keeping with the Republican outlook, a statement he made a week later on a new labor agreement in the building trades was even less so. On February 2, 1947, a contract was signed by several large construction unions and their managerial counterparts that was considered favorable to both sides. While leading Republican legislators were pleased with the outcome of these negotiations, they were also somewhat apprehensive, fearing that such favorable publicity might well temper the prevailing antilabor sentiment in America. Senator Homer Capehart of Indiana, a spokesman for conservative Republicanism, personified this belief, calling the agreement "a step in the right direction," but quickly added his hope that it would not stop Congress "from enacting constructive labor legislation."[18]

In almost a direct rebuttal to the Capehart statement, Senator McCarthy lauded the building trades agreement, claiming that it would negate much of the antiunion feeling in the nation and "make unnecessary . . . some of the drastic steps that have been proposed."[19] Not only did he realize the value of this new settlement in pacifying an aroused public, but by using the term "drastic steps" McCarthy seemed to indicate that much of the pending legislation was misguided and unfair.

A short while later, however, McCarthy changed his position by stating that if certain restrictive practices within the construction unions were not controlled, the government would have to intercede in the public's interest. At a hearing before the Senate Banking and

17. It is difficult to determine what motivated McCarthy to initiate his labor proposal. Possibly he was trying to win the favor of union leaders by authoring a bill that, while favorable to their interests, had no real chance for passage. But he may have had another motive in mind. Since the bill was doomed from the very outset, it offered him an excellent opportunity to exert his legislative independence from Tom Coleman and other conservative state Republicans without doing any real damage to the conservative cause. Both of these theories were offered during interviews with George Haberman, Loren Norman, and Miles McMillin.

18. *New York Times*, February 2, 1947.

19. Ibid.

Currency Committee on the issue of public housing, the Wisconsinite accused several unions of drastically increasing the cost of housing. In what seemed to be an authoritative statement, he noted that restrictions on the size of brushes used by union painters, the failure of union plumbers to use sandpaper in the preparation of joints (because sandpaper increases the speed of output), and the demand of many unions that more than one journeyman be used on jobs that could easily be handled by a single man were but a few of hundreds of instances in which organized labor had purposely inflated the price of a home. His remarks precipitated a heated exchange with Boris Shiskin, AFL national housing director.

McCarthy. We are both concerned with creating more housing. Let me ask you: Do you know of any practices in the building trade unions that cause an increase in the cost of housing?

Shiskin. No. I have been the recipient of many charges emanating to a large extent . . . from the National Association of Home Builders and other lobby organizations that have been publicizing certain allegations in general terms.

McCarthy. We find, Mr. Shiskin, that when we attempt to eliminate those practices we are promptly dubbed as anti-labor. . . . You do not mean that you are not aware of all these restrictions and restrictive practices that are being indulged in by the building trades unions? . . .

Shiskin. What seems appalling to me is that at the time when a $3,000 home is being sold on the real estate market for $10,000 or $12,000 that the real estate people can get away with putting the blame for this high speculative price on labor.[20]

Although McCarthy was certainly correct in his assumption that many construction unions were increasing the cost of housing through their coercive practices, his failure to indict private builders for their skyrocketing prices enraged the labor movement. Worse still, the sketchy nature of his research left him open for a successful counterattack. Less than two weeks after the initial confrontation, Shiskin revealed that all of McCarthy's charges were taken from two pages in a pre-World War II pamphlet published by the Brookings Institution and that the specific examples originated with the Cleveland Chamber of Commerce.[21] Although Shiskin took some delight in pointing out the folly of McCarthy's reliance upon outdated and obviously biased

20. U.S., Congress, Senate, Committee on Banking and Currency, *Hearings on Bills Pertaining to National Housing*, 80th Cong., 1st sess., 1947, p. 187.
21. *Madison Union Labor News*, May, 1947.

material, he could hardly have realized that the senator would shortly rise to a position of almost unchallenged authority by using similar tactics on a grander scale.

III

An analysis of Joseph McCarthy's participation in the deliberations leading up to passage of the Taft-Hartley Act is important because it offers yet another preview of the Communist-hunting techniques he was later to perfect. While the senator did not begin his investigations into domestic subversion until 1950, the possibility of exploiting this issue had occurred to him several times before. In the case of Taft-Hartley, however, only the strong argumentative powers of several senators, who were more concerned with constitutional safeguards on civil liberties than with alleged disloyalty, blunted McCarthy's initial probe.

The Taft-Hartley bill provided that union officials had to sign non-Communist affidavits each year. There had to be on file with the National Labor Relations Board "an affidavit executed contemporaneously or within each preceding twelve month period by each officer of such organization . . . that he is not a member of the Communist party . . . or that he does not believe in . . . the overthrow of the U.S. Government by force or illegal or unconstitutional means."[22] McCarthy wanted to amend the provision so as to allow members of individual unions to go before their employers in order to ask for the discharge of any employee who was removed from the union for Communist activities. "This amendment," McCarthy claimed, "was urged by a delegation of labor leaders who are interested in the rank-and-file of labor."[23]

Senator Warren Magnuson, the Washington Democrat, immediately called into question McCarthy's unclear definition of communism. Magnuson continued: "in my state there is a Communist party. . . . It does not receive many votes, but the party takes part in elections, and it is a legal political party and has a right to have its name on the ballot. . . . There are probably 2,000 or 3,000 who vote in the state of Washington. Would it [McCarthy's amendment] include them regardless of whether the party was legal?" Magnuson's question brought an angry response from the Wisconsinite.

McCarthy. What does the senator mean by legal? Does he refer to the fact that the party can have its name on the ballot?

22. 61 Stat. 146 (1947), section 9 (5), Taft-Hartley Act.
23. U.S., Congress, *Congressional Record*, 80th Cong., 1st sess., 1947, 93, pt. 4:4880. The following debate is included in pp. 4880–83.

Magnuson. It is a legal party in the United States.
McCarthy. I do not think the Communist party is ever legal. It may be legal to have the name "Communist" on the ballot.

McCarthy was in no mood to haggle over legal technicalities. As Senator Magnuson attempted to explain to him the subtle constitutional issues involved, McCarthy retorted: "I submit that any man who joins the Communist party knowing that the Communist party is dedicated to the overthrow of the government by force, is guilty of treason the minute he joins it, regardless of whether or not the state allows the Communist party on the ballot."

Still, his colleagues were skeptical of the amendment. Millard Tydings, Maryland's Democratic senator, told McCarthy quite sternly that his examination "might turn into a witch hunt." Republican Senator Joseph Ball of Minnesota was more concerned with the effect of the amendment on the right of each individual to earn a living. "I agree that the only way to handle Communist infiltration in a union is to kick the Communists out," he stated, "but I do not think the government of this country should go a step further and say that when an individual is thrown out of the union on that ground, he is no longer entitled to the right to earn a living at that particular job." Perhaps the most significant comment of all came from Senator Magnuson when, half in jest, he told McCarthy, "I think that the senator ought to advocate a bill outlawing the Communist party in America."

The defeat of Senator McCarthy's amendment did not, however, change his favorable attitude towards the Taft-Hartley bill. Not only did he cast ballots in favor of both the Senate version on May 13, 1947, and the joint Senate-House version on June 6, but he also helped to make the bill official by voting to override President Truman's veto on June 23. Furthermore, in the coming years he consistently opposed any amendment designed to weaken or delete sections of the act.[24] On Taft-Hartley, certainly the most important piece of labor legislation of that era, McCarthy remained a true Republican.

IV

Following the Taft-Hartley Act, few significant labor proposals were discussed by Congress. Senator McCarthy concerned himself with several issues indirectly affecting organized labor but took only two stands on basic labor matters, each with little success. In June of

24. See McCarthy's domestic voting record, pp. 83–85.

1949, he chastised President Truman for his "failure to re-create a strong Labor Department," claiming that he was "very much disturbed to find that the President . . . even though allegedly a friend of labor, had failed in this all-important task . . . when Congress gave him unlimited authority to do so."[25] McCarthy failed to mention, however, that he and his fellow Republicans had recently voted down Presidential Reorganization Plan Number 1, a program supported unanimously by organized labor, which would have given President Truman the power to do exactly what McCarthy claimed he was not doing: re-create a strong Labor Department with all of its former powers and subdivisions intact.[26]

Of greater importance was an amendment proposed by Senator McCarthy in May of 1949 to establish a minimum wage for all teachers in states receiving allotments for educational purposes from the federal government. The reason for such an amendment, he told Congress, was that "we cannot hope to get a sufficient number of high-grade teachers if we pay salaries presently being paid in some of the states."[27] McCarthy was criticized immediately by Senator Elbert Thomas, Democrat from Utah, "for interfering with the principle that the federal government shall make no prescriptions in regard to anything which specifically refers to persons in schools."[28] The amendment was overwhelmingly defeated.

Ironically, as was the case with his proposal concerning the Labor Department, Senator McCarthy's federal minimum wage for teachers was not in keeping with his past record. In 1948, for example, he was one of only twenty-one senators who voted against the Federal Education Bill, which provided $300 million in additional funds for the improvement of state educational facilities. Even such long-standing conservatives as Ohio's Senator Robert A. Taft voted for the bill because of the chronic shortage of trained personnel, buildings, and equipment in many of the poorer states.[29] Here again, the

25. U.S., Congress, *Congressional Record*, 81st Cong., 1st sess., 1949, 95, pt. 6:8018.
26. Under the presidential reorganization plan, the U.S. Employment Service and other subdivisions would have been kept in the Department of Labor.
27. U.S., Congress, *Congressional Record*, 81st Cong., 1st sess., 1949, 95, pt. 4:5594.
28. Ibid.
29. When the Federal Education bill was before Congress, Senator Taft stated: "I believe the federal government should aid education in those states in which the income is less than the national average." See, Caroline Harnsberger, *A Man of Courage: Robert A. Taft* (New York: Wilcox and Follett, 1952), pp. 298–305.

inconsistency between Senator McCarthy's voting record and the legislation he proposed is quite apparent. One wonders whether he took any of these labor proposals seriously; certainly his legislative colleagues did not.

V

During his first three years in Congress, Senator McCarthy became known for his work in behalf of the business lobbies. One national magazine claimed that in this period "he took an interest in ending sugar rationing, in five-percenters, got himself appointed vice-chairman of a joint committee on housing, and was viewed as a friend of the real estate lobby."[30] Because of his active involvement with lobbyists, McCarthy was forced into direct conflict with organized labor on several crucial issues. The most important of these concerned the necessity of federal intervention in the housing field. No one could deny that a severe housing shortage existed. The controversy centered around who could best remedy the situation; the government, private industry, or a combination of both. In siding with the real estate interests, and especially the private, prefabricated housing group, Senator McCarthy opposed all government-financed housing programs. Labor, on the other hand, was clamoring for more active federal participation in this area.

In 1946, senators Taft, Ellender, and Wagner attempted to bring the opposing forces together by virtue of a legislative compromise. They offered a comprehensive proposal that provided not only for public low- and middle-income housing projects and veterans' co-operatives, but also for lucrative subsidies to private builders.[31] Veterans' organizations, civic groups, and the entire labor movement lobbied for its passage. Opposition came mainly from builders, contractors, and manufacturers of prefabricated homes.

During reconversion, labor leaders and the labor press spoke constantly of the need for immediate government action in the housing field. In the first five months of 1947, for example, the *Kenosha Labor* had banner headlines reading: "Housing For Everyone," "City Housing Survey Advocated by American Veterans Committee," "Republicans Oust Bill From Program—Say Housing Not A Must," "Home For Veterans Drive Endorsed," "Kenosha Mobilizes Against Housing

30. "The McCarthy Controversy," p. 23.
31. Richard Davies, *Housing Reform During the Truman Administration* (Columbia: University of Missouri Press, 1966), pp. 40–42.

Crisis," and "Housing Main Subject At Legion Meet."[32] When the Taft-Ellender-Wagner bill finally passed the Senate, labor pressure became more intense. "S. 1592 is the key to your new home," the *Madison Union Labor News* reminded its readers. "Urge Henry [Representative Robert J. Henry] to vote favorably."[33] President William Green of the AFL sent telegrams to all local union leaders, stating: "The postwar housing program supported by the AFL is contained in the General Housing Bill, S. 1592. . . . Every union member must help make his Congressman act now."[34]

To the dismay of Green and his allies, Representative Jesse Wolcott, chairman of the House Committee on Banking and Currency, refused to act on S. 1592 until the sections relating to public housing and slum clearance were removed. He then joined with senators McCarthy and Chappie Revercomb of West Virginia to postpone action on the proposal by introducing a resolution creating a joint congressional committee to study the housing problem "from A to Z." "Wolcott's resolution blandly ignored the work of Taft's subcommittee and the hearings on the T-E-W bill," wrote one historian. "This last minute action . . . was a deliberate cover-up for the procrastinations of the Eightieth Congress . . . and passed both Houses without a dissenting vote."[35]

On August 19, 1947, the joint committee met to choose its chairman and vice-chairman. Because Charles Tobey of New Hampshire was the senior Republican member of the group, the unwritten rules of the Senate entitled him to the chairmanship. McCarthy, however, was determined to block the appointment at all costs; he knew too well Tobey's deep antipathy for the real estate lobby. By privately canvassing all committee members in advance, the Wisconsinite learned that Tobey held the proxies of six public housing supporters who did not plan to attend the session. With all of his own supporters present, McCarthy moved that no proxies be accepted; "Let's play out our cards on the table here," he told the flabbergasted Tobey.[36]

32. The headlines, in order, are March 27, 1947; April 24, 1947; May 8, 1947; June 19, 1947; July 10, 1947; July 30, 1947.

33. *Madison Union Labor News*, March, 1947.

34. William Green to Otto Solberg, June 3, 1946, Papers of the Eau Claire Building and Construction Trades Council, Wisconsin State Historical Society.

35. Davies, *Housing Reform During the Truman Administration*, p. 67.

36. Jack Anderson and Ronald May, *McCarthy: The Man, the Senator, the 'Ism'* (Boston: Beacon Press, 1952), p. 142. In a letter to Senator Charles Tobey (R. New Hampshire) McCarthy minimized the importance of the meeting and intimated that Tobey's presence there was of no great importance. See, Senator Joe McCarthy to Senator Charles Tobey, August 19, 1947, Senator Charles Tobey Papers, Box 116, Manuscripts Division, Dartmouth College Library. Along with the letter are the proxies Tobey gathered from

Since he now had a majority of attending members on his side, Senator McCarthy's motion to ignore the proxies passed. Representative John Gamble, a conservative New York Republican, was elected chairman, while McCarthy graciously accepted the vice-chairmanship. After the meeting, he told reporters assembled outside the committee room, "I frankly didn't want Tobey to be chairman. He thinks the sole answer to the problem is public housing. I'm for public housing but its only part of the answer." Tobey, meanwhile, stormed from the room claiming that McCarthy was "guilty of bad faith and that the real estate lobby was behind the whole thing."[37]

Labor leaders were quite disturbed over McCarthy's appointment. They remembered not only his bitter clash with AFL Housing Director Boris Shiskin, but also the substantial financial support he received during his senatorial campaign from several of Wisconsin's prefabricated housing tycoons.[38] McCarthy's motive in dumping Tobey was apparent to them. "Because Tobey was supposedly favorable to public housing," wrote syndicated columnist Bradford Carter, "Senator McCarthy, the reactionary *enfant terrible*, engineered a deal wherein Gamble, less favorable to public housing, was made chairman of the committee. . . . He certainly knew what he was doing."[39]

Several factors became readily apparent as the joint committee began a series of hearings in the major American cities. First, although Representative Gamble was the chairman, it was Senator McCarthy who directed the investigation. Gamble, in fact, did not even bother to appear at the hearings. The scope of McCarthy's authority was amply documented in a letter he wrote to Gamble, which accompanied his interim report.

> Dear Congressman Gamble:
>
> I am forwarding to you . . . a brief general report in accordance with your request to members of the committee that each of them submit to you such report upon specific tasks assigned to them. As you, of course, know, no specific task was assigned to me, but you requested

---

senators Glen Taylor, John Sparkman, Robert Wagner, and Ralph Flanders, and representatives Hale Boggs and Albert Rains.

37. Quoted in the *New York Times*, August 27, 1947.

38. During the 1946 elections, several Wisconsin builders, contractors, and prefabricated housing men contributed significant sums of money to McCarthy's personal campaign fund. The most prominent of these donors was Walter Harnischfeger, a Milwaukee industrialist and an arch-conservative who had long been opposed to any form of public housing. See, Secretary of State of Wisconsin, *Political Contributions to the 1946 Election*, Folder 2062.

39. *Kenosha Labor*, December 10, 1947.

that I attend and act as chairman of all those hearings which you personally were unable to attend. In the course of this work, which included both formal hearings and informal conferences, I visited practically every major city in the country, and covered approximately 30,000 miles.[40]

Second, while the hearings were held allegedly to listen to differing viewpoints and to gather information, Senator McCarthy used his position as vice-chairman to inform the nation about the evils of public housing. His antics at the Milwaukee hearings provided a classic example of this bias. After loading the schedule with real estate lobbyists, private builders, contractors, lumbermen, and prefabricated housing experts, the senator told a representative of the Milwaukee Board of Realtors: "To put it another way, if the federal government says it is going to spend $100,000,000 to help these thousands of . . . veterans . . . who cannot be properly housed, then how can we get the greatest number of low rental units for the money we have. . . . I don't think it is through public housing. I think it is the most inefficient and wasteful agency we have had."[41]

McCarthy also sought to discredit the testimony of witnesses who supported the public housing provisions of the Taft-Ellender-Wagner bill. When a member of Racine's Housing Authority spoke highly of S. 1592, McCarthy tore him apart.

McCarthy. Do you favor all parts of the bill? Do you know anything about the bill?

Nordstrom. I read the bill and the bill proposes a decent home for every American family and that is a good goal.

McCarthy. In other words, you favor the preamble, and I think we all do.

Nordstrom. Yes.

McCarthy. Do you know what is in the bill? If you know what is in the bill, that is all right.

Nordstrom. I am not familiar enough with the bill to go into detail.

McCarthy. That seems to be the prime prerequisite for testifying for the bill, not knowing anything about it at all.[42]

40. U.S., Congress, *Congressional Record*, 80th Cong., 2d sess., 1948, 94, pt. 2:2819.

41. U.S., Congress, *Hearings Before the Joint Committee on Housing*, 80th Cong., 1st sess., 1947–1948, 1:2426.

42. Ibid., p. 2433. Not surprisingly, letters of protest began filtering back to other committee members in Washington. After an acrimonious public hearing in Pittsburgh, an angry supporter of the Taft-Ellender-Wagner bill

The senator's personal feelings on public housing were not confined exclusively to the hearings. When addressing an American Legion convention at Columbus, Ohio, McCarthy predicted defeat for the Taft-Ellender-Wagner bill because of its stand on public housing; he later told a group of veterans who had gathered on the Capitol steps that prefabricated housing was the answer to their problems. According to the *Kenosha Labor*, "the veterans replied with Bronx cheers."[43]

Third, the hearings were often marked by antiunion outbursts from McCarthy and his handpicked witnesses. When one Milwaukee builder, Francis Schroedel, charged local construction unions with certain illegal and coercive practices, the senator complimented him for his courage and honesty in bringing these facts to light. "I must say, Mr. Schroedel, without attempting to comment upon the testimony," McCarthy retorted, "that this is the type of material that ordinarily is offered to us behind closed doors or in secret sessions, and regardless of what I might think about the accuracy of what you say, I certainly have a lot of respect for a man who will come out and say publicly what most people are trying to give us behind closed doors or in secret sessions."[44] Unfortunately for McCarthy, Schroedel's testimony caused such an uproar that the builder was forced to come back that same afternoon in order to clarify some of the statements he had made in reference to the hiring practices of local carpenters, masons, cement finishers, and common laborers.[45]

McCarthy himself was alternately hostile and patronizing to his labor witnesses. He made headlines in Milwaukee by intimating that the scarcity of skilled labor in the building trades was due to the restrictive union apprenticeship programs, and he noted that the diverse Milwaukee building codes were responsible for "adding to the cost of building and standing as a definite roadblock in the way of mass production."[46] When an official of the Wisconsin Industrial Union

---

wrote to Senator Tobey: "I wish to protest the un-American manner in which Senator McCarthy conducted the housing probe in our city. He left no doubt that he is opposed to the TEW bill. . . . He was gracious with real estate and building representatives, but unfair and arbitrary with those who tried to present the real problems in housing . . . and the means with which to remedy the situation." Elizabeth Hutson to Senator Charles Tobey, October 29, 1947, Senator Charles Tobey Papers, Box 116, Manuscripts Division, Dartmouth College Library.
43. *Kenosha Labor*, March 4, 1948.
44. *Hearing Before the Joint Committee on Housing*, 1:2380.
45. Ibid., p. 2381.
46. Ibid., pp. 2404–5.

Council told the senator that the Milwaukee codes were, in fact, widely known for their fairness and efficiency, McCarthy informed him that "you can say what you like in the record, but I don't want you to stick your neck out unless you know what you are saying."[47] The labor representative claimed he knew exactly what he was saying and would gladly defer to the Joint Action Committee for Better Housing in Milwaukee—a nonpartisan organization composed of nineteen different labor, veteran, and civic groups—for corroboration. McCarthy replied that since he was running the hearing, he would defer to no one. And to prove his point, he quickly adjourned for the day.

The senator's partisan approach to the committee hearings was particularly disturbing to national building trades officials. They realized that the investigation was seriously damaging the image of the construction unions, and they were especially fearful that some of the disclosures might provide fuel for a building trades scandal of major proportions. In an effort to prevent such an occurrence, the Executive Council of the AFL Building and Construction Trades Department invited McCarthy to a private conference aimed at reducing the cost of housing.[48] Here Council President Richard Gray, a staunch conservative who was far less interested in public housing than he was in preserving the reputation of the construction unions, worked out a compromise with the senator whereby the joint committee would discontinue its attacks on labor in return for Gray's assurance to personally investigate charges of union coercion and rate-fixing.[49]

A joint statement was then issued. The Building Trades Department publicly agreed to rectify isolated cases of featherbedding and other abuses in order to bring about "orderly and economical progress," while McCarthy tempered his antiunion position by stating that "everywhere it has gone our committee has found a ready willingness among labor to produce. . . . There is no featherbedding in their minds, and if any remains . . . we have assurances that it will be cleaned out."[50]

Several months after this initial compromise was enacted, Richard Gray was called to testify before the joint committee. His performance, and that of Vice-Chairman McCarthy, exemplified the suc-

47. Ibid.
48. *Report of the Proceedings of the 40th Annual Convention of Building and Construction Trades Department, American Federation of Labor*, 1947, p. 170.
49. Interview with Joseph Keenan, April 10, 1970.
50. U.S., Congress, *Congressional Record*, 80th Cong., 1st sess., 1947, 93, pt. 9:11745.

cess of their earlier meeting. Gray read a long, disjointed statement that discussed the possibility of coercive action among union workers but dismissed it as "no more numerous, no more flagrant than any other group in society." He noted further that labor abuses in the housing field had been blown out of proportion, not by the real estate lobby but more generally by "sinister forces" seeking to discredit the working man.[51] To which McCarthy replied benignly: "I think I should state . . . that we found a number of cases of local unions—not too many—engaging in restrictive practices . . . but . . . I have called them to the attention of Mr. Gray . . . and without reservation he succeeded in correcting the local situation."[52] In sum, the compromise had proved to be beneficial to both concerned parties: McCarthy effectively shed (at least temporarily) his antiunion image, while the construction unions reduced the possibility of unfavorable publicity emerging from future committee hearings.

Still, Senator McCarthy's successful agreement with the Building Trades Department did not alter the opinions of most labor leaders or progressive legislators about the need for immediate government action in the housing field. In March, 1948, Republican senators Tobey and Ralph Flanders of Vermont joined with Democratic committee members in issuing a majority report that provided for low- and middle-income housing projects, veterans' cooperatives, and funds for slum clearance. "It is a matter of common knowledge," they stated, "that millions of American families are forced to live in slum dwellings which constitute a menace to their health and decency. The whole disparity between the rents which low-income families can pay and the price at which private industry can supply decent housing, either new or second hand, is so great that public aid must be made available if these families are to be decently housed."[53] This massive act of insubordination so disturbed Representative Gamble that he reportedly sat down and wept.[54]

McCarthy simply refused to acknowledge the majority report. On March 15, he made public his views on the housing problem. The senator asked that the two most vital sections of Taft-Ellender-Wagner—public housing and slum clearance—be eliminated. "Present public housing projects," he wrote, "should be available only to

51. *Hearings Before the Joint Committee on Housing*, 5:5108–9.
52. Ibid. Following these hearings, Gray and McCarthy continued their amicable relationship. Indeed, the construction unions were almost alone among labor groups in their support for McCarthy's later anti-Communist crusade. See, Chapter 7, pp. 124–25.
53. Joint Committee on Housing, *Final Majority Report*, 80th Cong., 1st sess., March 15, 1948.
54. Anderson and May, *McCarthy*, p. 150.

low income groups."[55] The financing of these projects could best be accomplished by inducing private capital to enter the field through abatement of federal corporation taxes and grants by municipalities of land and utilities. As for the problem of slum clearance, McCarthy simply asked that it be discussed at a later date. In short, his entire program for public housing was identical to the one proposed by the real estate lobby. By vetoing the idea of middle-income housing and veterans' cooperatives, McCarthy greatly expanded the market for private dwellings; and by having the government literally ensure a profit to those builders who invested in low-rental projects, he encouraged them to enter a field that once held little hope for their monetary advancement.

Once McCarthy released his report, he did everything possible to secure its ratification by the Senate. In fact, the senator and a few of his cohorts began associating support for public housing with communism and socialism. At a dinner meeting of the Army and Navy Club in Washington, Representative Gamble stated that "comment on public housing would be incomplete without references to the fact that in city after city, Communists were boisterous in the advocacy of more and more public housing."[56] McCarthy took a similar approach. To his thinking, the people who actively supported government housing for the middle classes were extremists. "The aim of such professional public housers," he wrote, "is to socialize all housing under the guise of providing housing for the underprivileged."[57] Most labor newspapers not directly associated with the building trades were quick to condemn McCarthy's smear tactic approach. One Wisconsin journal noted that "by his not too subtle comparison . . . the large cross-section of the American public which favors substantial public housing is now in a class with the Communists."[58]

The factional debate over the two committee reports provoked fierce debate in the Senate. Under the sharp cross-examination of Senator Tobey, McCarthy actually claimed that he supported the principle of public housing. The real problem, he concluded, was that the sections relating to it in S. 1592 were too complicated and all-encompassing. "I held hearings from one end of the country to the other on the Taft-Ellender-Wagner bill," he stated, "and people came forward and vigorously opposed the . . . bill because of one fea-

55. U.S., Congress, *Congressional Record*, 80th Cong., 2d sess., 1948, 94, pt. 2:2823–24.
56. Ibid., p. 1230.
57. Ibid., p. 2823.
58. *Kenosha Labor*, December 18, 1948.

ture, the public housing feature. . . . I know to be frank that if we continue public housing with the remainder of the badly needed legislation, there is going to be a great deal of opposition to the whole bill, solely because of the misunderstanding as to what public housing is."[59]

Senator Tobey attacked McCarthy's report by appealing to the political instincts of his Republican colleagues. "We have an election . . . in November," he noted. "If our party wants to appeal to the rank-and-file of the great common people . . . we cannot present a finer program . . . than to pass legislation which will encourage the building of housing and will provide for slum clearance and for low cost public housing."[60] Tobey's warning struck a responsive chord with the legislators, and they decided to send S. 1592 back to the House with its public housing and slum clearance sections intact.

As expected, the recalcitrant Wolcott again tabled the Senate proposal. S. 1592 was quickly returned to the upper chamber. In its place, McCarthy sponsored a substitute that struck out the sections on public housing and slum clearance. The bill also gave federal loans to private builders and guaranteed a profit of at least 2.75 per cent to any insurance company that invested in private housing.[61] President Truman signed the McCarthy proposal into law on August 11, 1948, although he was clearly upset with the obvious deletions. "Because it will be of some help in meeting the critical housing shortage, I am giving it my approval," he said, "but the people of this country should understand that it falls far short of the legislation which could and should have been enacted."[62]

Organized labor roundly condemned the McCarthy law. By limiting public housing to the indigent, the senator had excluded millions of Americans who desperately needed housing but could not afford to pay the going market prices. "The indigent are not the only people incapable of paying more than $10,000 for a house or renting an apartment for 75 dollars a month," claimed a writer for one union weekly. "That being true, the large majority of our citizens are indigent."[63] Another labor reporter called the act "a financial proposition designed to aid banks unload their mortgage holdings on the government."[64] Furthermore, the very idea of having the government

59. Ibid.
60. U.S., Congress, *Congressional Record*, 80th Cong., 2d sess., 1948, 94, pt. 8:9857–62.
61. Ibid.
62. *New York Times*, August 11, 1948.
63. *Kenosha Labor*, December 10, 1948.
64. *CIO News*, August 16, 1948.

guarantee a profit to private business seemed highly unethical. Mc-Carthy, it continued, "will be surprised to learn that private enterprise, according to the sane use of the English language, is not consistent with the taxpayers making up its losses."

*   *   *

Early the next year, Senator McCarthy revealed that the rights to a pamphlet he had written on the housing shortage had been purchased by the Lustron Corporation, a large prefabricated housing concern. The pamphlet, entitled *Wanted: A Dollar's Worth of Housing For Every Dollar Spent*, was designed ostensibly to acquaint veterans with the complicated federal legislation dealing with home financing. McCarthy told reporters that the fee was "embarrassingly small." "Besides," he continued, "I have split it with ten people who helped me."[65] Although the senator's statement went largely unnoticed, there was some doubt expressed as to why the vice-chairman of a congressional committee on housing would accept a fee from such an interested party.[66]

In June of 1950, a reporter looking through the records of the Lustron Corporation found a canceled check for $10,000 made out to Joseph R. McCarthy. The large amount of money seemed to conflict with the senator's earlier claim that the fee for his pamphlet was embarrassingly small. Moreover, a study of McCarthy's state income tax form for 1949 revealed that he had not split the fee with anyone; the $10,000—for 100,000 copies of the pamphlet at $0.10 per copy—was duly recorded as taxable income. By now, a serious question of ethics had been raised. "McCarthy," noted one popular magazine, "has turned the results of his committee work and a 30,000 mile junket through the United States into a neat profit. . . . And his fancy author's fee is enough to raise eyebrows."[67]

As the months passed, the Lustron-McCarthy controversy unfolded in spectacular fashion. In February, 1951, CIO official Leo Goodman charged that McCarthy had assigned a member of his staff, Miss Jean Kerr (later to become Mrs. Joseph McCarthy), to have the Federal Housing Authority provide detailed answers to specific questions on mortgage financing and other housing problems.

65. *Milwaukee Journal*, March 1, 1949.
66. Ibid.
67. "Author, Author," *Time* 55 (June 26, 1950): 16.

The senator then allegedly used this information to make a substantial profit with Lustron. In a letter to the Senate Committee on Banking and Currency, FHA Administrator Raymond Foley substantiated Goodman's accusation. Wrote Foley:

> Miss Jean Kerr indicated that Senator McCarthy was considering the possibility of converting the information and data into a series of articles for magazine publication. It was our understanding that the articles were to be offered to the periodicals without charge. . . . The arrangements for publication by the Lustron Corporation apparently were worked out later, as the possibility was not mentioned during the time the FHA was providing assistance.[68]

When the Reconstruction Finance Corporation foreclosed a $37 million mortgage guaranteed by the floundering Lustron Corporation, a full investigation was begun by the Banking Committee.[69] One witness testified that Lustron President Cal Strandlund had often loaned money to McCarthy at suburban racetracks and had, upon occasion, torn up the senator's repayment check. When Strandlund was questioned about these incidents he claimed to be unclear as to the dates when the checks were cashed and the amounts involved but stated that several small checks had been torn up after McCarthy substituted a new one with a larger total.[70] The most interesting part of Strandlund's testimony, however, was his assertion that he did not know who McCarthy was at the time the checks were cashed. "It was just an accommodation and I didn't even know the senator," he told the committee. "I probably wouldn't have cashed his checks, but his colleagues were also a little short of funds so I volunteered."[71] Although the committee accepted Strandlund's explanation without question, there must have been some surprise that the president of one of the largest prefabricated concerns in the nation (and one accepting large sums of money from the govern-

68. U.S., Congress, Senate, Subcommittee of the Committee on Banking and Currency, *Hearings on the Defense Housing Act*, 82d Cong., 1st sess., 1951, p. 458.

69. U.S., Congress, Senate, Subcommittee of the Committee on Banking and Currency, *Hearings on a Study of the Reconstruction Finance Corporation*, 82d Cong., 1st sess., p. 2389.

70. U.S., Congress, Senate, Subcommittee on Privileges and Elections of the Committee on Rules and Administration, *Hearings to Determine Whether Expulsion Proceedings Should be Instituted Against Senator Joseph R. McCarthy*, 82d Cong., 1st sess., 1952, p. 156.

71. Ibid.

ment) did not realize that he was cashing a check for the vice-chairman of a congressional committee on housing. The story seemed even stranger when considering the fact that McCarthy signed his contract with Lustron several weeks after Strandlund cashed his checks.

Strandlund also admitted why McCarthy's pamphlet was of such enormous importance to his company. "It had great value with him being the author and vice-chairman of the combined . . . Housing Committee," he claimed, ". . . and it tied in at a time when we were introducing a new project to meet the needs of those without housing. . . . It added to the value with his name on it." Since the Lustron Corporation was interested in eliminating the public housing sections of the Taft-Ellender-Wagner bill while promoting its own prefabricated brand of housing, Strandlund readily accepted the senator's pamphlet. "McCarthy wanted to name the price," he recalled. "He wanted $10,000. We thought it was worth it to us."[72]

Senator McCarthy probably was worth the price, for in writing a pamphlet that pointed to the shortcomings of public housing while glorifying the private, prefabricated kind, he had used the prestige inherent in his position as vice-chairman to mold and persuade a confused public opinion. Strandlund said it well: "He gave us more than Joe Blow writing the article."[73] Although the Senate decided that McCarthy's conduct did not merit an official rebuke, there were many Americans who believed the Wisconsinite had violated a public trust by using a high elected office to further his own financial position.

VI

Senator McCarthy's voting record on domestic legislation from 1947 through 1949, especially legislation directly affecting industry and labor, stamped him as a true conservative Republican. According to statistics provided annually by CIO-PAC, McCarthy's voting record was, to its way of thinking, one of the poorest in the Senate. During this period he voted consistently for restrictive labor legislation, the lifting of price and quantity controls on consumer goods, tax cuts for higher income groups, and smaller federal budgets. On the other hand, he voted against federal aid to education, public housing, and public power appropriations.

72. Ibid., p. 161.
73. Ibid.

Table 6. Voting Records of Senators Taft and McCarthy on
Legislation Affecting Industry and Labor, 1947–1949

1947 Bill	McCarthy	Taft	CIO
Taft-Hartley Senate version May 13, passed	yes	yes	no
Taft-Hartley Conference version June 13, passed	yes	yes	no
Taft-Hartley Veto vote June 23, passed	yes	yes	no
Wage-Hour Amendment (banned portal-to-portal wage suits) March 17, passed	yes	yes	no
Taylor Rent Control Amendment (extended rent control for another year) June 2, defeated	no vote	no	yes
Reed-Bulwinkle Bill (freed railroads from antitrust statutes) June 18, passed	yes	yes	no
1948			
Presidential Reorganization Plan No. 1 (reorganized Labor Dept. with all subdivisions intact) March 16, defeated	no	no	yes
Barkley Price Control Amendment (gave Truman power to control prices on certain scarce commodities) December 18, defeated	no	no	yes
O'Mahoney Tax Amendment (heavier taxes on corporations) March 19, defeated	no	no	yes

1948 Bill	McCarthy	Taft	CIO
Knutson Tax Bill Veto vote (heavy cuts for high-income groups) April 2, passed	yes	yes	no
Cain Housing Amendment (removed public housing sections from S. 1592) April 21, defeated	yes	yes	no
McClellan Rent Control Amendment (forced federal rent control authorities to accept proposals of local boards) May 9, defeated	absent	no	no
Federal Education Bill (gave $300 million in federal aid to states for educational purposes) April 1, passed	no	yes	yes
Reed-Bulwinkle Veto vote (overrode Truman's veto) June 16, passed	yes	yes	no
Gearhart Social Security Bill (removed 750,000 persons from S.S. rolls) June 13, passed	yes	yes	no
Public Power bill (additional appropriation for TVA) March 11, defeated	no	no	yes
1949			
Lucas Amendment (repeal of Taft-Hartley emergency injunction provision) June 28, defeated	no	no	yes

1949 Bill	McCarthy	Taft	CIO
Taft-Hartley Injunction Plan (left injunction section unchanged) June 28, passed	yes	yes	no
Taft-Hartley Reendorsement June 30, passed	yes	yes	no
Ellender Minimum Wage bill (called for $.65 hour wage when Administration wanted one for $.75) August 31, defeated	absent	absent	no
Department of Interior Allocation (budget cut for dept.) August 23, defeated	no	yes	no
Fulbright Rent Control Amendment (local autonomy for boards) March 22, passed	no	yes	no
Taft Housing Amendment (eliminated loans to farmers for housing improvements) April 21, defeated	yes	yes	no
McClellan Budget Cut (required Truman to cut federal spending by at least 5 per cent) July 1, defeated	yes	yes	no
Anti-Filibuster bill August 3, defeated	no	no	yes

SOURCE: Congress of Industrial Organizations, *CIO News*, 1947–1949.

In an effort to place Senator McCarthy's voting record into some political perspective, a comparison between it and the voting records of his fellow senators is necessary. Of the seventy-five senators who remained in continuous service from 1947 through 1949, sixty-six had better records from the standpoint of the CIO. Senator McCarthy was tied with Robert A. Taft of Ohio, dean of the conservative Republicans, both being ninth from the bottom.[74] A tabulation of their votes on twenty-six domestic bills and amendments considered most important by the CIO-PAC showed each man voting correctly only twice. It is interesting to note, however, that Senator Taft received widespread criticism from labor journals for his antiunion position while Senator McCarthy emerged relatively unscathed. This was due, no doubt, to the fact that Taft, as chairman of the Senate Committee on Labor and Public Welfare (and probably the most influential Republican in the Senate) had initiated and encouraged legislation that the labor movement found offensive. McCarthy, a relatively obscure freshman senator, was to the labor movement simply one more unfriendly face in a sea of hostility. He was soon, however, to remove his mask of anonymity.

74. The senators with records "worse" than McCarthy's were John Bricker (Republican, Ohio); Hugh Butler (Republican, Nebraska); Harry Byrd (Democrat, Virginia); Zales Ecton (Republican, Montana); Burke Hickenlooper (Republican, Iowa); Edward Martin (Republican, Pennsylvania); Eugene Milliken (Republican, Colorado); and A. Willis Robertson (Democrat, Virginia).

Chapter 6.

Organized Labor in the "McCarthy Years":
The CIO's Response

I

On a bleak February day in 1950, Joseph McCarthy told the Ohio County Women's Republican Club of Wheeling, West Virginia, that he had in his hand "a list . . . a list of names that were made known to the Secretary of State as being members of the Communist Party and who nevertheless are still working and shaping policy in the State Department." Two nights later in Reno, Nevada, the senator, according to one of his critics, "took the square root of his original number 205 . . . multiplied it by four for good measure," and claimed that he now had "57 cases of individuals who appear to be either card-carrying members or certainly loyal to the Communist Party." To add further to the confusion, McCarthy told his legislative colleagues a week later that his principal concern was neither the 205 Communists, nor the 57 sympathizers, but rather the 81 "security risks" still shaping policy for the government. While his arithmetic was more than enough to baffle a competent mathematician, McCarthy had again struck a responsive chord with the American public.[1]

Playing heavily upon public apprehension over the recent fall of China, the loss of America's atomic monopoly, and a rash of sensational espionage trials throughout the free world, Senator McCarthy cleverly orchestrated a massive anti-Communist barrage against the traditional enemies of conservative Republicanism—including, among others, New Dealers, Fair Dealers, labor unionists, intellectuals, career diplomats, and the editors and columnists of many of the nation's leading newspapers and journals. With a feeling of absolute power that made no challenge seem beyond his capabilities, the Wisconsinite impugned the loyalty of generals George C. Marshall and Ralph Zwicker; Representative to the American Delegation at the United Nations Philip Jessup; Secretary of State Dean Ache-

1. Earl Latham, *The Communist Controversy in Washington* (Cambridge: Harvard University Press, 1966), pp. 269–84. William Buckley and L. Brent Bozell, *McCarthy and His Enemies* (Chicago: Regnery, 1954), p. 50. Jack Anderson and Ronald May, *McCarthy: The Man, the Senator, the 'Ism'* (Boston: Beacon Press, 1952), p. 174. Richard Rovere, *Senator Joe McCarthy* (Cleveland: World Publishing Co., 1960), pp. 125–30.

son; and, by insinuation, President Harry S. Truman. His investigations into subversive activities ranged from the "Voice of America" to the Government Printing Office to the United States Army. In an attempt to silence all journalistic criticism, he claimed that Communists were very possibly running the *New York Times, New York Post, St. Louis Post-Dispatch, Washington Post, Milwaukee Journal,* and *Madison Capital-Times.* His senatorial critics were treated even more rudely; Senator Robert Hendrickson of New Jersey was referred to by McCarthy as "a living miracle in that he is without question the only man who has lived so long with neither brains nor guts," while Ralph Flanders of Vermont was called "so senile [that] they should get a man with a net and take him to a good quiet place."[2] Inherent in these charges was the quality that placed McCarthy above all other Red-hunters: his incredible arrogance.

From the point of view of organized labor, McCarthy's anti-Communist crusade came at a most inopportune moment. In recent years, unions had been viewed as potential breeding grounds for subversives. In fact, several labor organizations, particularly within the CIO, were following a pro-Soviet editorial policy and threatening mass work stoppages in government agencies and defense plants. Worse still, popular magazines, newspapers, congressional committees, independent politicians, business organizations, and many virulent anti-Communist labor leaders spoke often about the dangers of unrestricted left-wing unionism. The United States Chamber of Commerce, in a pamphlet on Communist infiltration in America, exemplified the feelings of much of the nation when it wrote: "The tremendous power of labor today permits no . . . complacency. When a businessman or industrialist finds that nothing he does can please his union, he tends to form a sour view of organized labor. But as he becomes more sophisticated, he realizes that his difficulties may not arise from his own workers, who usually understand his problems, but from outside forces controlling his local union. The Communists' demands are insatiable because they thrive on trouble."[3]

As the Cold War took on more ominous proportions, fears were aroused that much of the labor movement could not be trusted in periods of international crisis. "This country, racing to re-arm, is finding out how easy it is for one well-placed, well-disciplined union to throw the arms program into a tailspin," reported a writer for the *U.S. News and World Report.*[4] The article listed a group of unions—

2. Latham, *The Communist Controversy in Washington,* p. 402.
3. Chamber of Commerce of the United States, *Communist Infiltration in the United States,* 1946, pp. 21–22.
4. "Defense Worry: Damage Four Key Unions Could Do," *U.S. News and World Report* 31 (September 7, 1951): 62.

among them the International Union of Mine, Mill and Smelter Workers, the International Longshoremen's and Warehousemen's Union, the American Communications Association, and the United Electrical Workers of America—which merited special attention. Other sources were quick to agree.[5] Confronted with the extremism of communism on the one side and McCarthyism on the other, organized labor knew that the time for action had come.

II

The focal point of national concern over Communist infiltration and subversion within organized labor was the Congress of Industrial Organizations. Within its loosely knit structure resided the alleged culprits, a group of affiliates whose loyalties to the American government were highly suspect. By 1945, it was estimated that fifteen such unions, comprising approximately 20 per cent of the CIO's total membership, were under Communist domination.[6]

From its inception, the CIO had provided Communists with an unprecedented opportunity to establish themselves in the new industrial unions. In 1936, CIO President John L. Lewis made it known that he would accept aid from any group willing to recruit workers. Although Lewis had a long history of Red-baiting within his own union, the United Mine Workers, he sympathized with the Communists' belief that the growing class militancy of unorganized and unskilled workers should be encouraged, not crushed. Unlike Sidney Hillman of the Amalgamated Clothing Workers Union, or Philip Murray of the United Steelworkers of America, Lewis felt that a large degree of rank-and-file insurgency was vital to a movement employing mass organizational techniques.[7] And Lewis realized that few groups in America could identify with this working-class mili-

5. U.S., Congress, House, Special Subcommittee of the House Committee on Education and Labor, *Hearings into Communist Infiltration in the Fur Industry*, 80th Congress, 2d sess., 1948; Special Subcommittee of the House Committee on Education and Labor, *Hearings into Communist Infiltration of the United Electrical Workers*, 80th Cong., 2d sess., 1948. "Stalinists Still Seeking Control of Labor in Strategic Industries," *Saturday Evening Post* 223 (February 24, 1951): 12. "Leftist Unions: Defense Risk?" *U.S. News and World Report* 31 (December 14, 1951): 62–66. Daniel Seligman, "UE: The Biggest Communist Union," *American Mercury* 69 (July 1949): 35–45.

6. Max Kampelman, *The Communist Party vs. the CIO* (New York: Praeger, 1957), pp. 45–49.

7. Saul Alinsky, *John L. Lewis: An Unauthorized Biography* (New York: Vintage Books, 1949), pp. 370–76. James Green, "Working Class Militancy in the Depression," *Radical America* 6 (November–December 1972): 1–30.

tancy better than the Communists. During the depression's early years, the party had organized regional councils that sought to radicalize the jobless through massive demonstrations for more relief. These councils were also instrumental in preventing the eviction of rentless tenants and in organizing gas and electric squads to turn on these utilities after they had been shut off by local companies.[8] On the labor front, the most dramatic strikes of this period—including the bloody walkouts at Toledo, Minneapolis, and San Francisco and the sit-downs at Flint and Cleveland—were led by Stalinists and Trotskyists. As Len DeCaux, a well-known labor radical, so well put it: "The Communists brought misery out of hiding in the workers' neighborhoods. They paraded it with angry demands through the main streets to the Public Square, and on to City Hall. They raised particular hell."[9]

While this initial commitment to working-class militancy, which was coupled with a superb sense of organizational discipline, made the Communists top-flight labor recruiters, their effectiveness within the CIO still varied greatly from union to union. In the established affiliates, like Lewis's United Mine Workers, that were well-organized and controlled by strong leaders, the Communists made no headway at all. Indeed, it is one of the great ironies of labor history that at the very time Lewis was recruiting Communists as CIO organizers, his own union had a law on the books barring them from membership. Similarly, the CIO's new unions in steel, textiles, and meatpacking, which began as national organizing committees governed from the top by Murray, Hillman, and Van Bittner, proved difficult to penetrate. By 1938, in fact, Hillman and Murray had quietly removed all known Communists from their organizations. The Communists did succeed, however, among such affiliates as the Fur and Leather Workers and the Mine, Mill and Smelter Workers that had a legacy of radicalism, and among several industrial unions—particularly the United Automobile Workers and the United Electrical Workers —whose devotion to the principle of local union autonomy precluded any CIO attempt to organize them from above.[10]

In the CIO's early years, the tenuous relationship between the

8. Bernard Karsh and Phillips Garman, "The Impact of the Political Left," in Milton Derber and Edwin Young, *Labor and the New Deal* (Madison: University of Wisconsin Press, 1957), p. 87.

9. Len DeCaux, *Labor Radical* (Boston: Beacon Press, 1970), p. 162.

10. Karsh and Garman, "The Impact of the Political Left," pp. 105–7. Kampelman, *The Communist Party vs. the CIO*, pp. 28–50. David Oshinsky, "Labor's Cold War: The CIO and the Communists," in Robert Griffith and Athan Theoharis, *The Specter* (New York: Franklin-Watts, 1974), pp. 118–51.

left-wing and right-wing factions was based on their common desire to organize mass production workers and to unite in a popular front against Hitlerism. Temporarily, at least, basic political and ideological differences were cast aside. From a political standpoint, this meant that both sides unanimously endorsed the New Deal's alleged commitment to industrial unionism, its social welfare programs, and its obvious sympathies for the Soviet Union and the western democracies in their relations with the Axis powers. The main difference was that those on the right truly believed in the social-reformist philosophy of the New Deal and were determined to channel the CIO's political power through the Democratic party in an effort to make their voices heard, while the Communists believed the concept of a government–labor coalition was anathema to the interests of the working class.[11] Only the Stalinist line of class collaboration, coupled with Roosevelt's enormous popularity among industrial workers, kept most Communist trade unionists in the New Deal camp.

Because the Communists in the CIO adhered so rigidly to the Stalinist line, they were often forced into dangerous political situations. A good example of this occurred in 1939 when the Soviet Union signed a nonaggression pact with Nazi Germany. As one labor historian noted: "The self-effacing affability of the Communists came to an end with the . . . pact. The Communists stopped deferring to the Roosevelt administration and the liberal CIO leadership and began once again to articulate rank-and-file demands."[12] More specifically, the Communists now viewed Roosevelt's foreign policy, as well as his mobilization program, as a thinly veiled attempt by Wall Street interests to involve the nation in an unwanted, utterly senseless foreign conflict aimed at protecting the imperialist interests of England and France. And they responded with a series of wildcat strikes in the defense industries, most notably at Allis-Chalmers and North American Aviation.[13]

To many right-wing CIO leaders, the Communists' failure to support Roosevelt and his defense program became the perfect excuse for a major campaign to expel them from the CIO. In 1939, David

11. Art Preis, *Labor's Giant Step: Twenty Years of the CIO* (New York: Pioneer Publishers, 1964), p. 46.
12. James Prickett, "Communism and Factionalism in the United Automobile Workers, 1939–1947," *Science and Society* 32 (Summer–Fall 1968): 260.
13. Walter Galenson, *The CIO Challenge to the AFL* (Cambridge: Harvard University Press, 1960), pp. 184–92. Donald Schwartz, "The 1941 Strike at Allis-Chalmers," M.A. thesis, University of Wisconsin, 1943. For a firsthand account of both strikes by one of the UAW's leading left-wing participants, see, Wyndham Mortimer, *Organize* (Boston: Beacon Press, 1972).

McDonald, secretary-treasurer of the Steelworkers Organizing Committee, warned his followers that "agents of the Communist Party quite naturally would like to turn SWOC into an instrument for their own use.... We will not subscribe to any political or economic theory which is anti-union or anti-American." At the 1940 and 1941 UAW conventions, the Reuther brothers rammed through a series of resolutions opposing both the strikes at Allis-Chalmers and North American Aviation and the "brutal dictatorships and wars of aggression of the totalitarian governments in Germany, Italy, Russia and Japan."[14] Similar results were achieved at the conventions of the Clothing Workers, the Steelworkers, and the Rubber Workers of America.[15]

In this particular case, the matter of expelling the Communists was complicated by the imposing figure of John L. Lewis. Since 1938, the CIO president had consistently taken issue with Roosevelt's foreign and domestic policies; and, after resigning from Labor's Non-Partisan League in protest against its subservience to the Democratic party, he made his famous speech endorsing Wendell Willkie for the presidency. It was difficult, therefore, to condemn the Communists for not supporting Roosevelt without also condemning Lewis —a step that few CIO leaders were willing to take. Moreover, Lewis believed that an attempted purge of the Communists would destroy the CIO, and he did everything possible to prevent it.[16]

The issue was finally resolved at the CIO's 1940 national convention when the resolutions committee drafted a carefully worded statement that condemned the "Communist menace" but virtually denied its existence within the CIO. The statement was so contradictory that Tom Kennedy, the committee chairman, moved immediately to close debate on the subject. At this point, Philip Murray, Lewis's handpicked successor, called for a standing vote and declared the convention's "unanimous approval."[17]

Those on the right viewed this resolution as a great victory. It was, they believed, the first step in a program to eliminate Communist influence from the CIO. Those on the left took a more guarded approach. To their thinking, support for the resolution was necessary to prevent a showdown they could not hope to win. Most CIO members,

14. *Steel Labor*, July 28, 1939. *Proceedings of the Fifth Annual Convention of the United Automobile Workers*, 1940, pp. 292–93. *Proceedings of the Sixth Annual Convention of the United Automobile Workers*, 1941, pp. 83–84, 328–32.
15. DeCaux, *Labor Radical*, pp. 330–31.
16. Ibid., p. 379.
17. *Proceedings of the Third Constitutional Convention of the CIO*, 1940, p. 192.

however, could agree on one basic point: The power and prestige of John L. Lewis had kept this internal dissension from assuming the proportions of a civil war.

*   *   *

All attempts to deal with the Communist problem were postponed by the German attack on Russia and America's subsequent entry into the war. As soon as Russia was invaded, the pro-Communist unions discarded their opposition to the defense program by promising an all-out effort to increase production and to decrease the possibility of labor-management disputes. Yet even after the political differences dividing the two factions were temporarily put aside, disputes arose over the extent to which organized labor should moderate its demands to conform with the war effort. In this case, it was the Communists who became the most ardent defenders of wartime cooperation. While both sides generally endorsed the no-strike pledge, for example, several prominent Communist union leaders ignored national CIO policy by supporting the Smith-Connally Act, which advocated the prohibition of strikes in defense industries and jail terms for strikers, as well as Roosevelt's own proposal for a labor conscription act covering all workers between the ages of 18 and 65. Indeed, Harry Bridges told a meeting of Longshoremen in San Francisco that strikes were treason; that the government should "refuse to give consideration to the demands of any section of labor on strike"; and that "the strike weapon is overboard, not only for the duration of the war, but after the war too."[18]

This strict adherence to the concept of wartime cooperation took other forms as well. The Communists actively supported contracts calling for speedups, incentive pay, and the reintroduction of piecework; they were also particularly adamant in their determination to break wildcat strikes at the local level. Since these policies were often in direct conflict with the wishes of the workers, the left-wing leadership was forced to discard the concept of local union autonomy in favor of strict consolidation at the national level. By war's end, the Communist-controlled unions could hardly claim to be more demo-

---

18. Irving Howe and Lewis Coser, *The American Communist Party* (Boston: Beacon Press, 1957), pp. 411–12. Preis, *Labor's Giant Step*, p. 222. Joel Seidman, "Labor Policy of the Communist Party During World War II," *Industrial and Labor Relations Review* (October 1950), pp. 55–69.

cratic than any of the other CIO affiliates; to the contrary, their war-time "sellout" of the rank and file was soon to serve as a pretext for expelling them from the CIO.

*　　　*　　　*

As CIO delegates moved into Atlantic City for the 1946 national convention, the Communist issue clearly dominated their thoughts. In the wake of the 1946 congressional elections, in which Republicans won control of Congress with a campaign stressing New Deal subversion and Soviet aggression, the CIO was in a most precarious position. As the major power base for domestic Communists, it was becoming a prime target for Red-baiters, legislative committees, and the right-wing press. The choice facing CIO leaders seemed ominous indeed. On the one hand, they could turn on the Communists, thereby encouraging a factional dispute that might destroy the federation; on the other, they could ignore them, waiting helplessly as the albatross of treason was hung around their necks.

At the convention, the leadership could not reach immediate agreement upon a suitable course of action. The more vehement anti-Communists, headed by Walter Reuther and James Carey, wanted a showdown on the issue; the pro-Communists, headed by Ben Gold of the Fur and Leather Workers and James Mattles and Julius Emspak of the United Electrical Workers, were trying desperately to avoid one. And somewhere in the middle was CIO President Philip Murray, who wanted some sort of national policy or statement that would publicly confront the issue without alienating either side.

Murray's primary concern at this time was the preservation of unity within his organization. Although he was known to harbor strong anti-Communist feelings (just two months before the convention he told an informal gathering that labor "wants no damn Communists meddling in our affairs"), he also refused to give his blessing to the Red-baiting assaults of the CIO's right wing. Moreover, he seemed to respect many of the left-wingers for their ability to run sound trade unions. A few weeks earlier, he had publicly congratulated Mattles and Emspak for their "splendid support . . . for all national CIO policies"; and in a particularly revealing private conversation with radio commentator Martin Agronsky, Murray answered a pointed question about Ben Gold's Communist connections by stating: "Mr. Gold is an estimable gentleman. He runs an excellent trade union along good trade union lines. He is highly regarded by the employers of his industry."[19]

In an attempt to reach some sort of compromise on the issue, Murray appointed a special committee, which was composed of three right-wing and three left-wing executive board members, to respond to "the allegations contained in the newsprint [which Murray termed "wild and wholly irrational"] . . . that this organization of ours . . . is Communistically inclined." For its part, the committee finally decided on a resolution stating that the CIO "resents and rejects efforts by the Communist Party or any other political party and their adherents in the affairs of the CIO." However, as was the case at the 1940 national convention, no mention was made of the fact that Communists were presently working within the CIO, and Murray was careful to note that the resolution "should not be misconstrued to be a repressive measure, calculated to do things of a repressive nature."[20]

By 1947, however, as relations between the United States and the Soviet Union continued to decline, America's liberal community began to feel the effects of the Cold War. Already two opposing groups had been formed: the Progressive Citizens of America and

19. Kampelman, *The Communist Party vs. the CIO*, p. 129; DeCaux, *Labor Radical*, p. 239.

20. *Proceedings of the Eighth Constitutional Convention of the CIO*, 1946, pp. 111–13. When considering the hostile political climate surrounding the convention, a resolution that condemned Communist interference but took no action against the Communists themselves seems surprisingly mild. In fact, it was supposed to be mild, and for several good reasons. First, the majority of CIO leaders feared that a purge of known Communists would tear the organization apart. Indeed, it was only after the overwhelming defeat of Henry Wallace in 1948 that most of them realized the CIO could survive such a purge. Second, more than a few CIO leaders were concerned about the constitutional issues involved. They knew that since the Communists were legally elected by the rank and file of a given affiliate, the CIO could only remove them by expelling the union itself; by this process the CIO could have lost as many as a million members. Third, the rival factions seemed to be in general agreement on the one issue that usually divided them, foreign policy. In 1946, the CIO was nearly unanimous in its opposition to Truman's handling of foreign affairs. The Communists, of course, were highly critical of his new "get tough" policy towards Russia, and advocated a return to the "more progressive thinking" of Franklin Roosevelt. Interestingly enough, most non-Communist CIO leaders also felt Truman was moving away from his predecessor's policy of cooperation with Russia in favor of Churchill's proposed Anglo-American alliance against communism. See, for example, *Proceedings of the Fifteenth Biennial Convention of the Amalgamated Clothing Workers*, 1946, p. 96; *Proceedings of the Sixteenth Biennial Convention of the Fur and Leather Workers Union*, 1946, p. 253.

the Americans for Democratic Action. The PCA, an outgrowth of an earlier Conference of Progressives attended by Philip Murray and several members of the CIO's Political Action Committee who resigned soon after, was organized primarily to oppose Truman's handling of domestic and foreign policies—especially his failure to perpetuate "the progressive global thinking of Franklin Roosevelt." The ADA, supported by Walter Reuther and James Carey, was also critical of Truman's domestic failings but excluded Communists from membership. Indeed, as one sympathetic journalist noted, "it was in large part set up as a counterpoise to PCA—to provide a rallying ground for anti-Communist liberals who rejected all associations with Communists."[21]

Although the CIO Executive Board refused to endorse either organization at its general meeting in February, 1947, and issued a statement "deploring the division in the liberal movement," this attempt to remain apart from the conflict proved of short duration. In the months that followed, Truman began winning back many disenchanted CIO leaders by his veto of the Taft-Hartley bill and his espousal of the Marshall Plan. While the ADA applauded Truman's efforts, the PCA, with strong Communist backing, bitterly attacked the Marshall Plan and set out to organize a third-party movement around the candidacy of Henry Wallace. By the summer of 1947, the CIO's Communist faction was marching in step to the drums of Gideon's Army.

The repercussions caused by this opposition to the Marshall Plan and support for the Wallace movement were particularly damaging to the left. Philip Murray, who had been on record many times against the formation of a third party, was so disturbed by these incidents that he told the CIO Executive Board members in July, 1947: "It is high time the CIO leaders stopped apologizing for Communism. If Communism is an issue in any of your unions, throw it to hell out, and throw its advocates out along with it. When a man accepts office . . . to render service to the workers, and then delivers that service to other outside interests, that man is nothing but a damned traitor." Two months later, Murray demanded the resignations of four suspected Communists on his staff and then made plain his support for Truman by inviting Secretary of State George Marshall to address the CIO's national convention.[22]

21. Mary McAuliffe, "The Red Scare and the Crisis in American Liberalism, 1947–1954," Ph.D. dissertation, University of Maryland, 1972, pp. 52–116. Norman Markowitz, *The Rise and Fall of the People's Century* (New York: Free Press, 1973), pp. 231–97. Irwin Ross, *The Lonliest Campaign* (New York: New American Library, 1968), p. 146.
22. Preis, *Labor's Giant Step*, p. 337. Murray also made his pro-Marshall

While the pro-Communist faction was badly shaken by the strong support given to the Administration's foreign and domestic policies in 1947, its final defeat came the next year with Truman's stunning reelection. From the very outset, the CIO made it clear that it expected every affiliate to work within the Democratic party and that support for Henry Wallace would be interpreted as a deliberate attempt "to create confusion and division within the labor movement." Some pro-Communists, like Mike Quill of the Transport Workers Union of America, took the warning to heart. "If being for Wallace will split the CIO, the price is too great," he claimed. "I'm a trade unionist first." A few days after his statement, "Red Mike" broke openly with the third party and began criticizing "the crackpots of the Communist Party." Other left-wingers, however, including Mattles, Emspak, Gold, and Bridges, were not so easily intimidated. They argued that according to the CIO constitution the national office had no right to interfere in the political activities of the various affiliates. And Bridges declared that he would vote for Truman only if the CIO conducted a referendum to determine whether a majority of the rank and file supported him over Wallace.[23]

The CIO responded with a campaign to deprive Wallace of mass labor support by portraying him as a fellow traveler and by harassing his followers. In March, 1948, Murray ousted Bridges from his post as CIO regional director for Northern California; two months later, he openly advocated the ouster of any regional council that either condemned the Marshall Plan or supported the third party effort. CIO-PAC, which spent slightly over $1 million in "voluntary contributions" to put Truman and other Democratic candidates over the top, cooperated with the ADA in distributing thousands of copies of a *Speakers' Book of Facts*, in which the question "Is Henry Wallace being supported by Communists?" was to be answered with the statement: "Yes. The Communist Party National Chairman, William Z. Foster, who is under indictment for conspiracy, . . . announced that the Party will endorse and will support Wallace."[24]

Truman's resounding pluralities in the labor areas, coupled with the disappointing Wallace turnout, provided the final impetus for the Communist expulsions. To begin with, the results indicated (at

---

Plan feelings very clear at this convention. See, *Proceedings of the Ninth Constitutional Convention of the CIO*, 1947, p. 292.

23. Kampelman, *The Communist Party vs. the CIO*, p. 143. Preis, *Labor's Giant Step*, pp. 345–46; 369–70. *New York Times*, February 11, 1948.

24. *New York Times*, March 6, 1948. *CIO News*, March 8, 1948. CIO-PAC, *Speakers' Book of Facts*, 1948, p. 12. See, also, CIO-PAC, *How Sincere is Wallace?*, 1948.

least to the CIO's national leadership) that the majority of CIO members identified strongly with the Democratic party, supported Truman's foreign and domestic policies, and rejected the pro-Soviet attitude of the Gold-Bridges-Mattles-Emspak faction. This meant, of course, that the left-wingers were guilty of acting against the political interests of their constituents. Moreover, unlike in their stand against Roosevelt, the Communists could not claim to be following the wishes of the CIO's president; indeed, their support for the third party was in direct defiance of Murray and national CIO policy. The Communists were trapped by Truman's actions.

*   *   *

The actual purges of the left-wing affiliates took place at the 1949 and 1950 national conventions. Here, they were charged with advocating policies that were "consistently directed to the achievements of the purposes . . . of the Communist Party rather than the objectives set forth in the constitution of the CIO." The charges themselves included opposition to the defense program prior to World War II, wartime collaboration with employers, failure to support the Marshall Plan, and opposition to the reelection of Truman in 1948.[25] Walter Reuther, one of the leaders of the Communist purge, told delegates to the 1949 national convention that the decision to oust these unions was "not a denial of the Communist Party's right to stand up in America and have its say" but rather a refusal to permit any longer "the peddling of the Communist Party line with a CIO label on the wrapper." Some, however, were more uncompromising in the militant anti-Communist outlook, as exemplified by President Philip Murray's statement that the expulsions were necessary "to fight Stalin, to fight Moscow, to fight imperialism, to fight aggression here at home," as

25. *Official Reports on the Expulsion of the Communist-Dominated Organizations From the CIO*, 1954, pp. 14–15, 26–27, 106–8. Nine affiliates—the International Union of Mine, Mill and Smelter Workers; the Food, Tobacco, Agricultural, and Allied Workers Union, the United Office and Professional Workers; the United Public Workers Union; the American Communication Association; the International Brotherhood of Fur and Leather Workers; the International Longshoremen's and Warehousemen's Union; the National Union of Marine Cooks and Stewards; the International Fishermen and Allied Workers Union—were expelled, while two others—the United Electrical Workers and the Farm Equipment Workers Union—departed before they could be removed.

well as to remove "the dirty, filthy traitors of American trade unionism from the CIO."[26]

These expulsions were carried out so quickly that the million or so members involved, most of whom were either oblivious to or unconcerned by the Communist affiliations of their leaders, were given little warning of what was to come. In fact, the CIO was far more interested in preserving its own image than it was in saving these workers from the dogmas of radicalism, for in only three cases did it attempt to recapture them by forming rival unions.[27] When the smoke had cleared, CIO leaders commended themselves on the thoroughness of the operation and for the irreparable damage done to the cause of domestic communism. "To put it bluntly," a *CIO News* writer boasted, "we have in a year broken the back of the Communist party in the United States."[28]

The Communist expulsions greatly altered the CIO's perspective in foreign and domestic affairs, since it was no longer forced to avoid ticklish political issues in order to portray a unified image. CIO journalists now wrote comfortably about the problems posed by Soviet expansion in Europe and Asia and by leftist influence in the American labor movement without fear of stinging rebuttals from their left-wing affiliates. To a large degree, the CIO replaced the remnants of its radical ideology with the more respectable rhetoric of American liberalism. Therefore, President Truman's often ineffective and contradictory policy of containment—including the formation of NATO, the Marshall Plan, the Truman Doctrine, the Korean counterattack, and the allied involvement north of the thirty-eighth parallel—was enthusiastically endorsed. As Paul Jacobs, a willing

26. The Reuther and Murray quotes are from *Proceedings of the Eleventh Constitutional Convention of the Congress of Industrial Organizations*, 1949, pp. 16, 270.

27. F.S. O'Brien, "The Communist-Dominated Unions in the United States Since 1950," *Labor History* 9 (Spring 1968): 204–5. Some historians have speculated that the national CIO was forced to expel the Communist unions because the anti-Communist factions within the various left-wing affiliates were unable to dislodge the Communists from power. This means, they contend, that the Communists were actually quite popular with the rank and file. See, especially, James Prickett, "Some Aspects of the Communist Controversy in the CIO," *Science and Society* 33 (Summer–Fall 1969); Frank Emspak, "The Break-Up of the Congress of Industrial Organizations, 1945–1950," Ph.D. dissertation, University of Wisconsin, 1972.

28. *CIO News*, November 20, 1950. To those who claimed that the CIO, by virtue of its recent Communist expulsions, had turned away from its crusading past, the *CIO News* retorted (March 6, 1950) that its position was still "left of center, but not to the extreme left, and that's a good place for a labor organization to be."

participant in the purges, later wrote: "An inevitable consequence of the expulsions was to bring all serious political debate within the CIO to a standstill. . . . Unions could be counted on to give automatic approval to any action undertaken by the government in its struggle with world Communism."[29]

III

On crucial domestic issues, CIO leaders unanimously supported the welfare programs initiated by the Democratic New and Fair Deal administrations. These unionists had lived through the Great Depression and had seen, first hand, how the party of Roosevelt encouraged both the growth of industrial unionism and the belief that organized labor was entitled to the respect and sympathy of federal agencies. For these reasons, the CIO aligned its fortunes with those of the Democratic party. This allegiance was significant in two major respects. First, as opposed to the more conservative, antistate position of the American Federation of Labor, the CIO looked to the federal government for help in organizing its unions and in alleviating the basic social and economic inequities of society. Second, this dependence upon government programs and agencies created a growing interest in the concept of partisan national political action.[30]

Beginning with the election of 1936, the CIO became one of the most powerful groups in the Democratic coalition. Indeed, political analysts attributed Roosevelt's victories in 1940 and 1944 to the efforts of organized labor. "The fundamental factor in the re-election of President Roosevelt was his hold on the labor vote . . . without which he could not have won," wrote Irving Bernstein. "In the strategic industrial states, the industrial unions were the sheet anchor of his victory. His debt to them is, indeed, great."[31]

By realizing immediately the immense political value of this union support, the Democratic party began to perform many of the

29. Paul Jacobs, *The State of the Unions* (New York: Atheneum, 1956), p. 263. For an excellent collection of pamphlets showing the CIO's devotion to Truman's foreign policy, see, Philip Murray Papers, Box A4–66, CIO-PAC Folder, Manuscripts Division, Catholic University of America.

30. See, J. David Greenstone, *Labor in American Politics* (New York: Knopf, 1969), pp. 40–52; Irving Bernstein, *Turbulent Years* (Boston: Houghton Mifflin, 1969), p. 778.

31. Irving Bernstein, "John L. Lewis and the Voting Behavior of the CIO," *Public Opinion Quarterly* 5 (June 1941): 249. Samuel Lubell, "Post-Mortem: Who Elected Roosevelt," *Saturday Evening Post* 213 (January 25, 1941): 91–93.

functions of a labor party.[32] Aside from its sympathetic legislative programs, the party did everything possible to bring union representatives into its own structure and the structure of the federal government. During World War II, for example, prominent labor leaders were appointed to the National Defense Advisory Commission, the Office of Production Management, and the War Production Board; and by 1945, almost 80,000 union members were serving on various local advisory committees throughout the country. Similarly, through its well-organized Political Action Committees, the CIO actually gained control of the Democratic party machinery in some seventy-five localities.[33]

Following World War II, however, when President Truman's domestic programs were floundering, some Communist and non-Communist CIO officials demanded that their organization free itself from the Democratic shackles and initiate independent political action on behalf of all deserving candidates. As noted earlier, such dissension provoked a fierce battle between pro-Wallace and pro-Truman unionists in 1948. Similar confrontations arose when affiliated unions like the United Automobile Workers bitterly debated whether Truman's domestic failings necessitated the formation of a new liberal party.[34] Yet, the vast majority of CIO leaders remained loyal to the Democrats, for they saw how readily their unions were accepted into the New Deal coalition and how influential CIO-PAC had become in making labor's voice heard in that party's inner circles.

During the 1948 elections, the CIO national office made support for the Democratic party a kind of political loyalty test for its affiliates. With the help of a massive PAC effort, Truman, like Roosevelt before him, captured the presidential election with the aid of a strong working-class turnout. According to one survey of the nation's ten most powerful CIO counties (in which CIO-PAC "clearly dominated the regular Democratic organization"), Truman actually fared better than Roosevelt had in 1944, and "the increase in Democratic support here was much greater than the increase of Democratic percen-

32. Greenstone, *Labor in American Politics*, p. 50. Joel Seidman, "Organized Labor in Political Campaigns," *Public Opinion Quarterly* 3 (October 1939): 653–54.

33. William Riker, "The CIO in Politics, 1936–1946," Ph.D. dissertation, Harvard University, 1948, pp. 30, 341–44. For a superb analysis of the close working relationship between the CIO and the federal government during the war, see, Nelson Lichtenstein, "Industrial Unionism Under the No-Strike Pledge: A Study of the CIO During the Second World War," Ph.D. dissertation, University of California, Berkeley, 1974.

34. *Proceedings of the Thirteenth Constitutional Convention of the United Automobile Workers . . . of America*, 1951, pp. 280–85.

tages in the strong Truman areas of the West and rural Midwest."[35] Following the impressive Democratic victory of 1948, most observers concluded that CIO-PAC was the most potent weapon in the Democratic party's political arsenal. Indeed, a widely distributed study of the voting patterns of CIO members during this period revealed that 78 per cent of them voted consistently for Democratic candidates.[36]

IV

It was not surprising, then, that the CIO was one of Joseph McCarthy's earliest critics. While others hesitated in an attempt to assess the political ramifications of an attack upon the senator, the CIO immediately mobilized its editorial resources against him. Within days after his controversial Wheeling speech, the national Political Action Committee was distributing reams of anti-McCarthy material that pictured the senator as an unscrupulous liar who was being manipulated by the conservative Republican forces in Congress. On February 27, 1950, PAC's weekly handout, *Political Action of the Week*, noted that McCarthy's blasts against the State Department reminded many observers of the Wisconsin State Supreme Court's blasts against McCarthy for his unethical activities as a circuit court judge. The senator was also credited with revising the traditional Republican slogan of "a chicken in every pot," to the more updated "a red under every bed."[37] Moreover, the names of Taft and McCarthy were often linked in an attempt to show that the reactionary forces in America were actually behind these vicious diatribes. At one point, Taft was mentioned as "the Edgar Bergen to McCarthy."[38]

Aside from these relatively personal attacks, the Political Action Committee also kept its affiliates well informed of the day-to-day activities centering around the latest Communist charges. Not only did the PAC cover the hearings of the Tydings Committee, but the statements of journalists, politicians, labor leaders, clergymen, and academicians were carefully scrutinized. Although *Political Action of the Week* was obviously biased in favor of McCarthy's liberal critics, its condemnations were directed at the senator's own blunders —his constantly changing numbers game and his broken promises about naming names and waiving senatorial immunity so that his

35. James Foster, "The Union Politic: The CIO Political Action Committee," Ph.D. dissertation, Cornell University, 1972, pp. 264–65.
36. George Gallup, "How Labor Votes," *The Annals of the American Academy of Political and Social Science* 274 (March 1951): 123–24.
37. *Political Action of the Week*, April 3, 1950.
38. Ibid., April 17, 1950.

charges could be tested in a court of law. To these political writers, at least, McCarthy was viewed not as an object of fear but rather as the perfect target for well-documented counterattacks.

Within a month's time, the *CIO News* was using this PAC material for its own forceful condemnations. On March 20, 1950, the newspaper chastised McCarthy for being oblivious to "the danger and folly of his guilt by association tactics." Claiming "not to be so silly as to declare that McCarthy won't dig up a person—or maybe two—in the State Department," it warned that "he has demonstrated a dirty method of making what he no doubt considers political hay."[39] In the following weeks, CIO publications were filled with anti-McCarthy articles and editorials. Headlines such as "Senator McCarthy Used Smear To Win Office," "McCarthy Act—Ho Hum—Runs Another Week," "Hit-Run Senator Leaves Smears," "McCarthy Should Receive Irresponsibility Award," "McCarthy Used Big Lie to Perpetrate Hoax," and "Too Much McCarthyism" became regular features of the *CIO News*.[40] Often, these articles criticizing the Wisconsinite were put on the same pages with condemnations of Communist aggression, so as to give the appearance that while the CIO supported responsible anti-Communist action, it believed that the unethical, headline-hunting techniques employed by Senator McCarthy served no purpose other than the political elevation of the Republican party.

The belief that McCarthyism was being manipulated by conservative, antilabor Republicans for their own political ends became a partial reality following the national elections of 1950. The victories of Robert Taft in Ohio, Richard Nixon in California, John Marshall Butler in Maryland, Everett Dirksen in Illinois, and Homer Capehart in Indiana were interpreted by many CIO leaders as an indication that the rhetoric of extreme anticommunism could effectively shift large numbers of Catholic and traditionally Democratic CIO voters into the Republican camp. In a confidential memorandum describing the influence of McCarthyism upon the 1950 elections, CIO-PAC Director Jack Kroll wrote that "it aroused and encouraged . . . antilabor sentiment in large parts of the country. . . . McCarthyism contributed to the Republican program for creating confusion in the minds of the voters by generally discrediting the Administration, and its techniques were applied in vicious attacks on labor and other liberal groups and programs, creating a long-term handicap for all liberal groups and ideas." To effectively counter this evil, Kroll

39. *CIO News*, March 20, 1950.
40. The dates of these headlines in order are, March 20, March 27, April 3, April 10, May 1, August 3, and September 11, 1950.

concluded, CIO members must be taught to differentiate between the principled anticommunism of Harry Truman, the ADA, and the CIO, and the unprincipled, reactionary anticommunism of right-wing Republican opportunists.[41]

V

As expected, almost all CIO affiliates accepted the prevailing negative opinion of McCarthy. Unlike the AFL, which prided itself on local union autonomy, the CIO-PAC often demanded a nominal adherence to nationally conceived political policies. Therefore, in the case of McCarthy, the difference in approach among the individual affiliates was one of degree, with the moderating force being the affinity of each union for the Truman Administration. Among avid Fair Deal supporters, McCarthyism was seen as a conservative plot to destroy crucial social welfare programs. *The Advance*, journal of the Amalgamated Clothing Workers, attacked McCarthy early in 1950 for using an emotional issue for political gain. However, it claimed, the American people were "too accustomed through the years to the callous tactics so often employed by the reactionary elements in the Republican party to be hoodwinked by these latest antics."[42] In a similar vein, *Textile Labor*, official publication of the Textile Workers' Union of America, stated that "history will demonstrate that McCarthy's maneuver was a monstrous, calculated scheme to divert the energies and attention of Congress and the people from the critical need to halt mounting unemployment and to attack wastage of our natural resources."[43]

On the other hand, a few affiliates believed that the failure of the Truman Administration to provide relief from pressing domestic problems actually encouraged right-wing demagoguery. The United Automobile Workers, for example, while forcefully condemning McCarthyism as "the work of politically-motivated Old Guard Republicans," claimed that the senator's increasing popularity was due, in

41. CIO-PAC Research Department, "Confidential Report on the 1950 Elections," Jack Kroll Papers, Box 7 (CIO-PAC Research Department Reports, 1949–1951), Manuscripts Division, Library of Congress.

42. *The Advance*, April 15, 1950.

43. *Textile Labor*, April 6, 1950. For the formal censure of McCarthy at the national conventions of these two unions, see, *Report of the Proceedings of the 18th Biennial Convention of the Amalgamated Clothing Workers of America*, 1952, p. 226; *Report of the Proceedings of the 7th Biennial Convention of the Textile Workers Union, . . . 1952*, p. 194.

part, to the widespread belief among working people that the Democratic party had turned its back on them. Indeed, while the Administration criticized the opposition party as reactionary and antilabor, it had little to show the average union member but broken promises and worn-out slogans.[44] Still, the UAW remained in the forefront of the anti-McCarthy movement, contributing large sums of money to the senator's Democratic opponent in the 1952 election, distributing pamphlets and fliers condemning his actions, and inviting prominent citizens, like Bishop Sheil of Chicago, to speak against him at its union meetings and conventions.[45]

One other affiliate, the Oil Workers International Union, was in complete agreement with the UAW, noting that unionists were "getting tired of pretty promises but no action from the present Administration." Instead of responding defensively to Republican charges of subversion, it continued, the Democrats would do better to concentrate on positive programs to cure unemployment and inflation. The time had now come to pay attention to the individual candidate rather than the party label.[46]

Most other unions, however, did not become involved in the controversy until after the national CIO's official condemnation of McCarthy in 1951. *The Packinghouse Worker*, which because of its large black audience was far more concerned with civil rights than civil liberties, carried an occasional feature scrutinizing McCarthy's antilabor record in Congress, while more politically disinterested publications such as *The United Rubber Worker* and *The Brewery Worker* relied almost exclusively upon material supplied by CIO-PAC.[47] However, several other affiliates, including the Steelworkers,

44. *Proceedings of the Thirteenth Constitutional Convention of the United Automobile Workers . . . of America*, 1951, p. 283. A minority report on political action called for the creation of a third political party, stating: "These so-called Fair Dealers have turned out to be fake dealers. . . . Truman has ceased giving even lip service to social legislation. The fight for a real Fair Deal depends upon labor and the party it must create." (pp. 280–85).

45. *The United Automobile Worker*, April, 1950; December, 1951; September and December, 1952; April, 1953; April, 1954. For UAW political contributions, see, Secretary of State of Wisconsin, *Political Contributions to the 1952 Senatorial Campaign*, Folder 5557, Wisconsin State Historical Society. For Sheil's speech see, *Proceedings of the Sixteenth Constitutional Convention of the United Automobile Workers*, 1953, pp. 11–14.

46. *The International Oil Worker*, July 12, 1950; August 4, 1952.

47. *The Packinghouse Worker*, October, 1951; October, 1952. *The United Rubber Worker*, October, 1952. *The Brewery Worker*, March 22, 1950; February 21, 1951; March 20, 1951. The Brewery Workers were also the only union to take exception to the CIO's stated policy of opposing all legislation designed to crack down on alleged subversion in the United States. In 1950,

the Transport Workers, and the International Woodworkers of America, issued formal and unanimous condemnations of McCarthyism at their respective national conventions.[48] The senator, claimed one such resolution, had "created an atmosphere of alarm and insecurity which, heightened by the worldwide conflict between democracy and aggressive Communism, seriously endangered every individual's democratic rights." In fact, only one major union, the National Maritime Union of America, failed to publicly censure McCarthy, although its official publication criticized reactionary legislators who used the Communist issue to subvert critical welfare programs.[49]

The only union that openly condemned the foreign policy of the Truman Administration was a former affiliate, the maverick United Mine Workers of America. Indeed, it actually endorsed McCarthy's views on the State Department without mentioning the senator by name. Wrote the *United Mine Workers' Journal*:

> Americans don't want to be continually called upon to refight battles they thought they had won to regain the status of victor—battles stupidly brought about by the blundering and inexcusable error chargeable to our statecraft's lack of knowhow of what to do to cement the victorious productive and military achievements of our people. . . . There is no denying that the man on the street is troubled, wondering if the Korean venture is necessary . . . to say nothing of the lateness of the decision to shield Formosa . . . after letting China go by the boards.[50]

Actually, this bitter criticism was not hard to explain. United Mine Workers' President John L. Lewis hated Truman because of his forceful handling of the mine strikes in past years. It was only after the Missourian had left office that the *United Mine Workers' Journal* would write: "Whatever else he may have been, we are confident Truman was a loyal American. To try to pin a Commie label on an old corncob like Truman, born and bred in the tradition of rough-and-tumble partisan politics, is just a bit too slick."[51]

---

against a specific national CIO recommendation, it asked the government to pass specific legislation outlawing the Communist party. See, *Proceedings of the Thirty-First Convention of the . . . Brewery Workers*, 1950, p. 421.

48. *Proceedings of the Sixth . . . Convention of the United Steel Workers*, 1952, p. 265. *Proceedings of the Seventh Biennial Convention of the Transport Workers Union*, 1950, p. 127. *Proceedings of the Eighth Biennial Convention of the . . . Woodworkers*, 1953, p. 183.

49. *The Pilot*, November 30, 1950; October 28, 1951.

50. *United Mine Workers' Journal*, July 15, 1950.

51. Ibid., November 15, 1953.

VI

Because of the CIO's nearly unanimous belief in the dangers of McCarthyism, the national organization lost little time in formally condemning the senator's actions. At the 1950 convention, a resolution on "Civil Liberties and Internal Security" was passed, which stated that "the irresponsible . . . activities of Joseph R. McCarthy have, unfortunately, created an atmosphere of alarm and insecurity." The next year, another resolution was accepted that read, in part:

We in the CIO have won the right to speak out for freedom. . . . Communist influence in the labor movement has been broken through the determined efforts of our organization. . . . We in the CIO know full well that the irresponsible actions of the McCarthys . . . and their ilk only aid the Communists and their stooges. . . . We shall not be moved by these attempts to smear all that is liberal and progressive. . . . As the way of the American people is lighted by the facts, the McCarthys will be flushed out of their dark alleys of reaction, and honest men will be able again to serve their country without fear of irresponsible attack.[52]

Many state CIO councils followed the course charted by the 1950 and 1951 national conventions. A sampling of twelve such bodies, most in well-populated and heavily industrialized states, showed nine formally condemning the senator's actions and three taking no position at all.[53] Not surprisingly, those voting for condemnation followed the same basic approach. The Michigan CIO Council passed a resolution that differentiated between "men who through lack of foresight reacted to the external threat [communism] in such a way as to endanger those institutions they sought to protect [and] men like McCarthy . . . who are in the category of expert character assassins."[54] In Ohio, the state CIO convention asked the United States Senate to check into McCarthy's finances, claiming that a man so easily corrupted by public life was unfit to lead a crusade against the Communist enemy.[55] The Illinois organization, which for years had been

52. *Proceedings of the Thirteenth Constitutional Convention of the Congress of Industrial Organizations*, 1951, p. 387.
53. The states surveyed were California, Connecticut, Illinois, Massachusetts, Michigan, Minnesota, New York, Ohio, Oregon, Pennsylvania, West Virginia, and Wisconsin. These were used because of the availability of their convention proceedings.
54. *Proceedings of the Fifteenth Convention of the Michigan CIO Council*, 1954, p. 150.
55. *Proceedings of the Fourteenth Convention of the Ohio CIO Council*, 1953, pp. 156–57.

warning the nation of its impending loss of civil liberties, was not even satisfied with the senator's censure. It told fellow members that "there is, indeed, grave danger that the congressional defeat of McCarthy will leave unscathed the vicious doctrines of McCarthyism."[56] Other condemnatory resolutions were passed in California, Massachusetts, Minnesota, New York, and Wisconsin. The Pennsylvania, Oregon, and West Virginia organizations failed to single out McCarthy for special censure, but all three issued resolutions in regard to the protection of civil liberties. Certainly the most important single factor here is that in no instance did the McCarthy issue evoke bitter dissension within these organizations. As we shall see, this was not at all the case with state AFL groups.

VII

The overall approach of the CIO to McCarthyism was at once pragmatic and disappointing. As good Cold War liberals, the majority of national CIO leaders viewed communism as a dangerous ideology that had to be contained abroad and destroyed at home. Not surprisingly, then, they vigorously supported government policies aimed at controlling Soviet expansion and carefully initiated a series of purges to eradicate Communist influence within the labor movement. In this sense, CIO policy was no different from many other fraternal, business, or political organizations of the postwar era.[57]

What made the CIO's position distinctive, though, was not simply its own close association with Communists in past years but also its strict adherence to the policies of the Truman Administration. By 1950, when McCarthy began his anti-Communist attacks on the national level, most CIO leaders were solidly in the Democratic camp and ready to do battle with any political adversary, including McCarthy, who attacked the Administration's handling of foreign and domestic affairs. To their thinking, at least, the Wisconsinite was not a dedicated anti-Communist but rather an extreme right-wing, partisan Republican who was attempting to destroy New Deal-Fair Deal programs by creating a dangerous mode of thinking in which progressive action was considered subversive and crucial social and

56. *Proceedings of the Twelfth Convention of the Illinois State Industrial Union Council*, 1955, p. 84.
57. Two recent dissertations that effectively cover the activities of various liberal (and other) organizations during the early Cold War era are, Peter Irons, "America's Cold War Crusade: Domestic Politics and Foreign Policy, 1942–1948," Ph.D. dissertation, Boston University, 1973; McAuliffe, "The Red Scare and the Crisis of American Liberalism."

economic issues became secondary in importance to those of alleged internal security.

This rigid conception of McCarthy had several major drawbacks. To begin with, by tying in the senator's anti-New Dealism so closely with his rabid anticommunism, the CIO often lost sight of the dangers of McCarthyism in a strictly civil libertarian sense. His attacks on innocent people were rarely seen as just that—attacks on innocent people. Rather they were viewed as thrusts at the New Deal, or Truman, or the Democratic party, or labor. One seriously questions whether the CIO would have attacked McCarthy as strenuously had he been a domestic liberal who supported Taft-Hartley repeal, public housing, and the like. By concentrating almost exclusively upon the antiprogressive nature of his crusade, the CIO frequently ignored a far greater issue—the potentially disastrous effect of a movement like McCarthyism upon a constitutional system of government.

Another disturbing aspect of this rigidity was the similar and unanimous nature of the CIO's condemnations. While almost every state and national body publicly censured McCarthy, in no case on either level did the real issues surrounding McCarthyism receive serious discussion. Considering now that the best available evidence points to a substantial minority of blue-collar workers who were swayed by McCarthy's rhetoric, these unanimous condemnations seemed not only unrealistic but unrepresentative as well. It was no secret that McCarthyism appealed to some very real fears among lower-class and lower-middle-class Americans—fears engendered by alleged status deprivations, communism, domestic subversion, and common insecurities.[58] The CIO might have done better to allow a full debate on the senator, his methods, his targets, and his effect on working people than to purposely sidestep these issues with blanket condemnations that were centrally issued and scarcely read.

Overall, however, the CIO's approach to McCarthyism was consistent with its own political philosophy. As one historian has written: "CIO leaders . . . clung to the belief that all union members could easily be converted to union voters. A union voter was but a labor liberal in the New Deal tradition. He could be depended upon to support the right candidates and the right issues. All that was required to convert labor's millions into union voters, in CIO eyes, was to fill the millions with a 'new awareness' of the political world."[59] To Jack Kroll, Philip Murray, and other CIO officials, at least, this new awareness meant teaching the rank and file that McCarthyism was actually "an extension of the GOP attack on the Fair Deal Adminis-

58. See Chapter 8, pp. 151–55.
59. Foster, "The Union Politic," p. 221.

tration."[60] Once the membership understood this point, they reasoned, it would unite to vote McCarthy and his allies out of office. Not unexpectedly, CIO leaders were soon to discover that the process of reeducating workers in Cold War America to the evils of McCarthyism was to prove a most demanding task.

60. *CIO News*, August 20, 1950; February 25, 1951.

Chapter 7

The AFL's Response

I

The American Federation of Labor, older, more solidly established, and certainly more politically conservative than the CIO, was better equipped to handle the problem of Communist infiltration into its ranks. Although there were, in the late 1940s, sensational exposures of Communists in the AFL "Hollywood unions" (the Talent Guilds and the Stagehands' Union) by the House Committee on Un-American Activities, the problem was minor compared with that of the CIO. Within the AFL, Communists were able to penetrate the local levels of a few affiliates but never achieved success at the national level. The majority of AFL unions were decidedly anti-Communist, and equally important, were considered as such by the American public.[1]

Long before Joseph McCarthy made his sensational charges, the American Federation of Labor was warning a complacent citizenry about the dangers of Communists in government. Indeed, the major issue at the 1946 AFL national convention was not labor legislation, or wages, or hours of work, but rather the infiltration of subversives into the State Department. "The entire story of this infiltration has not yet been told," claimed federation officials, "but it is known that members of the Communist party employed in government departments purloined secret state and other papers, many of which were photographed before being returned to the files, and photostats forwarded to Moscow."[2]

Historically speaking, the AFL took the view that American diplomats "made concessions to Stalin at Yalta that made possible his

1. For a general description of the AFL's traditional anticommunism, see, Lewis Lorwin, *The American Federation of Labor* (Washington: Brookings Institution, 1933), pp. 213–26; 259–68; David Saposs, *Communism in American Unions* (New York: McGraw-Hill, 1959), pp. 135–226; Philip Taft, *The AF of L from the Death of Gompers to the Merger* (New York: Octogon Books, 1959), pp. 430–36.

2. *Proceedings of the Seventy-Fifth Annual Convention of the American Federation of Labor*, 1946, p. 553–54. For still another exposé of communism in the State Department, see, *Proceedings of the Twenty-Sixth Convention of the United Brotherhood of Carpenters*, 1950, pp. 322–23.

bringing of continental Eastern Asia within the Russian orbit," and that "Stalin demanded and received concessions in Europe that enabled him to place Eastern Europe in his empire."[3] The federation also saw no hope for coexistence between the United States and the Soviet Union and openly condemned "those who think some kind of compromise can be evolved from two utterly conflicting philosophies."[4] George Meany, secretary-treasurer of the AFL, bluntly charged that too many Europeans were "soft on Communism" and that "only patriotic Americans were worried about it."[5]

The AFL often seemed unconcerned about the possible effects of the Communist issue upon basic civil liberties. Although its officials lobbied against congressional attempts to outlaw the Communist party, they still lauded the Supreme Court decision upholding the Smith Act in 1951, claiming that "punishing the enemies of America" was of primary importance.[6] Most AFL affiliates took similar posi-

3. *The American Federationist*, December, 1950, p. 16.
4. Ibid. See, also, the statement of AFL Vice-President Daniel Tobin in the *International Teamster*, April, 1951, pp. 2–3; and AFL Vice-President Matthew Woll in the *American Photo-Engraver*, November, 1953, pp. 1131–34. For an analysis of the AFL's active participation in foreign affairs during the Cold War, see, Ronald Radosh, *American Labor and United States Foreign Policy* (New York: Random House, 1969), pp. 304–47, 435–52; John Windmuller, "The Foreign Policy Conflict in American Labor," *Political Science Quarterly* 82 (June 1967): 205–19.
5. *AFL News-Reporter*, October 31, 1952.
6. Ibid., December 5, 1951. Perhaps the best example of the federation's official position concerning communism and civil liberties came from AFL President William Green's testimony before the House Committee on Un-American Activities. Green at this time was asking HUAC not to adopt legislation outlawing the Communist party. The testimony went in part:

Nixon. Mr. Green, I take it . . . that you oppose the Communist doctrine, but you do not agree with the methods that these two bills are using to combat this doctrine?
Green. That is right. . . . Human nature must be taken into consideration in formulating important legislation. It responds sympathetically to one who claims to be persecuted and one who is made a martyr. Now that may be the outcome of this legislation outlawing the Communist party.
Nixon. Could you comment generally as to whether or not Communists have succeeded in infiltrating labor unions in America?
Green. I can speak for the AFL. . . . They have not succeeded. There are provisions in our constitutions which prohibit Communists from being officers of our unions; and our constitutions provide that they cannot be delegates to our conventions.
Nixon. I gather you would not deny the right of membership in a union to Communists?
Green. No; but they can't serve as officers . . . nor can they attend conventions as delegates.
Nixon. In other words, you won't deny the Communists the right to a job . . .

tions. That same year, an editorial writer for the United Hatters, Cap and Millinery Workers (whose president, Alex Rose, was one of the founders of New York's Liberal party) claimed that both the CIO and the Americans for Democratic Action had "gone off the deep end on the Communist issue" by calling for repeal of the Smith Act.[7] Dave Beck, president of the International Brotherhood of Teamsters, wrote that "it is not necessary to prove that a member of our union is actually a member of the Communist party. If," said Beck, "he advocates a *philosophy* of Communism . . . we throw him out."[8] And *The Carpenter*, monthly magazine of the International Brotherhood of Carpenters, scoffed at a decision by the National Labor Relations Board to reinstate a worker accused of Communist beliefs, stating that "as we see it, the thing that is involved here is a principle, a principle involving the right of good, honest Americans to choose with whom they want to work."[9] The principle of each man's right to earn a living, religiously adhered to by the AFL, went strangely unnoticed.

II

Unlike the CIO, the AFL was not averse to an attack upon the Democratic Administration. Following its customary policy of politi-

---

but you feel that the danger is in allowing them to get positions of power in your unions.

Green. That is right.

In sum, suspected Communists were theoretically allowed in the AFL if they agreed to second-class citizenship in regard to their rights and duties. See, U.S., Congress, House, Committee on Un-American Activities, *Hearings Investigating Un-American Activities in the United States*, 1947, p. 62.

7. Quoted in *The United Hat Worker*, January 15, 1952. At the same convention in which the Hat Workers condemned the Mundt-Nixon bill as "dangerous to supporters of liberal and unorthodox causes," it also voted down a resolution allowing Communists to hold office in the union. "The Communists' contempt for the Democratic process . . . in favor of the interests of a foreign state," it wrote, "makes it imperative that we guard our union . . . against their treacherous machinations." *Proceedings of the Seventh Convention of the United Hatters, Cap and Millinery Workers' Union*, 1950, pp. 378, 411–12.

8. *The International Teamster*, January, 1953, p. 4.

9. *The Carpenter*, December, 1952, p. 26. At issue here was the forcible expulsion of an alleged Communist auto worker from a General Motors plant by his fellow unionists. In an angry memorandum to all UAW officials, Walter Reuther wrote of the incident: "Members of the UAW must not participate in unlawful acts such as walking alleged Communists . . . out of plants. Violent action that deprives individuals of their . . . rights is a weapon of totalitarians." See, Public Relations Department, *UAW-CIO Press Release* Union File, Sloan Library, Massachusetts Institute of Technology, n.d.

cal neutrality, the federation had not officially supported Truman in 1948, and there was neither a strong ideological commitment to the principles of the Democratic party nor the unanimous desire to perpetuate its twenty-year hold on the White House. The issue of whether to endorse political programs or candidates was left to the individual affiliates, and it was here that the political divisions within the AFL were clearly revealed.

Among old-line federationists—including Richard Gray of the Building and Construction Trades Department, Matthew Woll of the International Photo-Engravers Union of North America, and William Hutcheson of the Carpenters—the political philosophy of "voluntarism" still prevailed.[10] As enunciated by Samuel Gompers a half century before, it meant the freedom to pursue particular goals through economic means without governmental interference. In theory, voluntarism was an extreme antistate doctrine based on the premise that government was at its best when it sat back and let the free market forces of capitalism run their course; in practice, it was a ludicrous denial of political reality exemplified by the federation's formal opposition to New Deal measures like unemployment insurance and wage-hour laws.[11] As Matthew Woll wrote in 1953, with some historical perspective:

> Labor, as represented by the AFL, presents no apology for our system of individual and personal initiative and free enterprise. . . . Here we have developed a way by which the benefits and rewards of free enterprise are more generally . . . and equitably distributed. No one factor can definitely be responsible. . . . The growth of a strong, vital, and free trade union movement and the development of progressive management policies led to a great increase in wage rates and earnings. . . . High levels of employment for more than a decade increased annual family incomes. Social legislation had a contributory effect, *although to a lesser degree.*[12]

10. See, especially, Michael Rogin, "Voluntarism: The Political Functions of an Antipolitical Doctrine," *Industrial and Labor Relations Review* 15 (July 1962): 521–35; J. David Greenstone, *Labor in American Politics* (New York: Knopf, 1969), pp. 25–29.
11. To promote better competition, however, the AFL supported government efforts in the antitrust field. See, Joel Seidman, "Organized Labor in Political Campaigns," *Public Opinion Quarterly* 3 (October 1939), pp. 646–54; Henry David, "100 Years of Labor in Politics," in J.B.S. Hardman, ed., *The House of Labor* (New York: Prentice-Hall, 1951), pp. 96–100.
12. Italics mine. *Voice* (Journal of the United Cement, Lime and Gypsum Workers International Union), March, 1953, p. 23. Until recently, labor historians have tended to view voluntarism as a positive, pragmatic approach to unique American political and economic conditions. It has been lauded as a

To these federationsts, the New Deal represented a particularly dangerous political philosophy. On the one hand, they believed, its vast social welfare programs had weakened the worker's allegiance to his union by providing him with benefits normally derived through the collective bargaining process; on the other, its obvious favoritism toward massive industrial unions had decreased the economic and political leverage of skilled craft organizations. In sum, the Democratic administrations of Roosevelt and Truman had callously ignored the needs and wishes of conservative craft unionism. "Are we as a union, as building tradesmen, respected by the Democrats," asked the *AFL Building and Construction Trades Bulletin*. "The answer to this question, unfortunately, is no—we are neither feared nor respected." The only solution to this predicament, it continued, was to vote Republican in the hope that this symbolic act would "wake up . . . the Democrats and make them respect us."[13]

The Teamsters Union leadership was even more direct. "If some of my friends in the Democratic party, from the top brackets down, give you their word to be helpful," complained retiring President Daniel Tobin, "they will crawl into their private rooms after 5:30 and laugh and tell their associates how, with their clever political persuasions, they made labor believe they were friends of labor. . . . Don't tell me that we are given any real consideration by the Democrats."[14] In many cases, this open resentment prevented the AFL from either supporting New and Fair Deal programs or criticizing those who condemned them.

*　　　*　　　*

However, other AFL leaders, led by David Dubinsky of the International Ladies Garment Workers' Union, Alex Rose of the United Hatters, Cap and Millinery Workers, Al Hayes of the International

---

rejection of class-oriented, Marxist philosophies of European trade unions. See, for example, David Saposs, "Voluntarism in the American Labor Movement," *Monthly Labor Review* 77 (September 1954): 967–71. Moreover, they assumed that voluntarism was also popular at the state and local levels of the AFL. See, Marc Karson, *American Labor Unions and Politics, 1900–1919* (Carbondale: Southern Illinois University Press, 1958), pp. 118, 129–30. With the publication of *Labor's Search for Political Order* (Columbia: University of Missouri Press, 1973), however, Gary Fink has demonstrated that many state and local AFL leaders actively supported government welfare programs and various state and federal reforms affecting trade unions at the very time that prominent national AFL leaders were condemning them.

13. *AFL Building and Construction Trades Bulletin*, October, 1951, p. 8.
14. *International Teamster*, May, 1952, pp. 2–3; June, 1952, pp. 2–3.

Association of Machinists, and Joseph Keenan of the International Brotherhood of Electrical Workers, felt that precisely because the bargaining powers of labor and other groups were limited in scope and unequal in influence, the government had an obligation to provide critical social and economic services. These men viewed the New and Fair Deals as a welcome departure from the apathy or outright hostility of the political establishment towards the nation's working people. They applauded government attempts to formulate social welfare programs, to pass prolabor legislation such as the Wagner Act and the Fair Labor Standards Act, or to appoint prounion members to federal agencies like the National Labor Relations Board. In return, these leaders rewarded presidents Roosevelt and Truman with partisan political action aimed at perpetuating Democratic control of the country. Their rationale was that the domestic programs of the Democratic administrations were far more beneficial to unions than the sink-or-swim alternative offered by the opposition party.[15] As *The Electrical Workers' Journal* stated: "The New and Fair Deals and the Democratic party have come in for some pretty severe criticism recently. But before you join in . . . consider one question—are you better off today than you were in the last year of the old deal, say 1932?"[16]

This reliance upon concerted political action by individual affiliates gradually eroded the federation's nonpartisan outlook. Late in the 1930s, for example, when various AFL unions contributed large sums of money to the Democratic party and cooperated openly with the CIO in local and national campaign operations, President William Green angrily condemned their actions.[17] But by 1944, the personal support of federation leaders, including Green, for FDR's candidacy was unmistakable. Indeed, fifty AFL members attended the Democratic convention as official delegates, where they used their organization's influence to secure the vice-presidential nomination for Harry

15. Greenstone, *Labor in American Politics*, pp. 36–52. Alfred Braunthal, "American Labor in Politics," *Social Research* 12 (February 1945): 1–21.
16. *The Electrical Workers' Journal*, November, 1951, p. 37.
17. Louise Overacker, "Labor's Political Contributions," *Political Science Quarterly* 54 (March 1939): 59; Greenstone, *Labor in American Politics*, p. 50. The AFL's traditional policy of rewarding its friends and defeating its enemies implies only that labor could exert itself politically by first examining the attitudes of individual candidates towards vital union issues and then voting accordingly. However, as one labor historian has written: "It follows that the [AFL] should neither be permanently and exclusively tied to one of the existing parties. . . . The Gompers philosophy . . . implies temporary alliances with existing or emerging parties or political personalities . . . for it is only through the formation of such alliances that it is possible for labor to reward its friends and punish its enemies." Braunthal, "American Labor in Politics," p. 2.

S. Truman.[18] However, in response to pressure exerted by Woll, Hutcheson, and other conservatives, the federation refused to officially endorse the Democratic slate.[19]

III

Shortly after the enactment of Taft-Hartley, the AFL formed Labor's League for Political Education. This committee, headed by Joseph Keenan of the Electrical Workers, was created allegedly to channel labor's political power for repeal of this new law, to counteract the considerable influence exerted by CIO-PAC, and to help finance the federation's various political activities.[20] As expected, several conservative affiliates were wary of the LLPE's motives, fearing that a centralized body would discourage local political action and degenerate into a mouthpiece for the Democratic Administration. Although Keenan publicly disavowed any partisan political notions, several prominent unionists let it be known that they would not contribute to, or be bound by, league policy.[21]

One of the first political problems confronting the LLPE concerned the handling of the McCarthy controversy. Keenan decided upon a direct approach from the beginning. Less than two weeks after the senator's Wheeling speech, the league examined his allegations at length. In a private memorandum to all national AFL officials, it confirmed the worst suspicions of conservative unionists by linking McCarthy with the reactionary, antilabor elements in the Republican party. "The Truman program is the target of the men most active in the developments of February, 1950," wrote Keenan. "In the McCarthy group, besides himself, are Senators Taft, Brewster, Mundt, Ferguson and Wherry. All that one has to do is to look up any voting scorecard whether prepared by labor or anybody else to see that these senators have been in the forefront of those who

18. Matthew Josephson, *Sidney Hillman: Statesman of American Labor* (Garden City: Doubleday, 1952), pp. 615–25.

19. Taft, *The AF of L from the Death of Gompers to the Merger*, pp. 307–9.

20. *Proceedings of the Sixty-Sixth Convention of the American Federation of Labor*, 1947, p. 407. *The American Federationist*, August, 1947, p. 3. Morton Leeds, "The AFL in the 1948 Elections," *Social Research* 17 (June 1950): 207–18.

21. Interview with Joseph Keenan, April 10, 1970. The most recalcitrant AFL officials were Gray, Beck, and Hutcheson. See, Sam Romer, *The International Brotherhood of Teamsters* (New York: Wiley, 1962), pp. 78–79; Morris Horowitz, *The Structure and Government of the Carpenters' Union* (New York: Wiley, 1962), pp. 83–86.

have fought the Truman administration at every step."[22] Several weeks later, Keenan sent his colleagues a final four-page summary of the McCarthy charges in which he claimed that the senator had done little "but throw 'red herrings' to divert public attention from his bad voting record and the real issues before Congress. . . . We must keep our eyes on the record," he warned, "and not on the 'red herring.' "[23]

On March 27, 1950, the *League Reporter*, official organ of the League for Political Education, issued its first formal statement on the senator's actions. In an article entitled "McCarthy's Mess," it wrote that "if the senator is as wrong about Communism in the State Department as he was about Taft-Hartley, TVA, public housing and minimum wage, there's not a Commie within a thousand miles of the place."[24] In the following weeks, the *League Reporter* carried out a series of well-planned attacks against McCarthy. The senator was accused of making fact out of fiction and of intimidating respectable witnesses with his classic bullyboy tactics. The journal also attempted to place McCarthy in a class with the most conservative legislators by noting that "no prominent reactionary of either party has protested McCarthy's series of character assassinations . . . not one."[25] Other attacks were directed at the senator's dealings with the Lustron Corporation and his censure by the Wisconsin State Supreme Court.[26]

Unfortunately, these reports proved totally ineffective in generating anti-McCarthy sentiment within the AFL. Both official national publications—the *AFL News-Reporter* and *The American Federationist*—ignored the press releases, printing not one word of criticism about the senator. The reason for this inaction was simple: Many top-ranking AFL leaders, knowing well the grave doubts of their conservative associates about the Democratic Administration's willingness to combat domestic subversion, felt that a strong stand for or against McCarthy would only divide the organization at a time when labor unity was especially vital for the upcoming battles against Taft-Hartley and other alleged legislative injustices.[27] In fact,

22. Committee on Political Education of the AFL, "The Senate Inquiry into State Department Personnel," AFL-CIO Papers, File B, Box 1, February, 1950, Wisconsin State Historical Society.
23. Ibid.
24. *League Reporter*, March 27, 1950.
25. Ibid., April 11, 1950.
26. Ibid., June 15, 1950.
27. Interview with Joseph Keenan, April 10, 1970; interview with David Dubinsky, October 9, 1969; interview with George Haberman, September 30, 1969.

the *League Reporter* soon discontinued its coverage of the senator's crusade, claiming "exhaustion of the subject matter." Further discussion, it concluded, would be left to the individual affiliates.[28]

*   *   *

Although the AFL continued in its attempt to ignore McCarthy, the increased belligerence of the Republican party toward organized labor (exemplified primarily by its adamant refusal to consider the issue of Taft-Hartley repeal) afforded the activist wing another opportunity to attack the traditional policy of political neutrality. Indeed, these leaders began lobbying for an official endorsement of the Democratic party in 1952—an endorsement that had not been given to a political party since the defeat of Robert LaFollette, Sr., in the presidential campaign of 1924.[29]

Keenan first broached the subject at the 1951 AFL national convention when he called for the defeat of McCarthy and eighteen other senators, fourteen of whom were Republicans, for their antilabor philosophies; however, because of the delicate nature of his appeal, Keenan did not condemn McCarthy for his attacks upon Truman or the State Department.[30] By the end of that year, many additional affiliates were dropping the banner of neutrality in favor of concerted political action. "In 1952, most members of the AFL will find them-

28. *League Reporter*, July 17, 1950. This failure to critically analyze McCarthy was often coupled with a peculiar insensitivity to the dangers presented by legislators of the McCarthy mold. Reporting on the outcome of the 1950 elections, for example, *The American Federationist* (December 1950): 3, wrote that it was disappointed "in that we failed to defeat some candidates hostile to effective unionism," but overall, "the election was gratifying in that it revealed the preponderance of American citizens who regard defense against the International Communist Conspiracy as the major issue before our government." The publication was, in effect, giving its blessing to the conservative wing of the Republican party, which according to the *New York Times* (November 7, 1950) had attacked "the Administration's softness on Communism in Washington" to increase the political chances of those "who opposed most vigorously the social, economic and foreign policies of the Administration." In rationalizing the victories of senators Taft, Butler, Dirksen, Capehart, and other conservatives, the AFL seemed to consider their attacks on communism to be of greater importance than their conspicuous antilabor records.

29. Taft, *The AF of L from the Death of Gompers to the Merger*, pp. 303–9. John Hicks, *Republican Ascendancy 1921–1933* (New York: Harper, 1960), pp. 79–106.

30. *Proceedings of the Seventieth Convention of the American Federation of Labor*, 1951, p. 435.

selves . . . in the midst of one of the biggest name-calling political campaigns to be waged in a long time," wrote one former neutral. "We have long shied away from partisan politics. . . . But with the continued oppression of Taft-Hartley and the constant rise of living costs, the Federation must take action at the ballot box to defend Labor's bargaining and living rights."[31]

Although the choice of the Democratic party was a foregone conclusion, the AFL placated its Republican followers by sending labor delegations to both political conventions. As expected, the Democrats received the Meany-led contingent with open arms, afforded it a full hearing before its platform committee of twenty-one senators, governors, and congressmen, and promised to work for repeal of the Taft-Hartley Act. The Republicans, on the other hand, represented only by Senator Wiley of Wisconsin and a single delegate from Idaho, told Meany that there was little hope of revising the party's stand on Taft-Hartley, a higher minimum wage, and other vital labor issues.[32] Therefore, at its 1952 national convention, the AFL Executive Committee endorsed the Stevenson-Sparkman ticket but stressed that "the affiliated unions . . . and each and every one of their members are free to make their own individual political decisions without any compulsion on our part."[33]

*   *   *

The decision to support the Democratic slate greatly altered the AFL's attitude towards Senator McCarthy. By December, 1951, when the federation began its cautious attack upon the conservative wing of the Republican party, the senator was criticized publicly for the first time by its official publications as he and ten of his colleagues were elected to the AFL's "All-American Reactionary Team."[34]

31. *Voice* (January 1952): 4. See, also, Sidney Lens, "Labor and the Election," *Yale Review* 41 (June 1952): 567–78; "The AFL and Politics," *Newsweek* 40 (September 29, 1952): 32–33.
32. *The Electrical Workers' Journal* (August 1952): 16.
33. *Proceedings of the Seventy-First Convention of the American Federation of Labor*, 1952, p. 511. In the alleged spirit of fair play, both Dwight Eisenhower and Adlai Stevenson were invited to address the national convention. Following the speeches, however, the Executive Committee released a statement noting that the Democratic party was "responsive to the desires of liberal-minded and working people," while the Republican party was "responsive to the demands of the ultra-conservative, anti-union elements in the nation." (p. 310)
34. *AFL News-Reporter*, December 12, 1951.

Similarly, on February 10, 1952, a small article appeared in the *News-Reporter* informing the reader that Joseph McCarthy had been voted worst United States Senator by the American Political Science Association. It was not until the middle of 1952, however, when the federation threw its official support to the Democratic party, that a concerted attack was initiated against McCarthy for his abuses in the field of civil liberties. From July of 1952 until the election in November, the senator came under constant criticism from both officials and publications of the AFL. The *News-Reporter* now viewed him as "a symbol of political smear tactics," while George Meany, speaking on the television show "As We See It," claimed that "the junior senator from Wisconsin, in my opinion, is a tool of the Communists, whether he intends to be or not."[35] There were, however, strong counterbalancing factors; the AFL still made no official attempt to censure the senator's conduct, and Richard Gray went as far as to acclaim "McCarthy's impressive job."[36]

IV

The AFL's early facade of neutrality on the McCarthy issue masked a great and bitter diversity of opinion among the various federation affiliates. The so-called liberal wing, led by David Dubinsky's International Ladies Garment Workers' Union and Alex Rose's United Hatters, Cap and Millinery Workers, came out in immediate opposition to the senator but also stressed the need to control subversive activities in a more orderly fashion. These unionists, who had previously defeated Communist attempts to infiltrate New York's clothing industry, believed that the entire issue of Communist infiltration into American society had been usurped by the McCarthyites simply because too many liberals were more interested in protecting the civil liberties of alleged subversives than they were in combating the real dangers posed by domestic subversion. As Dubinsky stated: "In the struggle against Communist tyranny there can be no neutrals. In the United States, organized labor—particularly within the AFL and our union—has always realized the acute menace of Communism. We can only wish that a lot of the people who get red in the face shouting that they are liberals would be as wide awake

35. Ibid., August 12, 1952.
36. In addition, several prominent AFL leaders—including Gray, Hutcheson, Beck, and William McFetridge of the Building Service Employees Union —endorsed the national Republican ticket in 1952.

to this great threat to our liberties."[37] Therefore, while the ILGWU was critical of McCarthy "for bringing an honest crusade to the level of a vaudeville show," it constantly sought alternative methods for dealing with the Communist problem. Finally, in 1953, the union advocated the formation of a nonpartisan commission, chosen by the President, to investigate allegedly dangerous organizations and then to hold its findings open for public scrutiny.[38]

The Millinery Workers went even a step further by censuring strict civil libertarians for their paranoia over the entire Communist issue. The problem with these people, it seemed, was that they wasted too much moral energy defending the " 'I am not a Communist but' crowd, particularly the articulate members among them who peddle . . . canned liberalism at so much a slug."[39] Until responsible liberals took it upon themselves to repudiate this latter group and to respond positively to the very real threat of Soviet aggression, *The Hat Worker* noted, men like McCarthy would continue to degrade, and ultimately destroy, the anti-Communist movement in America. To unionists like Dubinsky and Rose, this was the true danger of McCarthyism: its lack of honest commitment in fighting the Communist menace.[40]

A few affiliates, however, viewed McCarthyism primarily in terms of its antiprogressivism. The International Association of Machinists, which had long supported New Deal programs and candidates, often criticized AFL leaders for not realizing that "anti-Communists of the McCarthy mold have never put human values first in their thinking."[41] These "right wing charlatans," it believed, had turned

37. Max Danish, *The World of David Dubinsky* (Cleveland: World Publishing Co., 1957), p. 242. Dubinsky was not the only liberal to criticize his ideological colleagues for being oblivious to the dangers of communism and therefore becoming overly sensitive to the persecution of alleged subversives. See, Sidney Hook, *Common Sense and the Fifth Amendment* (New York: Criterion Books, 1957); Irving Kristol, "Civil Liberties—1952: A Study in Confusion," *Commentary* 13 (March 1952): 228–36.

38. *Proceedings of the Twenty-Eighth Convention of the International Ladies Garment Workers' Union*, 1953, p. 371. In an article for the *New York Times Magazine* ("Instead of the McCarthy Method," July 26, 1953), Dubinsky wrote of McCarthyism: "It fails completely to serve as a means of converting Communists to the Democratic way of life since its primary weapons are threats and terror. . . . It fails completely to cut down the influence of Communists . . . since instead of clearly identifying and isolating them . . . it confuses the issue by tagging non-Communists as Communists. . . . It induces an ultimate cynicism by cheapening an honest crusade to the level of . . . a politician's catch-all."

39. *The Hat Worker*, February 15, 1952.

40. Ibid., July 15, 1951.

41. *The Machinist*, April 3, 1952. For the Democratic leanings of the

many federationists against the Democratic Administration by mis-representing its stand on the issues of domestic subversion and foreign policy. Many people "have embraced McCarthyism and are taking the line that our foreign policy was one of appeasement of Russia," wrote *The Machinist*. "Nothing could be further from the truth." To prove its point, the union invited Dean Acheson to address its 1952 national convention, where the Secretary of State defended the Administration's position to rousing ovations.[42]

Ironically, when the IAM condemned "the vicious doctrine of McCarthyism" at that same convention, it experienced difficulty not from rabid anti-Communists, but rather from delegates of Scotch and Irish descent, who claimed that the term McCarthyism cast negative aspersions upon their nationalities. In response to this ticklish charge, a member of the resolutions committee replied with good humor: "We wish to assure you that we had no intention of demeaning any nationality. But this THING cannot be designated by the roll of a drum, bookety—doop—doop—doop, but must have a name. Following custom, it bears the name of its foremost exponent."[43] The Scotch and Irish delegates seemed quite satisfied with the explanation.

A similar approach was followed by the American Federation of State, County and Municipal Employees, which in April, 1950, turned over the editorial page of its monthly journal to staff members residing in Wisconsin so they could "better inform the membership throughout the country about our junior senator, Joe McCarthy." In this issue were the standard analyses of McCarthy's censure by the Wisconsin State Supreme Court, his well-known income tax troubles, and his antilabor record in the Senate.[44] Few other affiliates, however, directed any real criticism towards the senator. In fact, only a handful of journals—*The American Pressman, The Electrical Workers' Journal, The Butcher Workman, The Boilermakers Journal,* and *The Painter and Decorator*—even bothered to avail themselves of the anti-McCarthy material distributed by the League for Political Edu-

union and its members, see, Mark Perlman, *The Machinists* (Cambridge: Harvard University Press, 1961) pp. 274–76; John Dean and Edward Suchman, "The Political Role of Labor Unions and Other Organizations," in Bernard Berelson, Paul Lazarsfeld, and William McPhee, *Voting* (Chicago: University of Chicago Press, 1954), pp. 46–49.

42. *The Machinist*, September 21, 1950; September 4, 1952. See, also, Dean Acheson, *Present at the Creation* (New York: Norton, 1969), p. 690.

43. *Proceedings of the Twenty-Third Grand Lodge Convention of the International Association of Machinists*, 1952, p. 170.

44. *The Public Employee*, April, 1950.

cation, although many others printed league statements on less controversial subjects like voter registration or increased labor participation in civic affairs.[45]

＊　　　＊　　　＊

Public support within the AFL for Senator McCarthy was centered primarily in the Building and Construction Trades Department, the last remaining bastion of conservative, craft-oriented unionism. In July and August of 1953, the *Building and Construction Trades Bulletin* featured a two-part editorial, which claimed "the time is long past due for someone in the American labor movement to set forth . . . an unbiased analysis of the aims and purpose of Senator Joseph McCarthy in his unrelenting fight to expose Communists holding influential positions in America . . . and the results he has achieved."[46] The editorial took for granted the sincerity of McCarthy's anti-Communist crusade, centering its attention instead upon the senator's controversial methods. They were, the *Bulletin* concluded, entirely justified in the face of such obvious dangers to the American way of life.

We of organized labor have more to lose than any other segment in American society. Our high standards of living have been achieved mainly through the efforts of organized labor made possible by the American free enterprise system. Communism would destroy the free enterprise system. . . .

We would suggest that the critics of McCarthy's tactics realize that the Communist battle is one in which we must fight fire with fire. Failure would be inevitable if we were to employ kid glove rules of play. . . . As we all well know, Communists lie, deceive, and even swear allegiance to our flag and country while at the same time plotting to deal America a fatal blow.

Somehow . . . we just can't find sympathy for those bleeding hearts who with pious indignation point their accusing finger at Senator McCarthy and shout for all the world to hear, "Persecution, Persecution."[47]

45. *The American Pressman*, April, 1951, p. 6; June, 1951, p. 4. *The Butcher Workman*, September, 1952, p. 8. *The Electrical Workers' Journal*, September, 1952, p. 17; November, 1952, pp. 34–35. *The Boilermakers' Journal*, October, 1952, pp. 225–26. *The Painter and Decorator*, March, 1951, pp. 8–10; June, 1951, pp. 31–32.
46. *AFL Building and Construction Trades Bulletin*, July, 1953, pp. 3–4.
47. Ibid.

The first part of this editorial brought such intense criticism from labor and liberal sources that the *Bulletin* quickly modified its position: "Certain elements of our free press in America in commenting on last month's issue . . . did their darndest to misconstrue the real purpose of these two articles. Many had us endorsing McCarthy's methods—this in our opinion beclouds the real issue of Communism in America."[48] However, in an attempt to vindicate McCarthy, the *Bulletin* presented an allegedly impressive list of printed material showing "the tremendous extent to which . . . Communists . . . have infiltrated our government, our colleges, our writing profession, industry, labor unions, etc." And the list was "impressive"—indeed notoriously so—for it relied almost exclusively upon the investigative findings of such professional Red-hunters as A. Mitchell Palmer, Clayton Lusk, Martin Dies, John Rankin, Pat McCarran, William Jenner, and McCarthy. The *Bulletin* also encouraged its membership to read the pamphlets of the House Un-American Activities Committee, including *100 Things You Should Know About Communism in Education*, *100 Things You Should Know About Communism in Government*, and *Spotlight on Spies.*[49]

*   *   *

Not surprisingly, McCarthy's post-1952 assaults upon both the Eisenhower Administration and a group of cherished symbols and institutions—including public libraries, Protestant religious organizations, and the United States Army—alienated several conservative unions that had previously refrained from condemning his behavior. In the spring of 1953, for example, an affiliate of the AFL's Metal Trades Division severely criticized the senator for attempting to hire, as chief of staff for the McCarthy Subcommittee, a man who claimed that American Protestant churches were filled with thousands of Communist and pro-Communist ministers. Adding its voice to a storm of protest raised by hundreds of labor, religious, and political organizations, the union "condemn[ed] the effects of McCarthyism" and sternly rebuked the senator for actions detrimental "to the very Communist cause which he purports to champion."[50] Sensing the unusually hostile reaction to his proposed attacks on organized religion, McCarthy decided to look elsewhere for a new chief of staff.[51]

48. Ibid., August, 1953, pp. 6–7.
49. Ibid.
50. *The Metal Polisher, Buffer and Plater*, July, 1953, p. 7.
51. The individual in question was J.B. Matthews, a "professional" anti-

Later that year, *The International Teamster* went out of its way to praise General George C. Marshall, who, as Secretary of State and Secretary of Defense under President Truman, had been repeatedly attacked by McCarthy as "a front man" for traitors. When Marshall received the Nobel Prize in 1953, the journal applauded his selection and lauded him as a dedicated anti-Communist and a man of peace.[52]

Far more damaging criticism of McCarthy followed reports of controversial "book burning" episodes at scattered sites throughout the nation and at State Department-operated libraries abroad. While hard proof of such incidents was often lacking, there was little doubt that volumes by "suspicious" authors were being removed from library shelves across America. And, in response to McCarthy's charge that State Department libraries contained some 30,000 books by Communists and pro-Communists (including, McCarthy claimed, the works of Arthur Schlesinger, Jr., Brooks Atkinson, Edna Ferber, John Dewey, and Stephen Vincent Benét), Secretary of State John Foster Dulles summarily banned material "by all Communist authors [and] any publications which consistently publish Communist propaganda."[53]

Ironically, the most eloquent defense of the freedom to read came from the International Brotherhood of Carpenters, a conservative, tough-talking, anti-Communist affiliate. In a particularly sensitive article, "No Book Burning for Us," *The Carpenter* noted that many libraries were removing books by Communist sympathizers even though the subject matter had nothing to do with politics. To follow such a course was sheer folly, for it deprived book lovers of the joy of reading many fine novels, mysteries, and adventure stories. Even

---

Communist who had been the director of Research for the House Committee on Un-American Activities from 1938–1945. From 1945 until his selection by McCarthy, Matthews had been working as a consultant to the Hearst corporation. A former Methodist minister, Matthews had written an article for the July, 1953 issue of *American Mercury* ("Reds in Our Churches") that began: "The largest single group supporting the Communist apparatus in the United States today is composed of Protestant clergymen." As might be expected, the announcement of Matthews's appointment aroused immediate protest. The Democratic members of McCarthy's committee demanded that Matthews be fired at once; clergymen across the nation mobilized against the appointment, and President Eisenhower issued a statement condemning the "generalized and irresponsible attacks that sweepingly condemn the whole of any group of citizens." Under the circumstances, McCarthy had no alternative but to let Matthews go. See, *New York Times*, July 3 and 4, 1953; Herbert Parmet, *Eisenhower and the American Crusades* (New York: Macmillan, 1972), pp. 264–67.

52. *The International Teamster*, December, 1953, p. 14.

53. Robert Donovan, *Eisenhower: The Inside Story* (New York: Harper, 1956), p. 90. Parmet, *Eisenhower and the American Crusades*, pp. 259–63.

more distressing was the fact that volumes by non-Communists and anti-Communists were being taken off the shelves simply because they were controversial or because right-wing vigilantes did not happen to agree with the author. The burning or the removal of a book from a library, the piece concluded, "is a wicked symbolic act. . . . It is not an act against that book alone; it is an act against free institutions."[54] To further emphasize the point, Carpenters' President William Hutcheson, a lifelong Republican known for his fierce anticommunism, stated publicly that McCarthy's shameful conduct merited no defense from organized labor.[55]

More than any other single event of that era, however, the army-McCarthy hearings of 1954 brought home to millions of Americans a complete, uncensored version of demagoguery in action. The senator's vicious, personal attacks upon General Ralph Zwicker, his persistent browbeating of Secretary of the Army Robert Stevens, his statements belittling the political courage of President Eisenhower and the intelligence and integrity of Republican and Democratic senators alike combined to portray McCarthy as a publicity-seeking bully who would stop at nothing to advance his own career.[56] McCarthy and his cohorts, noted one AFL journal during the army hearings, were "making a mockery" of sacred American institutions. If they were not quickly slapped down, their ultimate target—democracy—might well be destroyed.[57]

Other longtime McCarthy critics within the federation viewed the hearings in more positive terms. After years of warning skeptical colleagues about the dangers of McCarthyism, they were finally being vindicated—and by McCarthy himself. According to *The Electrical Workers' Journal*, the senator's daily televised performances were providing the American people with the "ultimate educational experience."

> Up until the advent of the Army-McCarthy hearings, there were many citizens . . . who were convinced that McCarthy was a knight in shining armor . . . carrying on a brilliant crusade against Communism. . . . We are convinced that the American people are pretty smart and after watching the current antics on television—Senator McCarthy in operation— . . . they are not inclined to be fooled by Senator McCarthy any

54. *The Carpenter*, August, 1953, p. 23, 29–30.
55. Maxwell Raddock, *Portrait of an American Labor Leader: William Hutcheson* (New York: American Institute of Social Science, 1955), p. 319.
56. See, especially, Michael Straight, *Trial by Television* (Boston: Beacon Press, 1954), entire; Richard Rovere, *Senator Joe McCarthy* (Cleveland: World Publishing Co., 1960), pp. 205–22.
57. *AFL News-Reporter*, March 12, 1954.

longer. If the hearings awakened the American people to the fact that McCarthyism does not defeat Communism and that a better and more effective way must be found to deal with the threat, then they will not have been in vain.[58]

Many heretofore silent affiliates seemed to agree. "We can all get a lesson out of the show as it has run thus far," commented one AFL journal. "If this country is to be saved from Communism it will not be because of McCarthy. It isn't necessary to make a racket like a banshee to get things done. It isn't necessary to threaten and browbeat . . . to accomplish a purpose." And, the *Foundry Workers' Journal* concluded in a sarcastic reference to former McCarthy staff member G. David Schine, "above all it isn't necessary to try to keep a rich young man out of the army."[59] The disappointment with McCarthy's televised showing was aptly summarized by *The Boilermakers' Journal*: "If ever a young man had an opportunity in government to really serve his country and bring honor to himself, McCarthy was given that opportunity, but instead he has become an affliction for which there seems to be no cure."[60]

V

The first attempt by the AFL to formally condemn Senator McCarthy came at the 1953 national convention. It was here that A. Philip Randolph, president of the Brotherhood of Sleeping Car Porters, proposed a resolution "condemning and repudiating . . . congressional investigations by rule of thumb of McCarthyism as being a deadly thrust at the very heart of democracy . . . since it is the essence of the police state."[61] In a clear move to avoid the issue, the Committee on Resolutions, which was headed by Matthew Woll, refused to allow its passage, noting that the AFL rarely, if ever, singled out an individual for special censure. However, in "the spirit of compromise" a substitute resolution was accepted that deleted all references to McCarthy. It read simply that the AFL "condemned the conduct of *some committee chairmen* who have completely abused their powers . . . by disregarding the rights of individuals to be heard in the due process of law with . . . appropriate safeguards for their rights and

---

58. *The Electrical Workers' Journal*, May, 1954, p. 29.
59. *International Molders' and Foundry Workers' Journal*, June, 1954, p. 24.
60. *The Boilermakers' Journal*, April, 1954, p. 78.
61. *Proceedings of the Seventy-Second Constitutional Convention of the American Federation of Labor*, 1953, p. 413.

interests."[62] Although it was quite obvious that the resolution was directed at McCarthy, the federation (in the months before the fateful army-McCarthy hearings) was still unwilling to officially condemn his actions.

Perhaps the great turmoil surrounding Senator McCarthy and his allegations can best be described by following the path of the resolution that finally condemned him. At the Massachusetts AFL Convention of 1954, delegate Kenneth Kelley of the Quincy Central Labor Union offered a statement to that body which read:

Whereas, on every one of the 33 issues affecting labor, he has worked against the interests of working people. . . .
Whereas, he has spurned the Democratic principles practiced by the American labor movement and has created disunity by his condemnations of loyal public officials. . . .
Resolved, that the 68th Convention of the Massachusetts Federation of Labor condemns the anti-labor record of Senator McCarthy and questions his sincerity as an opponent of Communism at home and abroad.[63]

Immediately, a Boston labor official protested the resolution, claiming that while no union could defend the senator's voting record there were millions of Americans who would gladly support his crusade against communism. After much commotion and charges that certain delegates were being denied the use of microphones, a representative of the Boston Central Labor Union took the floor to defend the resolution. He noted that the hysteria engendered by McCarthyism was as dangerous as the senator's conspicuous antilabor record; indeed, some four years had passed since the initial charges were made, and all McCarthy had done was to divide the nation. Following more heated debate, a former national legislative representative provided critics of the resolution with their most potent argument. "I . . . did lobby work in the Senate," he said, "and nobody knows McCarthy better than I do. But I don't want the Federation to become involved in this controversy because we have to get votes from pro-McCarthy people and anti-McCarthy people for the purpose of promoting our welfare. . . . We can't vote against McCarthy whether we like it or not because he is out in Wisconsin. Let the people of Wisconsin and the people in the United States Senate take care of this mess and we will be doing fine."[64] Although no further

62. Italics mine. Ibid., p. 400.
63. *Proceedings of the Sixty-Eighth Convention of the Massachusetts State Federation of Labor*, 1954, p. 51.
64. The McCarthy debate in ibid., pp. 51–56.

action was taken on the resolution, Kelley informed his colleagues that he would bring it up again at the national convention.

That same year, Kelley submitted his resolution to the AFL national convention in Los Angeles. He admitted that it had not been well received at his state convention, but insisted that the federation take a firm stand on the McCarthy issue.[65] This time, the pressure exerted by Keenan, Dubinsky, Rose, Meany, and other political activists was too great. They knew that the AFL had to take some action, for censure proceedings against McCarthy were already being conducted by the Senate in Washington, and a full-scale "Joe Must Go" recall petition drive was underway in Wisconsin. Yet, in a final effort to mollify the remaining McCarthy supporters, the Committee on Resolutions avoided any inflammatory statements or resolutions concerning the senator's conduct (including one of the latter, tabled immediately, which equated McCarthyism with Nazism).[66] The final resolution read that "having voted against the interests of the working people on every single issue . . . offers sufficient evidence that the senator's self-appointed role as America's champion against communism is not confirmed by the voting record. . . . Therefore," it concluded, "the AFL Convention hereby assembled condemn the conduct of Senator McCarthy as alien to the American tradition."[67]

What the committee had done was to question Senator McCarthy's sincerity as a champion against communism because of his antilabor record; it touched only lightly upon his inquisitorial methods. Since, the resolution noted, "Communism is able to grow by exploiting substandard conditions produced by low wages, insufficient education, slum housing, denial of civil rights, *including* denial and abuse of fair judicial processes," then Senator McCarthy and his reactionary colleagues were actually aiding the growth of communism, not fighting it. While the logic of this resolution was open to question, the resolution itself was noteworthy in that it was the first and only official condemnation by the AFL of Senator Joseph McCarthy.

*   *   *

On the state level, six of the twelve federations sampled debated the McCarthy issue at some length. In California and Wisconsin,

65. *Proceedings of the Seventy-Third Convention of the American Federation of Labor*, 1954, p. 377. Before Kelley left for Los Angeles, the Boston Central Labor Union passed a resolution asking him not to bring up the McCarthy issue at the national convention.
66. Ibid., pp. 374–75.
67. Ibid., p. 580.

forceful resolutions were passed condemning the senator for his anti-labor voting record and his abuses in the field of civil liberties.[68] In other states, the course was not nearly so smooth. At the Oregon convention, a resolution was submitted censuring McCarthy for "smearing many of America's noblest public servants," and for "instilling fear in the hearts of the American people for personal aggrandizement." After some debate, the chairman of the Committee on Resolutions offered a milder substitute that omitted all references to the senator and stated simply that the convention agreed in principle with the notion of fair treatment for all citizens before congressional committees. The delegates overruled the committee chairman in favor of the original resolution, however, even after hearing a personal plea for moderation by the state federation president.[69] In Connecticut, the federation was confronted with the issue when a member petitioned the convention in 1953 for a formal condemnation of McCarthy. No action was taken, as the resolution was quickly withdrawn.[70] The very next year, a strongly worded statement comparing McCarthyism to Hitlerism was passed over in favor of a less inflammatory one claiming that "McCarthyism is an attack upon basic American freedoms and the free labor movement."[71] Anti-McCarthyites in Minnesota met with the rudest treatment of all. In 1954, after four years of silence, they offered a modest resolution calling upon the state federation to urge the U.S. Senate to sustain the Watkin's Committee report recommending McCarthy's censure. After very little debate, the resolution was turned over to a legislative committee and never heard from again.[72] The federations in Illinois, Michigan, New York, Pennsylvania, Ohio, and West Virginia ignored the controversy altogether.

In a sense, these state bodies reflected the AFL's true sentiment

68. In California, the resolution read: "Whereas, a new smear technique, not unlike that employed in totalitarian countries, has taken hold in our country under the name of McCarthyism; Resolved, we go on record against McCarthyism in its various forms and call upon all Democratic elements in both the Republican and Democratic parties to energetically aid in its eradication." *Proceedings of the Fifty-First Convention of the California State Federation of Labor*, 1953, p. 341. For the reactions of the Wisconsin State AFL, see Chapter 8.

69. *Proceedings of the Fifty-Second Annual Convention of the Oregon State Federation of Labor*, 1954, pp. 94–95.

70. *Proceedings of the Sixty-Eighth Annual Convention of the Connecticut State Federation of Labor*, 1953, p. 160.

71. *Proceedings of the Sixty-Ninth Annual Convention of the Connecticut State Federation of Labor*, 1954, pp. 145–46.

72. *Proceedings of the Seventy-Second Annual Convention of the Minnesota State Federation of Labor*, 1954, p. 205.

on McCarthy. A small segment wanted to condemn his actions; an even smaller one wanted to praise them. The majority, however, believed that a decisive stand on this issue was not worth the obvious consequence: bitter internal dissension.

VI

The AFL's response to the political phenomenon known as McCarthyism reflected more than an attitude toward a particular public figure. It represented, in a larger sense, another example of the federation's careful rejection of long-held, monolithic perceptions about the role of organized labor in politics.

It was not surprising that McCarthy's most ardent supporters within the federation came from the conservative, craft-oriented unions. Here, to be sure, were the men whose intense personal anxieties about the threats of Soviet expansion and New Deal socialism were ripe for exploitation. For years they had preached the virtues of rabid anticommunism, of voluntarism, and of pride in a free and independent labor movement; and for years their voices were heard and respected. But as the small, highly skilled organizations—once the cornerstone of power and prestige in the labor movement—declined in influence, a group of younger, politically minded trade unionists began to take control. Moreover, they joined forces with government bureaucrats and politicians to push an alien philosophy upon the federation. The AFL now found itself endorsing welfare programs, expanded government participation in the economy, and partisan political action in favor of the Democratic party. In short, the labor movement had forfeited its role as an effective, independent force in American society to become one more arm in a massive, government-dominated coalition of leftist politicians, social theorists, and intellectual malcontents—the very coalition whose loyalty to America McCarthy seriously questioned. As Joseph Keenan so well described it:

> When I heard Dick Gray and others talk up McCarthy, I understood their concern. They felt that the government was full of Communists and Socialists and people who sat on their rumps all day thinking up ways to destroy this country. . . . And they were concerned that labor's involvement with these people would end the independence of our movement and make us like them. Gray felt that we had taken the easy way out by going to the government with our problems and now we'd all have to pay the price.[73]

73. Interview by the author with Joseph Keenan, April 10, 1970.

To some political activists, however, the social welfare programs of the New and Fair Deals were responsible for the economic security and material well-being enjoyed by most working people in America. They therefore viewed with great alarm the rise of McCarthyism, a force capable of destroying or at least severely weakening labor's profitable relationship with the government. These unionists feared that the senator was using the frustrations and anxieties of the American people to create an atmosphere in which liberal-minded citizens were afraid to express their opinions, and in which the peripheral issues of internal security and subversion took precedence over those of domestic reform. McCarthyism, in sum, represented both the mindless political repression of its namesake and the ultimate destruction of the New Deal concept of social welfarism.

Somewhere between these two positions was the majority federation opinion—a perception of McCarthyism that differed markedly from those expressed by conservatives and liberals. Most AFL unionists supported New and Fair Deal programs and therefore were critical of the senator's antiunion, probusiness outlook. However, their loyalty to the Democratic Administration did not blind them to that party's apparent shortcomings in the areas of foreign affairs and internal security. Many federationists, for example, refused to believe that McCarthy's broadsides against Truman and his colleagues were motivated solely by a desire to destroy domestic reform. Indeed, as vehement anti-Communists, they themselves had often expressed open resentment at the President's "shabby handling" of the problems posed by Soviet expansion and subversion in government. The feeling most prevalent during the early McCarthy years (1950–1951) was that the senator should be given every opportunity to prove his allegations. If they were true, the country would owe him a debt of gratitude; if they were false, he would be found out soon enough. To officially condemn his actions before the verdict was in, however, simply to protect the reputation of an Administration that had often ignored the dangers of communism, seemed both unreasonable and unpatriotic.

So the federation waited, deftly avoiding a showdown on the McCarthy issue, busily confronting the important problems of Taft-Hartley repeal, the proposed CIO merger, and the formal endorsement of the Democratic party. As time passed, however, and McCarthy's irresponsible actions became obvious to all but his most loyal supporters, the AFL was forced to abandon its self-imposed position of neutrality. "The issue was a very emotional one . . . and we felt originally that we could deal with it in our own unions, in our own way," concluded David Dubinsky. "But by 1954, just about every

Chapter 8

Wisconsin Labor Views the "New" McCarthy

I

Organized labor in Wisconsin had undergone several significant alterations since the senatorial election campaign of 1946. Of primary importance was the expulsion of the Communists from the state CIO after more than a decade of control. By 1947, both the Milwaukee and Wisconsin Industrial Union Councils had purged themselves of all "Red" leadership. The period of Communist domination had been a calamitous episode, for, as Thomas Gavett reported, "the fruits of some ten years of Communist influence . . . were violence, the suppression of union democracy, and the misuse of union funds."[1] The CIO, free at last from the scorn of public opinion and the shackles of political radicalism, moved once again in the direction of trade union respectability.

The expulsion of the CIO Communists coincided with another important political shift in Wisconsin. When the Progressive party disbanded in 1946, the Democrats moved in quickly to fill the void. As the new haven for liberals, the Democratic party established itself as a major political force in Wisconsin. Almost by default, labor unionists gravitated towards this organization and found a cordial reception, to no one's surprise. Essentially urban in outlook, the Democratic party stressed domestic reforms that invariably were in line with working-class demands. In fact, by 1952, organized labor controlled many local party organizations, placed three representatives on the Executive Board of the Democratic Organizing Committee, and came close to electing one of its own leaders, George Molinaro, to the chairmanship of that body.[2] So began a working political alliance that kept alive much of the Progressive tradition indigenous to Wisconsin.

*   *   *

1. Thomas Gavett, *The Development of the Labor Movement in Milwaukee* (Madison: University of Wisconsin Press, 1965), p. 196.
2. Donald Kommers, "Organized Labor's Political Spending and the Catlin Act," M.A. thesis, University of Wisconsin, 1957, p. 44; *The Wisconsin Democrat*, October, 1951.

Contrary to developments on the national level, where the AFL and CIO differed widely on their basic approaches to McCarthyism, both state labor organizations—the Wisconsin State Federation of Labor and the Wisconsin State Industrial Union Council—were vehemently opposed to the senator's anti-Communist crusade. In fact, they felt a special responsibility for McCarthy's political rise, since it was then widely acknowledged that organized labor had brought about Bob LaFollette's defeat in 1946. An example of this personal guilt was displayed at the national convention of the International Typographical Union, when the Madison local offered a resolution apologizing for the part Wisconsin labor had played in McCarthy's previous election victory and promising never to let it happen again.[3]

Within a short time after McCarthy's explosive Wheeling address, union journals in Wisconsin warned the public to beware of a hoax. "It need hardly be recalled," wrote the *Milwaukee AFL Labor Press*, "that the 'valiant' McCarthy loudly proclaimed at the start of the probe that he could name a large number . . . of Reds in the State Department. He dwindled these down to a comparative few, and even these have been absolved. Politically . . . Little Joe has proved . . . a blabbermouth."[4] Similarly, the *Wisconsin CIO News* described the senator as the "most outstanding example of our loss of civil liberties. His guilt by association technique was used successfully by both Hitler and Stalin . . . his big lie technique is decidedly Communist and Fascist."[5] Organized labor's strong antipathy for its junior senator was officially expressed in 1950 by the formal condemnations of both state labor organizations.[6]

*   *   *

The year 1952 was of particular interest to organized labor in Wisconsin because Joseph McCarthy was up for reelection; the man who had been labeled the "buffoon assassin" by one local labor paper and "Slippery Joe" by another was coming home to face the people. As labor mobilized its forces for the November confrontation there was a general feeling that far from being invincible, the senator was

---

3. *Milwaukee AFL Labor Press*, August 6, 1950.
4. Ibid., July 20, 1950.
5. *Wisconsin CIO News*, September 21, 1951.
6. *Proceedings of the Fifty-Eighth Annual Convention of the Wisconsin State Federation of Labor*, 1950, p. 324. *Wisconsin CIO News*, September 2, 1950.

actually quite vulnerable to a sustained attack on his record. Not only had the Democratic party increased itself numerically since 1946, but there seemed to be thousands of Republicans and independents who would gladly vote to retire McCarthy from office. It was widely believed in Wisconsin that "almost every group . . . with the exception of the real estate lobby and the large businessmen had at one time or another in the past six years been let down by McCarthy."[7] James E. Doyle, chairman of the Democratic Organizing Committee of Wisconsin, summed up the situation best when he told reporters that while there was some doubt as to whether McCarthy could be beaten, he would most assuredly run behind the rest of the Republican ticket in the state.[8] This prediction soon proved itself to be prophetic.

The first major organizational decision to be considered by the state labor movement was whether to involve itself in the senatorial primary, thereby risking a dissipation of precious financial resources and a possible factional dispute over the selection of nominees, or to wait until the senatorial election to throw its considerable political leverage behind a single Democratic candidate. Wisconsin unionists were badly split on this issue. Some wanted to rush into the Democratic primary to ensure the nomination of a decidedly prolabor candidate; others desired a strict policy of neutrality; a few even urged the use of union resources in the Republican primary to support the candidacy of Len Schmitt, a former Progressive who seemed to have an outside chance of defeating McCarthy for the GOP senatorial nomination.

At the very outset, labor's political predicament was minimized by the fact that only one major Democratic candidate, Henry Reuss, appeared willing to enter his name in the senatorial primary. Reuss, a Milwaukee lawyer well known for his prolabor sympathies, had the strong support of union leaders and journals along the industrial lakeshore.[9] He was soon visiting local and regional labor meetings, speaking at picnics, banquets, and other functions, and generally making a favorable impression among blue-collar workers. Moreover, by May of 1952, with no other Democratic challenger in sight, both state labor organizations—AFL and CIO—gave him their official endorsement.[10]

7. John Frank, "The Team Against McCarthy," *The New Republic* 126 (March 10, 1952): 17.

8. Ibid.

9. *Wisconsin CIO News*, July 11, 1952; August 1, 1952. *The Wisconsin Democrat*, November, 1951; January, 1952; June, 1952.

10. Some unionists, led by Harold Newton, editor of the *Kenosha Labor*, began a movement to draft Gaylord Nelson, then a young state senator, but

The trouble began on June 16 when, after repeatedly denying his intention to run in the Democratic senatorial primary, Madison's popular Thomas Fairchild entered the race. This eleventh-hour move again fragmented the labor community. Many unionists, remembering Fairchild's great drawing power among moderate Republican and independent voters in the 1950 elections, felt he would be the strongest possible candidate against McCarthy; others believed it was simply unconscionable to desert Reuss at such a late date.[11] In the end, the state AFL and CIO bodies (and the majority of regional and local councils) remained loyal to their original choice, although the decision was based mainly on pragmatic grounds. Having already printed hundreds of thousands of pamphlets and fliers supporting Reuss and having publicly endorsed him at various gatherings throughout the state they had neither the time nor the money to work for another candidate.[12]

On September 9, 1952, the Democratic voters of Wisconsin chose Thomas Fairchild to oppose Joseph McCarthy in the November senatorial election. Fairchild, a soft-spoken New Dealer, a proven liberal, and a strong critic of the Taft-Hartley Act, worked quickly to solidify his position with state labor leaders. His first move was to accept the unionist conception of McCarthy. "It has been continually said of our junior senator," he noted, "that he has hidden his poor attendance record and his votes for the privileged few behind the smokescreen of his violent attacks against the Administration. However, I don't think there is any smokescreen thick enough to cover his failure in the field of labor legislation."[13] As expected, Wisconsin union officials now claimed to be doubly pleased with Fairchild's nomination, for they not only had a candidate with the ability to beat McCarthy but also one who would provide them with representation.[14]

On the other hand, Wisconsin's Republican senatorial primary proved disastrous for GOP liberals. Although Schmitt ran an energetic, well-managed campaign, he was simply overwhelmed by the McCarthy forces. The junior senator had decided to use this primary as a testing ground for the popularity of the Communist issue; and, quite obviously, the Republican electorate was favorably impressed.

soon switched to the Reuss camp. See, *The Wisconsin Democrat*, December, 1951.

11. Fairchild had run on the Democratic ticket against incumbent Senator Alexander Wiley in 1950 and had come within 70,000 votes of unseating him.

12. *Wisconsin CIO News*, July 18, 1952.

13. *Madison Union Labor News*, September, 1952.

14. *Wisconsin CIO News*, September 28, 1952.

Advertisements for McCarthy dotted the Wisconsin countryside with slogans like:

FELLOW TRAVELER
PARLOR PINK
IS THERE A PLACE FOR THEM IN OUR GOVERNMENT?
THE AMERICAN PEOPLE SAY "NO!"

Another read: "America Loves Him for the Enemies He Has Made. Who are the Enemies . . . Joe Stalin, The Pinks, The Reds—Fearless Joe McCarthy Pulls No Punches, Names Them All."[15] Although Schmitt took out much expensive television time to explain to the voters the venomous nature of the senator's charges, he was drubbed by a margin of two to one. "They [voters of Wisconsin] didn't vote *for* anyone," the exasperated loser told one reporter, "they voted *against* Joe Stalin."[16]

While organized labor now had a favorable candidate to contest McCarthy in November the primary results were still disheartening, for they revealed a widespread acceptance among blue-collar workers of the senator's anti-Communist appeal. In Milwaukee's working-class wards, for example, 47 per cent of those voting in the primary cast their ballots for Republican candidates (as opposed to the city average of 61 per cent). However, these same workers (or members of their families) who voted Republican gave McCarthy 71 per cent of their ballots (as opposed to the city average of only 63 per cent). In the city's six strongest blue-collar wards, comprising much of the Fourth Congressional District, McCarthy ran well below his city average of 38.7 per cent but still managed to come in second in a field of four supposedly strong candidates.

Various interpretations have been forwarded to explain McCarthy's surprising strength in these labor strongholds. Among some Wisconsin unionists, the belief was that many Democrats purposely entered the Republican primary to support McCarthy because they felt he would be easier to defeat in November than a former Progressive like Schmitt, who could make deep inroads among the state's liberal voters. As one railroad labor leader wrote: "It is hard to tell just how the November election will come out. I know four people in my neighborhood that are Democrats that voted for McCarthy. I asked them why and . . . they said, 'He'll be an easier man to beat than Schmitt.' Just how many thousands of others did the same thing

15. Campaign Handout, Committee on Political Education of the American Federation of Labor, AFL-CIO Papers, File B, Wisconsin State Historical Society.

16. Italics mine. "Wisconsin Testifies Against McCarthy," *The Nation* 175 (August 30, 1952): 166.

Table 7. Primary Voting—Milwaukee Labor Wards, September 9, 1952, for Senator

Ward	Percentage nonwhite	Percentage ethnicity of foreign born		McCarthy	Schmitt	Reuss	Fairchild	Total vote
6	55	25	German	27.4	13.5	34.1	25.0	3,894
		18	Italian					
12	1	44	Pole	21.8	11.2	39.0	28.0	4,918
		15	German					
5	0	28	Slav	29.9	17.5	30.3	22.3	5,678
		16	Austrian					
10	20	25	German	30.0	22.3	32.0	15.7	4,675
		51	Pole					
14	0	81	Pole	20.9	9.9	43.3	25.9	7,002
		11	German					
8	0	47	Pole	30.7	12.4	33.3	23.6	5,972
		25	German					
	14.7	41	Pole	26.6	14.1	35.7	23.6	32,139
		35	Central European					
		16	German					
City average	3.6	17	Pole	38.7	22.6	24.4	14.3	202,488
		29	Central European					
		29	German					

SOURCE: *Twenty-second Biennial Report of the Board of Election Commissioners of the City of Milwaukee*, 1953, p. 104. U.S., Bureau of the Census, *Census of the Population: 1950. Milwaukee Census Tracts.*

is a question to be considered."[17] However, in a more candid moment, the same individual wrote that "McCarthy has us beat, at least temporarily. . . . I was not surprised that he won the nomination; the only thing that surprised me was the majority he got."[18]

In reality, this substantial labor support for McCarthy was not unexpected. Many Democratic unionists, especially Catholics of Polish, Italian, and Czech extraction who were clustered along the industrial lakeshore, were registering their protests not only at the

17. Roy Empey to John Reynolds, September 12, 1952, Roy Empey Papers, Wisconsin State Historical Society.
18. Roy Empey to William Evjue, September 14, 1952, in ibid.

standard McCarthy targets like the Eastern Establishment but also at a foreign policy that had failed to stop the rise of communism in Eastern Europe and had resigned itself to the proposition that Soviet expansion might only be contained, not rolled back. As labor leaders viewed these primary results, they realized all too clearly that their attacks upon McCarthyism as a threat to vital civil liberties held little or no appeal for these workers; in fact, it seemed as if most union members might well have supported any program, no matter how abhorrent to the American legal tradition, that would have reversed their government's alleged apathy toward both the Soviet Union and the American officials responsible for such a "treasonous" policy.[19] As the *Wisconsin CIO News* wrote in a postmortem of the September primary: "The Cavemen won a victory at the polls last Tuesday and it is obvious that many CIO members helped bring this about."[20]

With the primary elections behind them, state labor leaders reflected seriously upon their course of action. They decided, first, that although 1952 was the year of presidential, congressional, and gubernatorial elections in Wisconsin, the McCarthy-Fairchild contest would occupy their almost exclusive attention. The AFL's Committee on Political Education, for example, solicited all financial contributions on an anti-McCarthy basis by informing prospective donors that their money was being used for the campaign against the senator.[21] These leaders knew well that McCarthy was the issue in Wisconsin, and they were willing to exploit that issue in order to properly confront it.[22] Second, Wisconsin unionists were unwilling to

19. See, Samuel Stouffer, *Communism, Conformity and Civil Liberties* (Garden City: Doubleday, 1955), pp. 22–67; Seymour Lipset, "Three Decades of the Radical Right," in Daniel Bell, *The Radical Right* (Garden City: Doubleday, 1964), p. 400; Martin Trow, "Right Wing Radicalism and Political Intolerance: A Study of Support for McCarthy in a New England Town," Ph.D. dissertation, Columbia University, 1957, pp. 153–69; Kevin Phillips, *The Emerging Republican Majority* (New Rochelle: Arlington House, 1968), pp. 157–59.

20. *Wisconsin CIO News*, September 12, 1952.

21. *Proceedings of the Sixtieth Annual Convention of the Wisconsin State Federation of Labor*, 1952, p. 170.

22. Not surprisingly, the Democratic Organizing Committee of Wisconsin also centered its attack in 1952 on McCarthy. As Richard Haney has written: "Every aspect of the 1952 Democratic campaign . . . centered around the single issue of defeating McCarthy. Congressional candidates . . . ran against McCarthy. The Proxmire campaign for governor was conducted against McCarthy. Even the presidential campaign was used in a way to bring down McCarthy rather than to elect Stevenson." Richard Haney, "A History of the Democratic Party in Wisconsin Since World War II," Ph.D. dissertation, University of Wisconsin, 1970, p. 179.

repeat Schmitt's mistake by challenging McCarthy directly on the issue of Communists in government. Instead, they decided to stage a vigorous counterattack aimed at the senator's most serious weaknesses: his day-to-day performance as a legislator, his domestic voting record, and the nature and source of his political support.

At the regional PAC meetings, discussions were held on how to generate voter enthusiasm. It was decided that in addition to the standard procedures, the regular union meetings, picnics, and informal gatherings could be related to "some angle on politics." Wherever possible, Tom Fairchild was to be invited. Local "Fairchild Days" were urged, where the candidate would come to a city to have breakfast, brunch, lunch, or dinner with as many union members as possible. It was even suggested that the "union-citizen funds for education" be exhausted for registration and voting drives or other forms of direct political action.[23] However, because state leaders were sensitive about Republican charges of "delivering the labor vote" to Democratic candidates, they warned local officials against unnecessary arm-twisting. Harold J. Thompson, secretary of the Racine Political Action Committee, sent a note to all PAC workers that read: "Please keep in mind that the members of our locals should not be ordered to vote in a certain way. Politics should be discussed in terms of bread and butter issues and how the candidates stand on those issues. The members, after education and discussion, should be free to vote as they wish."[24]

By the summer of 1952, the labor campaign was in high gear.[25] Each local Political Action Committee formed an organizational hierarchy with a "labor alderman" assigned to each ward and a "labor assemblyman" to each district. These individuals were given the responsibility of breaking down the union membership lists into ward and precinct units and of assigning volunteer workers to distribute literature door to door. This policy, which had been in operation for some years in Milwaukee, Kenosha, and Racine, was extended for the first time into the cities of Sheboygan, Oshkosh, Beloit, and Janesville. Large telephone campaigns were also initiated in the major cities to contact workers and their families and inform them

23. *Racine Labor*, October 3, 1952.
24. Ibid., September 5, 1952.
25. Information on the labor campaign against McCarthy was derived from interviews with state labor leaders George Haberman, George Hall, Loren Norman, and George Poreden; Committee on Political Education of the AFL, File B, AFL-CIO Papers; Wisconsin Industrial Union Council Papers; and state and regional newspapers, including the *Madison Union Labor News*, *Kenosha Labor*, *Milwaukee AFL Labor Press*, *Wisconsin CIO News*, and *Racine Labor*.

of the crucial importance of voting against McCarthy. These phones were manned by volunteers, usually the wives and relatives of union members. In most areas, arrangements were made to provide transportation to the polls, and in Milwaukee and Kenosha, the Democratic party let the labor unions take over the traditional roll of poll watching.

State and regional labor leaders often banded together into "truth teams" to attend civic and club meetings for the purpose of leading political discussions, while union wives held card parties and raffles (attended usually by Mrs. Fairchild or Mrs. Doyle) to raise money for the campaign. Furthermore, special anti-McCarthy supplements were distributed by the thousands. The state AFL reprinted a brochure entitled *Inside McCarthy* (written by *Capital-Times* correspondent Miles McMillin), which centered on the senator's anti-labor record, his fondness for big business, and especially his unethical conduct. Articles appeared on his fraudulent state income tax returns, his censure by the Wisconsin State Supreme Court for destroying vital case records while a circuit court judge, and his allegedly dishonest endeavors in connection with various congressional lobbyists.[26] Similarly, the state CIO introduced a fifteen-page pamphlet, *Smear Incorporated: The Record of Joe McCarthy's One Man Mob Operation,* which contained features on almost all the same subjects—his unethical conduct as a judge, his "little favor" for the real estate lobby, his income tax scandal, and his strong endorsement by Senator Taft.[27] And, on the final day of the campaign, CIO-PAC bought an hour of radio time on thirty-one stations throughout the state for "a thumping, anti-McCarthy address" by Senator Hubert Humphrey of Minnesota.

Time and again, the state labor journals forcefully attacked McCarthy as antilabor and pro-big business. The *Milwaukee AFL Labor Press,* for example, began a series of articles entitled "Case of the People Versus Slippery Joe McCarthy" in which this theme was greatly exploited. On July 24, the first article appeared, stating in part: "And while McCarthy was helping to handcuff labor, he was serving as a 'water boy' for Big Business. His dealings with the Lustron prefabricating interests became a national scandal. His preferences for and friendship with Senator Robert Taft and the Big Business crowd is well known. Labor-hating Taft has endorsed McCarthy for re-election."[28] On August 7, the newspaper again leveled

---

26. Committee on Political Education of the AFL, File B, AFL-CIO Papers, Wisconsin State Historical Society.
27. Ibid.
28. *Milwaukee AFL Labor Press,* July 24, 1952.

the charge. "The junior senator's services to industrialists," it stated, "have come in the form of firm support of the Taft-Hartley Act and other anti-labor legislation. Private utility interests are happy over the senator's vote to cut public power appropriations. He sided with the oil interests on the Tidelands oil bill. . . . He has served the privileged interests in preference to the people back in Wisconsin."[29] Labor leaders took similar public stands. George Haberman, president of the Wisconsin State Federation of Labor, told *The Nation* that his organization "was not in favor of the re-election of a senator whose voting record was in opposition to labor 81.3% of the time on labor bills and in opposition to the public interest 72.2% on social legislation," while Theodore Kurtz, secretary-treasurer of the Wisconsin State Industrial Union Council, pointed out that "McCarthy's vote for restrictive labor laws and against minimum wage shows he is no friend of the working people."[30]

In the campaign's final stages, the political battle was intensified to a level in which hysterical charges by both sides became accepted as an integral part of the campaign. While McCarthy kept busy impugning the loyalties of men like Adlai Stevenson, Archibald MacLeish, and James Wechsler, the labor journals retaliated with equal force. It was charged in the *Milwaukee AFL Labor Press* that the senator's vote against the federal education bill was proof of his inherent dislike of children; moreover, while commenting on his votes against housing and social security, it added: "Do you hate the old folks, just as you apparently hate the youngsters, Joe?"[31] Although union newspapers dealt with McCarthy in a manner as crude as his own, they were successful in impressing upon the electorate the fact that its junior senator had no constructive program for the betterment of the people of Wisconsin.

*   *   *

Certainly, a factor worthy of serious consideration is the amount of money spent by national, state, and local labor organizations in

29. Ibid., August 7, 1952. Of course, the labor press made no secret of the fact that many of the state's largest and most antiunion employers—including F.R. Bacon of Cutler-Hammer, Henry Talboys of the Nordberg Company, John Sensenbrenner of Kimberly-Clark, Walter Harnischfeger of Harnischfeger Industries, and William Grede, president of the National Association of Manufacturers and president of Grede Foundries—were solidly in the McCarthy camp. See, for example, *Wisconsin CIO News*, June 6, 1952.
30. "Wisconsin Testifies Against McCarthy," p. 166.
31. *Milwaukee AFL Labor Press*, July 24, 1952.

the campaign against McCarthy. On the national level, fifteen major union groups contributed approximately $1,630,473 during the entire election year, virtually all of which went to Democratic candidates. Of this sum, somewhat less than half, or $797,555, was used to finance national campaign activity, and the rest, or $832,918, was transferred to other groups on the state level. Wisconsin received a substantial amount of this money, $21,000, ranking ninth highest among the forty-eight states. However, this figure is misleading, for it does not include the contributions that were funneled from these fifteen major labor groups to organizations like the Americans for Democratic Action (which used the money in Wisconsin against McCarthy), nor does it consider any of the $797,555 that may have been diverted back to state and local labor bodies by organizations like the AFL's League for Political Education or the CIO's Political Action Committee. Finally, this $21,000 figure totally excluded the substantial sums of money originating within state and local labor organizations that were used for campaign purposes.[32]

The situation is further complicated by the fact that the Wisconsin secretary of state demands financial statements not from individual contributors but rather from the organizations to which they contribute. This system makes it difficult to locate the various political contributions of any given labor organization; and, therefore, to attempt this task for a wide range of national, state, and local union groups is strenuous indeed. Moreover, unions that engage in political activities do not consider themselves "political committees" and are not legally obligated to file financial reports in Wisconsin. As one student of Wisconsin politics reported:

> Complete and accurate reports of campaign finances (by labor organizations) are always difficult to obtain because of the ambiguous wording of corrupt practice laws, archaic limits imposed on campaign spending, prohibitions against certain types of contributions (such as union dues being used for political purposes in federal elections), and a general reluctance on the part of politicians and labor leaders to disclose information concerning the financing of campaigns.[33]

However, to simplify this situation, two crude financial barometers can be used. The first is organized labor's public support for the Fairchild campaign, as seen, for example, through its political contributions to the Thomas Fairchild for Senator Club, a large, statewide organization that was the candidate's greatest source of financial

---

32. This analysis of labor's financial participation in politics is from a pamphlet, *Money in Politics*, n.d., prepared by Professor Alexander Heard of the University of North Carolina.

33. H. Gaylon Greenhill, *Labor Money in Wisconsin Politics*, 1964, p. 23.

support. From the beginning of June until the election in November, this committee spent approximately $66,000, almost 20 per cent of which was donated by various labor organizations.[34] Indeed, the only contributors who gave sums exceeding $1,000 were the Americans for Democratic Action (which was funded partially by national and state labor bodies), the AFL's League for Political Education, the CIO's national Political Action Committee, the International Ladies Garment Workers' Union, the Amalgamated Clothing Workers Union, and the Hotel and Restaurant Employees and Bartenders International Union.[35] Similarly, on the local level, the various regional councils, particularly the United Automobile Workers' councils and the CIO county Political Action Committees, contributed heavily to the numerous Fairchild for Senator Club affiliates. Donations ranging from $100 to $1,500 were received from such groups in Racine, Kenosha, Milwaukee, and Madison.[36]

The other barometer is the amount of money spent by the labor movement exclusive of direct contributions to the Fairchild campaign. In 1952, the state AFL and CIO organizations spent a total of almost $100,000 for political action, with most of this being used to discredit the legislative record of the incumbent junior senator. Funds were allocated to publish brochures, pamphlets, tabloids, and fliers; to buy radio and television advertising; and to finance a series of statewide Labor for Fairchild committees. Indeed, labor's deep financial involvement was most clearly shown by the fact that the state AFL's Political Education Fund, which, by virtue of its monthly one cent tax on all Wisconsin federation members could not be diverted to partisan political activities, was nevertheless used to print up a barrage of anti-McCarthy material.[37] Because state AFL leaders decided that "the money spent on this material was of an educational purpose which we consider not to have been political," an additional $14,636 was freed for the campaign.[38] The state CIO, on the other hand, listed $13,757 as its campaign expenditures for 1952, but one leader, Herman Steffes, claimed that the real figure was closer to $40,000.[39] In sum, while the exact amount of labor's financial

34. Secretary of State of Wisconsin, *Political Contributions to the 1952 Senatorial Election Campaign*, Folder 5557, November, 1952, Wisconsin State Historical Society.
35. Ibid.
36. Ibid.
37. Ibid., Folder 5639 (Wisconsin State Federation of Labor, Political Education Fund).
38. Ibid.
39. Kommers, "Organized Labor's Political Spending and the Catlin Act," p. 51.

involvement remains a mystery, the various national, state, and local union groups constituted the largest single monetary force in the effort to prevent Senator McCarthy's reelection in 1952.

*   *   *

When election day came to Wisconsin in November, 1952, the majority of union members voted against McCarthy; whether they did so because of the political activities of their labor organizations is another matter. The senator was carried to victory by a relatively narrow margin and, as was predicted by James Doyle, trailed the rest of the Republican ticket. In fact, political analyst Louis H. Bean stated that but for the Eisenhower landslide, McCarthy undoubtedly would have lost.[40]

Table 9. Republican Vote, 1952 Wisconsin General Election

Candidate	Vote	Percentage of total vote
Secretary of state (Zimmerman)	1,039,000	66
Governor (Kohler)	1,009,000	65
Lieutenant governor (Smith)	995,000	64
Treasurer (Smith)	992,000	64
President (Eisenhower)	980,000	61
U.S. senator (McCarthy)	870,000	54

SOURCE: Karl Ernest Meyer, "The Politics of Loyalty," Ph.D. dissertation, Princeton University, 1956, p. 204.

Furthermore, an analysis of selected wards in urban Wisconsin revealed the senator's miserable showing among working-class voters. In the heavily industrialized sections of Milwaukee's Fourth Congressional District, for example, Fairchild overwhelmed McCarthy; while the Democratic candidate captured 63.4 per cent of the total city vote, his percentage zoomed to 75.3 per cent in these blue-collar areas. The figures were even more impressive when compared with Adlai Stevenson's respective percentages of 51.5 per cent (city) and 68.5 per cent (labor wards).

40. Louis H. Bean, *Influences in the 1954 Mid-Term Elections*, 1954, p. 17. It is interesting to note that Secretary of State Fred Zimmerman, who headed the Republican vote getters in Wisconsin, ran on an anti-McCarthy platform.

Table 10. Election Statistics for Milwaukee Labor Wards, November 4, 1952, by Percentage and Total Vote

Ward	Male blue collar	Fairchild	McCarthy	Total vote	Stevenson	Eisenhower	Total vote
6	71.5	79.2	20.8	8,064	76.5	23.5	8,033
12	72.1	77.5	22.5	7,206	70.5	29.5	7,122
5	69.2	70.7	29.3	8,655	64.1	35.9	8,663
10	70.1	72.1	27.9	7,858	63.8	36.2	7,786
14	70.7	79.9	20.1	10,050	71.4	28.6	9,947
8	69.6	71.7	28.3	8,534	63.6	36.4	8,446
	70.5	75.3	24.7	50,367	68.5	31.5	49,997
City Total	59.7	63.4	36.6	308,901	51.5	48.5	305,305

SOURCE: *Twenty-second Biennial Report of the Board of Election Commissioners,* Milwaukee, 1953, pp. 370, 394.

The association between the percentage of blue-collar workers in a given ward and support for McCarthy in that ward can be more clearly demonstrated by the following scatter diagram of the six most pro-McCarthy and the six most anti-McCarthy wards in Milwaukee.

The six most pro-McCarthy wards (18, 3, 19, 22, 26, and 15) had relatively low percentages of employed male blue-collar workers; indeed, all of them were well below the citywide mean of male blue-collar workers in the labor force (59.7 per cent). They ranged from a low of 32.8 per cent in Ward 18 to a high of 51.1 per cent in Ward 3. On the other hand, the six most anti-McCarthy wards in Milwaukee (14, 6, 12, 24, 10, and 8) all had male blue-collar percentages above the citywide mean. They ranged from a high of 72.1 per cent in Ward 12 to a low of 61.1 per cent in Ward 24. In fact, five of the six most anti-McCarthy wards ranked at the very top of the city's twenty-six wards in percentage of employed male blue-collar workers. Obviously, the single variable most clearly associated with the McCarthy vote in Milwaukee was occupation.[41]

41. By superimposing census tracts over ward maps in Milwaukee, similar tests were run in these twelve wards to determine the effect of variables like level of education, median income, and ethnicity on support for McCarthy. There seemed to be absolutely no association between level of education or median income and support for McCarthy. The ethnic variable, however, showed some association. In general terms, the McCarthy vote dropped as the percentage of foreign-born Polish in the ward increased, and it rose when the level of foreign-born German increased. Poles, then, seemed to be the most

Figure 1. Scatter Diagram: Plot of McCarthy Vote and Percentage of Blue-Collar Voters

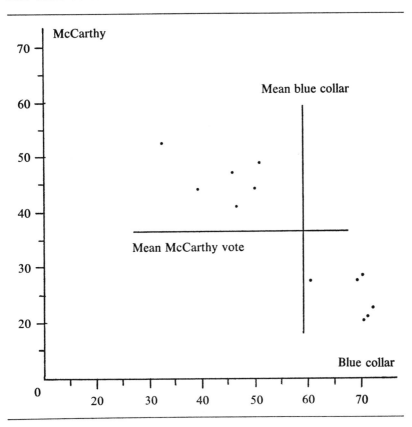

Nor was this anti-McCarthy sentiment among blue-collar workers prevalent only along the industrial lakeshore. In Madison, long a stronghold of Progressive Republicanism, the results were equally impressive. Throughout the city, where the *Madison Capital-Times* and other liberal Republican and Democratic sources carried out an intensive campaign aimed primarily at the senator's lack of integrity and his poor domestic record, the voters went narrowly for Eisenhower but overwhelmingly for Fairchild. Quite obviously, Madison's vast Progressive following, which had been badly fragmented by both the Portage convention and the senatorial campaign of 1946, had come together once more to roundly condemn a man whose political style was so alien to the LaFollette tradition.

anti-McCarthy ethnic group in the city, while Germans seemed to be the most pro-McCarthy.

In the city's labor wards, where the Democratic party was more firmly entrenched, these trends were greatly accentuated. Here, Adlai Stevenson's total increased by a full 13 per cent (from 48.2 per cent to 61.2 per cent), while Fairchild's percentage rose from 62.0 per cent to 71.4 per cent.[42]

Table 11. Election Statistics in Madison Labor Wards, November 4, 1952, by Percentage and Total Vote

Ward	Fairchild	McCarthy	Total vote	Stevenson	Eisenhower	Total vote
9	78.4	21.6	1,175	72.0	28.0	1,151
16–2	73.1	26.9	2,313	60.1	39.9	2,223
17	74.2	25.8	1,456	65.3	34.7	1,408
18–1	64.2	35.8	1,619	52.1	47.9	1,561
18–2	71.1	28.9	1,719	62.0	38.0	1,667
18–3	69.5	30.5	2,139	59.9	40.1	2,093
	71.4	28.6	10,421	61.2	38.8	10,103
City Total	62.0	38.0	44,177	48.2	51.8	42,848

SOURCE: *Madison Capital-Times*, November 5, 1952.

Even in Republican Janesville, where political action by the various labor unions was not fully developed and where the influential *Daily Gazette* consistently praised McCarthyism as the antidote to "years of Red influence under the Democratic administration," the labor wards bucked the prevailing political mood by giving Stevenson and Fairchild a majority of their votes.[43] In fact, Stevenson's total jumped from a low of 38.3 per cent for the city as a whole to a more respectable 51.6 per cent in the working-class areas, while Fairchild, who had received only 44.3 per cent of the city vote, captured a strong 54.7 per cent of the ballots in these labor wards.

Although the *Daily Gazette* claimed that the large Fairchild total in the city's west end (or blue-collar district) "was obviously a protest vote against Senator McCarthy . . . rather than representing Democratic party strength," the strong outpouring of support for Stevenson

42. Further evidence of McCarthy's poor showing in labor areas is shown by the fact that he ran dead last (behind all other Republican candidates) in every labor ward in Milwaukee and Madison.

43. *Janesville Daily Gazette*, November 1, 1952.

Table 12. Election Statistics in Janesville Labor Wards, 1952, by Percentage and Total Vote

		Fairchild	McCarthy	Total vote	Stevenson	Eisenhower	Total vote
Ward	*7*	53.5	46.5	874	48.9	51.1	867
	8	50.3	49.7	702	47.5	52.5	695
	9	51.2	48.8	625	50.1	49.9	631
	10	55.0	45.0	529	52.0	48.0	523
	11	62.5	37.5	666	60.8	39.2	633
	12	56.4	43.6	521	52.1	47.9	512
		54.7	45.3	3,918	51.6	48.4	3,861
City total		44.3	55.7	12,386	38.3	61.7	12,277

SOURCE: Janesville Daily Gazette, November 5, 1952

in these wards, especially in light of the fact that his opponent was an extremely popular political moderate, showed clearly that the Democratic organization had arrived as the workingman's party in Wisconsin.[44]

II

Much has been written about the affinity of the working class in America for right-wing extremism. The subject was carefully considered in 1954 when a group of distinguished social scientists, including Daniel Bell, Richard Hofstadter, Seymour Lipset, Talcott Parsons, and Nathan Glazer, collaborated on a series of essays entitled *The New American Right*.[45] Hofstadter, in his work "The Pseudo-Conservative Revolt," expressed the theme. He noted that throughout their history, Americans have experienced two kinds of processes, inextricably connected with one another: "*interest* politics, the clash of material aims and needs among various groups and blocs; and *status* politics, the clash of various projective rationalizations arising from status aspirations and other personal motives."[46] In periods of depression, economic turmoil, or national emergency, he continued, politics becomes clearly a matter of interests. In times of prosperity, however, status considerations become paramount.

44. Ibid., November 5, 1952.
45. Bell, *The New American Right*.
46. Richard Hofstadter, "The Pseudo-Conservative Revolt," in ibid., p. 43.

According to this hypothesis, America underwent a massive "status revolt" during the late 1940s and early 1950s, and McCarthyism was simply one of the forms of noneconomic protest through which Americans expressed their status dissatisfactions. During an era of unparalleled prosperity, when the real incomes and consuming powers of most citizens reached enormous heights, the lower and lower-middle classes discovered that their new material wealth could not buy them the respect they so badly needed. Among the sons and daughters of first- and second-generation Americans who make up the majority of the working class, these frustrations were particularly acute.[47] Their nagging insecurities over social status were hopelessly intertwined with strong fears about second-class citizenship. As Hofstadter wrote: "Status problems take on a special importance in American life because a very large part of the population suffers from one of the most troublesome of all status questions: unable to enjoy the simple luxury of assuming their nationality as a natural event, they are tormented by doubts as to whether they are really and truly and fully American." These anxieties, he concluded, often produced an affinity for the superpatriotic, antiestablishment appeals of Senator McCarthy.

Backed up by Gallup polls and surveys relating to civil liberties, communism, and authoritarianism, these social scientists believed that a large segment of the American working class was attracted by men of the McCarthy mold. Being of predominantly immigrant stock (in many cases Catholic), low but rising socioeconomic status, and with poor educational attainment, the blue-collar worker was taken in not only by the senator's anticommunism but also by his vicious slaps at Establishment figures—prominent government officials, social theorists, and Harvard-type intellectual snobs. The basic reason provided for this attraction was "status deprivation." "The support which a large section of the American working class gives to right-wing extremism," wrote Lipset, "may be related to the greater sense of status deprivation felt by 'failures' in periods of prosperity. . . . Workers who fail to get ahead while some friends, classmates, and fellow workers do, are likely to feel embittered." However, while

47. In his essay, Hofstadter clearly differentiates between the status deprivation of old-stock as opposed to immigrant Americans. He wrote: "Paradoxically the intense status concerns of present day politics are shared by two types of persons who arrive at them . . . from opposite directions. The first are found among some types of old family, Anglo-Saxon Protestants, and the second are found among many types of immigrant families, most notably among the German and Irish, who are frequently Catholic. The Anglo-Saxons are most disposed toward pseudo-conservatism when they are losing caste, the immigrants when they are gaining" (p. 44).

concluding that the working class constituted "the largest section of the mass base of the radical right," Lipset noted that it was, in terms of power, the least significant. This was because too many workers who supported right-wing policies relating to civil liberties and foreign affairs were also economic liberals. Therefore, "the principal significance of lower class attitudes lay in their votes and responses to public polls . . . rather than in their potential utilization as part of a mass base for an organized movement."[48]

It was not until several years later that other social scientists considered the equally relevant question of why such a large majority of the working class *rejected* the appeals of McCarthyism. By largely replacing Gallup polls with voting statistics, these researchers concluded that the status deprivation theory left too much to the imagination. In 1960, for example, a political scientist at the University of Wisconsin claimed that party affiliation was far more important in determining support for McCarthy.

> I want to turn now to a . . . hypothesis which attempts to explain McCarthyism as a political phenomenon. It is surprising that analysts have discounted so heavily the purely political aspect of his success. Therefore, I want to review now the rather heavy evidence supporting the hypothesis that McCarthy succeeded at the grass roots primarily among Republicans. . . . Inspection of election returns bears out the thesis that McCarthy ran best where the Republican party was strongest (and worst where it was weakest). . . . The returns demonstrate that the McCarthy vote was concentrated in areas of Republican strength, and was neither scattered nor distributed in some pattern unique to McCarthy, nor particularly strong."[49]

This political analysis, suggesting that McCarthy's greatest strength came from traditionally Republican areas and his greatest weakness from traditionally Democratic ones, seemed particularly relevant to Wisconsin's working-class areas. Many studies had pointed up the

48. Seymour Lipset, "The Sources of the 'Radical Right,' " in ibid., p. 194. A later survey, conducted among automobile workers in Detroit during the mid-1950s amplified Lipset's final conclusion by finding that authoritarian workers were no less likely to support liberal political action than were non-authoritarian workers. "Our 'authoritarian attitude' scores indicate a disturbing amount of undemocratic spirit and authoritarian-type thinking among the workers interviewed," noted the researchers. However, "authoritarian tendencies in our sample bear almost no relationship to voting, to active identification with the union, or to pro-labor political orientation." Arthur Kornhauser, Harold Sheppard, and Albert Mayer, *When Labor Votes* (New York: University Books, 1956), p. 199.

49. Nelson Polsby, "Towards an Explanation of McCarthyism," *Political Studies* 8 (October 1960): 258–63.

Democratic leanings of urban, working-class voters, especially (as in Milwaukee, Kenosha, and Racine) among Catholics of East European descent.[50] However, even if one accepts the hypothesis that the majority of anti-McCarthy sentiment among Wisconsin workers was party oriented, it still leaves unanswered the question of why the senator ran behind the rest of the Republican ticket in these urban districts. If party affiliation were the sole barometer in determining support for McCarthy, he should logically have done no better or worse than the other GOP candidates on the ballot. As noted earlier, this was not the case.

In attempting to determine the reason for McCarthy's dismal showing among working-class voters, the subject of trade union affiliation must be carefully considered. It was first analyzed in 1956, when Martin Trow completed his dissertation, "Right-Wing Radicalism and Political Intolerance: A Study of Support for McCarthy in a Small New England Town."[51] Trow concluded that membership in a labor union was a major factor in shaping a worker's attitude toward McCarthy. By accepting the then fresh theory of status deprivation, he hypothesized that a union channeled the free-floating frustrations and anxieties within and social and political order into an institutional framework of group conflict—such as labor versus management—thereby making these emotions unavailable for exploitation by a man like McCarthy.

> Now, without attempting . . . to distinguish among the various local unions in Bennington, it is clear that men who identify with or were active in their union differed markedly in their attitude toward McCarthy, and in other political and social orientations, as compared with inactive union members and with non-union workers. . . . Here is fresh evidence that involvement and identification with a union tends to channel the manifold discontents that are generated among working-class people into the institutional frameworks—of party and pressure

50. For working-class affinity for the Democratic party, see, George Gallup, "How Labor Votes," *The Annals of the American Academy of Political and Social Science* 274 (March 1951): 123–24. For the special affinity of Catholics of East European descent for the Democratic party, see, Scott Greer, "Catholic Voters and the Democratic Party," *Public Opinion Quarterly* 25 (Winter 1961): 611–25; Oscar Glantz, "Protestant and Catholic Voting Behavior in a Metropolitan Area," *Public Opinion Quarterly* 23 (Spring 1959): 73–82.

51. Martin Trow, "Right-Wing Radicalism and Political Intolerance: A Study of Support for McCarthy in a Small New England Town," Ph.D. dissertation, Columbia University, 1957. The town Trow studied was Bennington, Vt.

group politics and labor-management relations—which are available in our society for the expression of discontent and the registration of collective political and economic demands, and the resolution of conflicts that ensue from conflicting demands. McCarthy was the heir to free-floating discontent within our social and political order—discontent felt by people who had neither institutional channels nor public spokesmen for the expression of their discontent.[52]

Trow's analysis, as Michael Rogin has noted, was both provocative and incomplete; for while focusing exclusively on the alleged status deprivations of these workers, he failed to emphasize their attachments to McCarthy's major targets. "It was not only that workers had unions through which to express their grievances," wrote Rogin, "they also could not be mobilized by an attack on Roosevelt and the New Deal Democratic party."[53] Here, in essence, was where the true political value of the labor unions came into play. By organizing one of the largest statewide labor campaigns in history, the unions portrayed McCarthy as an anti-New Deal conservative whose domestic shortcomings far outweighed his possible value as an anti-Communist. And, they seemed to convince not only Trow's active union members but the far larger body of passive ones that McCarthyism was not in the best interests of working people. In short, while the best efforts of labor to defeat Senator McCarthy were unsuccessful, it made his victory in every way unimpressive.[54]

III

On the night of March 15, 1954, a rural newspaper editor in central Wisconsin composed a column that again heightened the feverish emotional climate surrounding Senator McCarthy. He wrote:

52. Ibid., pp. 153–54.
53. Michael Rogin, *The Intellectuals and McCarthy* (Cambridge: M.I.T. Press, 1967), p. 95.
54. In their study of the social and political attitudes of automobile workers in the Detroit area, Kornhauser and his colleagues provided a good deal of data showing passive union members (those who rarely went to union meetings, voted in union elections, or came to union functions) still tended to support the political recommendations of their union almost as much as active union members. "On the whole," they wrote, "the evidence reported here indicates that among auto workers . . . there is a fairly strong backing of union political activities . . . although personal involvement remains at a rather low level. . . . Our findings point to the conclusion that large numbers of those who go along with the union on political matters do so in a relatively passive spirit." Kornhauser et al., *When Labor Votes*, p. 145.

The *Star* proposes a recall election in which the sole issue shall be the fitness of Joseph R. McCarthy to serve his nation, his Party, and the sovereign state of Wisconsin. . . . Our decision to call upon the voters in Wisconsin is no whim of the moment. We have pondered, even prayed over it for long, dismal weeks as the genial Irishman we once so greatly admired has showered increasing humiliation upon the Party and the state to which we have long been devoted.[55]

Leroy Gore and his *Sauk-Prairie Star* soon became front-page news throughout the country; the very thought of an obscure local newspaper editor taking on a national figure of such power and influence was both "highly romantic" and "daringly democratic." Wisconsin Republicans had found a conscience.[56]

While recall elections are exceedingly rare in Wisconsin, Article XIII, Section 12 of the state's constitution provides that "the qualified electors of the state or any county or any congressional, judicial, or legislative district may petition for the recall of any elected officer after the first year of the term for which he was elected, by filing a petition demanding the recall of such officer. . . . Such petition shall be signed by at least twenty-five percent of the vote cast in the previous election."[57] Since 1,656,000 votes had been cast in the 1952 senatorial election, Gore needed notarized petitions with over 400,000 signatures and, by law, was allowed only sixty days in which to collect them.

Actually, the labor movement in Wisconsin had tinkered with the idea of recalling Senator McCarthy long before Gore popularized it. Less than two months after the dramatic Wheeling speech, the *Wisconsin CIO News* asked that "the recall provisions for U.S. Senator in Wisconsin's state constitution be invoked against McCarthy."[58] A week later, the newspaper claimed that "despite the fact that it would take several hundred thousand signatures, there are probably more people than that in Wisconsin who want to rid themselves once and for all of this misrepresentative."[59] This call to arms was not pursued, however, and little came of the idea until the Gore campaign in 1954.

Ironically, when Gore initiated the recall movement he did not ask for labor's support. McCarthy, he claimed, was a problem to be

55. *Sauk-Prairie Star*, March 18, 1954.
56. David Thelen and Esther Thelen, "Joe Must Go: The Movement to Recall Senator Joseph McCarthy," *The Wisconsin Magazine of History* 49 (Spring 1966): 185.
57. *The Wisconsin Blue Book*, 1954, p. 255.
58. *Wisconsin CIO News*, August 17, 1950.
59. Ibid., August 24, 1950.

disposed of by Republicans. While the editor seemed at least partially sincere in his contention that only party members should decide the fate of their junior senator, other motives were apparent. First, as a country editor, Gore wanted to direct a campaign based upon the spontaneous outpouring of individual sentiment rather than one dependent upon the huge voting blocs of a few well-placed leaders. Second, as a pragmatic man, he was afraid of being branded a Communist sympathizer by zealous McCarthy supporters and decided, therefore, to exclude all left-wing organizations from his movement. By ignoring groups like the ADA, CIO, and even the Democratic party, Gore believed he would be less likely to have this charge leveled against him.[60]

State labor leaders actually expressed a sense of relief at Gore's selective approach. While many of them would have worked enthusiastically for a large, well-organized, nonpartisan movement to recall Senator McCarthy, they were clearly not interested in the editor's meager campaign. As keen practitioners of organizational theory, they knew that it could not possibly succeed. As one labor journal noted, "the sheer weight of organizational machinery necessary and the complicated procedure of distributing petitions and getting them notarized and returned when filed will doom the movement to failure."[61] With defeat already hanging over the plan, unionists were perfectly willing to view the proceedings from a safe distance.

In running a highly partisan campaign that excluded all non-Republicans, Gore based his chance for success on the dubious supposition that thousands of past McCarthy supporters would suddenly see the light, throw off the shackles of McCarthyism, and storm the polls in an effort to recall their former hero. His poor organizational methods notwithstanding, the fact that Gore envisioned some 400,000 Republicans who would sign a petition repudiating one of their own leaders adequately reflected his political naivete. As a disenchanted Republican who had supported McCarthy in 1952, the Sauk City editor, no doubt, knew of many people who held beliefs similar to his own; but for his recall movement to have been successful, approximately 50 per cent of those persons who voted for the senator in 1952 would have had to sign recall petitions. This was all but impossible.

As Gore himself realized that he could not muster the necessary support, he took a more realistic approach and decided to accept aid

60. Ted Cloak and Jane Cloak, "Joe Must Go: The Story of Dane County in the 1954 Recall Against McCarthy," unpublished document, n.d., Wisconsin State Historical Society.
61. *Madison Union Labor News*, May, 1954.

from all available sources. In fact, the country editor now claimed that he was counting heavily on the unions to bail him out. "If the Milwaukee, Racine and Kenosha . . . groups can produce the signatures," he stated, "then the 400,000 goal can be reached."[62] Labor leaders, however, turned a deaf ear to his sudden plea for help; they saw absolutely no chance for success and did not want to become involved. The *Kenosha Labor*, for example, after sending a reporter to Sauk City to interview Gore, remarked of its admiration for the editor's courage but refused to officially support his movement. In fact, it placed an editor's note in the middle of the Gore article that stated simply: "The *Kenosha Labor* is and has been vigorously opposed to Senator McCarthy and McCarthyism and fully agrees with . . . Gore that this cancerous growth should be stamped out of the public life of the great state of Wisconsin. We wish the best of success to Editor Gore and his associates in their drive for more than 400,000 signatures on the 'Joe Must Go' petition drive."[63]

This type of positivistic neutrality was also expressed by some state labor leaders. CIO President Charles Schultz commended Gore for his effort but claimed that the recall movement was probably unconstitutional and therefore a wasted, though well-intended, project.[64] Most AFL unionists refused comment, although a few expressed the opinion that labor's participation in such a campaign was forbidden by the political limitations of the Taft-Hartley Act.[65]

Much of the rank and file of labor took a different position. For years they had been told by their leaders that Joseph McCarthy was an enemy of trade unionism, and yet, when the opportunity arose to finally do something about him, these very leaders remained silent. As confusion turned to anger, the pressure from below began to mount. First, union members in Madison and Milwaukee asked for thousands of petitions; then the movement spread along the lakeshore and into the Chippewa Valley. In Dane County, the local Political Action Committee passed a resolution supporting Gore's crusade.[66] Within days, petitions were circulated in the work rooms of Oscar Mayer, Kipp Company, Ray-O-Vac, Ohio Chemical, and other industrial concerns. A notary public appeared at the AFL Labor Temple, and union volunteers offered to collect, notarize, and mail all "Joe Must Go" petitions. One volunteer from the University of Wisconsin noted that "most labor people here [in Madison] regard

62. *Milwaukee Journal*, April 18, 1954.
63. *Kenosha Labor*, April 11, 1954.
64. *Madison Capital-Times*, March 23, 1954.
65. Ibid.
66. *Madison Union Labor News*, April, 1954.

the recall as they might regard a strike. Once into action, you don't stop to weigh the chances of success, you put all your energy into winning."[67]

Other cities had similar responses. Union officials in Milwaukee set up a "Joe Must Go" office and were swamped with support; volunteers manned phones and mimeograph machines around the clock. At Eau Claire, CIO official Ernest Christiansen promised Gore 10,000 signatures.[68] Even the labor press began to come around. Under the banner headline, "Will Assist Republican Liberals in Ouster Attempt," the *Kenosha Labor* formally endorsed the recall, as did its counterparts in Madison, Milwaukee, and Racine. This statement appeared in the *Milwaukee AFL Labor Press:*

> There may be some constitutional question as to the legality of the recall election affecting members of the federal legislative branch of government. . . . Nevertheless, if sufficient petitions are signed, it will show the temper of Wisconsin citizens, and hasten into oblivion a man who has certainly been no credit politically to his state. . . . The more that sign, and the quicker, the sooner will the stench of McCarthy politics be swept away from Wisconsin.[69]

Still, the state labor organizations and many of the regional councils rigidly maintained their neutrality. They refused to enter a campaign that was, to their way of thinking, hopelessly beyond repair. Yet, state labor leaders realized that they were reneging on the moral commitment of doing everything possible to rid Wisconsin of Joe McCarthy. In an effort to pacify the rank and file, labor leaders enacted a compromise whereby union members were urged to sign and circulate petitions "as individual citizens."[70] Typical of this new policy change was the plea by state AFL President George Haberman, who, after failing to officially endorse the recall movement, stated, "If there is a drop of patriotism in your body, get every man and woman you know to sign a 'Joe Must Go' petition."[71]

Labor's belated concern could not salvage the floundering recall movement. Although Joe McCarthy was given the scare of his political life, the Gore campaign lacked the professional expertise to achieve its objective; the junior senator from Wisconsin lived to fight another day.

In his book, *Joe Must Go*, which described the recall movement,

---

67. Cloak, "Joe Must Go," p. 50.
68. *Milwaukee Journal*, March 24, 1954.
69. *Milwaukee AFL Labor Press*, April 16, 1954.
70. *Madison Capital-Times*, May 28, 1954.
71. Ibid.

Leroy Gore claimed that labor failed to act because it feared possible retaliation by Senator McCarthy. He wrote:

> The unions had a ticklish and important legislative battle ahead of them. They knew only too well how effectively and how brutally Joseph Raymond McCarthy could strike at them through an unfortunate prejudice against unions. . . . The CIO had unquestionably put its house in order. . . . But you may be sure that he wouldn't hesitate to point a finger of accusation at the CIO for a 1946 blunder to which he was a gleeful partner.[72]

Yet, earlier in his book, Gore admitted that when the recall movement was begun, McCarthyism as an established political entity was on the wane, its originator a political corpse.[73] Therefore, according to the editor's own logic, labor had little to fear from the senator and should have willingly aided in his burial. Moreover, it was well known that organized labor had consistently opposed McCarthy at the height of his political power, a time when it was truly dangerous to have done so.

Unfortunately, the resources of labor remained on the sidelines for reasons that Gore himself helped to bring about. As a party excluded originally from active participation in the campaign, the unions were suddenly called upon to bail out a Republican newspaper editor who would, no doubt, get a lion's share of the credit if McCarthy were somehow recalled. Furthermore, it seemed more reasonable to assume that regardless of any effort put forth by the labor movement, the campaign, in its present debilitated condition, could not succeed. Union leaders were simply unwilling to officially commit themselves to a campaign that faced almost certain defeat, especially when the underlying causes reflected no discredit upon organized labor. One campaign aide close to Gore recalled:

> We had no real state-wide organizational support. This is not a criticism, because for their individual reasons, state labor groups, the Democratic party and other . . . groups could not support this effort. It must be said though that labor—particularly in the Milwaukee-Kenosha-Racine area and the Dane area—did give valuable assistance in many ways. . . . However, the real heavy hand of labor did not support the effort.[74]

72. Leroy Gore, *Joe Must Go* (New York: Messner, 1954), p. 131.
73. Ibid., p. 15.
74. Memorandum of Ivan Nestisgen, June 21, 1954, in Committee on Public Education, File B, AFL-CIO Papers, Wisconsin State Historical Society.

Chapter 9

The Effects of McCarthy and McCarthyism upon the Labor Movement

I

For the past two decades, historians and other social scientists have disputed both the origins of McCarthyism and the basis of its support. Interpretations abound as to whether this phenomenon resulted from a Republican plot to recapture national power, a Democratic desire to "play tough" with the Russians, a neo-Populist revolt to dismantle the existing status hierarchy, or some combination of these factors.[1] Moreover, its supporters have ranged from grass roots Republicans to disenchanted working-class ethnics to descendants of old-line American families.[2] McCarthyism, in short, has been analyzed from every conceivable angle—class, ethnicity, religion, education, and party affiliation, among others—and has produced far more scholarly conflict than consensus.

Social scientists have generally agreed, however, that a strong corelation existed between McCarthyism and anti-New Deal conservatism.[3] To many Americans, it seems, McCarthy's vicious attacks

1. For an analysis of McCarthyism as essentially a Republican attempt to regain national power, see, Earl Latham, *The Communist Controversy in Washington* (Cambridge: Harvard University Press, 1966); Robert Griffith, *The Politics of Fear* (Lexington: University Press of Kentucky, 1970). Those who believe McCarthyism was fostered largely by Truman's intense anti-Soviet attitude include Athan Theoharis, *Seeds of Repression* (Chicago: Quadrangle, 1971); Richard Freeland, *The Truman Doctrine and the Origins of McCarthyism* (New York: Random House, 1972). For the standard accounts of McCarthyism as a status revolt by frustrated Americans, see, Daniel Bell, ed., *The New American Right* (Garden City: Doubleday, 1954); Seymour Lipset and Earl Raab, *The Politics of Unreason* (New York: Harper and Row, 1970). A withering rebuttal to the Bell-Lipset approach can be found in Michael Rogin, *The Intellectuals and McCarthy* (Cambridge: M.I.T. Press, 1967).

2. See, especially, Rogin, *The Intellectuals and McCarthy*, pp. 216–60; Nelson Polsby, "Towards an Explanation of McCarthyism," *Political Studies* 8 (October 1960): 258–63; Lipset and Raab, *The Politics of Unreason*, pp. 209–47.

3. See, Lipset and Raab, *The Politics of Unreason*, pp. 221–35; Griffith, *The Politics of Fear*, pp. 30–48; Rogin, *The Intellectuals and McCarthy*, pp. 220–27; Latham, *The Communist Controversy in Washington*, pp. 270–315;

upon "subversives" in the Truman Administration were perceived as an attempt to rescue the nation from a group of New Deal reformers who had worn thin the vital fibres of Americanism. McCarthy, the opportunist, represented to a multitude of frustrated citizens a final barricade against the "massive conspiracy" that had delivered half the world to communism and most of America to stifling bureaucracy, welfare programs, labor leaders, and leftist politicians. When, in a dispute over foreign policy, the senator impugned the loyalty of Dean Acheson, he was also reinforcing the subversive New Deal image portrayed by the secretary of state. "I look at that fellow," the conservative Hugh Butler of Nebraska exploded, "I watch his smart-aleck manner and his British clothes and that New Dealism, everlasting New Dealism in everything he says and does, and I want to shout, 'Get out, get out, you stand for everything that has been wrong with America for years.' "[4]

According to many prominent conservative spokesmen, the New Deal had placed the nation in the hands of a group of smug intellectual reformers whose ideas were alien to American tradition. Rather than reaffirm the heritage of Thomas Jefferson, these visionaries (who all held key nonelective positions) created a massive federal bureaucracy that encouraged fiscal irresponsibility, class conflict, and the destruction of the free enterprise system. Worse still, they scoffed at the likes of Senator Robert A. Taft of Ohio, whose slogan "Keep America Solvent and Sensible" was the essence of true Americanism. Senator John Marshall Butler of Maryland, a McCarthy creation, claimed that nowhere in the country could one find a group "more completely devoted to the supposition that business and businessmen are bad and necessarily must be controlled and regimented by the Government, that private ownership is selfish and corrupt, and that public ownership is good and should increasingly supplant privately owned industries and institutions."[5] After surveying a list of

---

Ronald Lora, "A View From the Right; Conservative Intellectuals, the Cold War and McCarthy," in Robert Griffith and Athan Theoharis, *The Specter* (New York: Franklin-Watts, 1974), pp. 42–70.

4. Quoted in Eric Goldman, *The Crucial Decade* (New York: Knopf, 1956), p. 125.

5. U.S., Congress, *Congressional Record*, 83d Cong., 1st sess., 1953, 99, pt. 5:6512. Joseph McCarthy became known as the creator of Senator Butler because of the prominent role he played in Butler's 1950 senatorial election campaign against Senator Millard Tydings. See, U.S., Congress, Senate, Subcommittee on Privileges and Elections of the Senate Committee on Rules and Administration, *Hearings on the Maryland Senatorial Race of 1950*, 82d Cong., 2d sess., 1952.

"dangerous radicals" that President Roosevelt brought into the federal government, Senator Taft bitterly noted that "if Roosevelt is not a Communist today he is bound to become one."[6]

While viewing business as selfish and corrupt (the conservative argument continued) these New Dealers fostered a climate in which militant industrial unionism prospered. With encouragement from these collectivists, the labor movement began what was, according to the Chamber of Commerce of the United States, a struggle "replete with class consciousness, hatred for employers, and designed to intensify the class struggle—things foreign to most Americans."[7] One prominent right-wing publication went a step further by inventing a web of subversion where Communists controlled the CIO-PAC, which, in turn, dictated domestic policy to the New and Fair Deal administrations. Even the American Federation of Labor, no great friend of New Deal politicians and policymakers, was somehow thrust into the Communist camp.

> How could the AFL be captured by the Communists? It had a great tradition, but in the face of CIO's "gains," its leaders thought they had to "do something." And the Communists were ready and waiting to tell them what to do—policies nicely hidden behind the cloak of higher wages, more benefits, but still fitting perfectly the symbols laid down to guide policy-makers by Earl Browder.[8]

Not surprisingly, the allegation that the federal bureaucracy was riddled with subversives served to link conservative fears of communism and the Soviet Union with a deep antipathy to domestic reform. And, while many conservatives held sincere anti-Communist beliefs, they were well aware that by equating New Dealism with subversion, the spread of liberal, reform-minded ideas could be severely retarded. If, for example, a labor leader pressed for higher wages, a civil rights leader for stronger legislation, or a college professor for greater academic freedom, there was a distinct possibility that their cries for progressive action would be met with conservative counterclaims of subversion. Often this tactic took on absurd proportions, as exemplified by the statement of one legislator that "if a person says that in this country Negroes are discriminated against, or there is

6. James Patterson, *Mr. Republican: A Biography of Robert A. Taft* (Boston: Houghton Mifflin, 1972), p. 157.

7. Arthur Eggleston, "Labor and Civil Liberties," *The Nation* 174 (June 28, 1952): 647.

8. Edna Lonergan, "Anatomy of the PAC," *The Freeman* 1 (November 27, 1950): 137–39.

an inequality of wealth, there is every reason to believe that person is a Communist."[9]

Unfortunately, the more irrational assaults were often encouraged by some respected conservative constitutionalists. Senator Taft, dean of the Republican party during the early 1950s, clearly saw McCarthy's opportunism for what it was but decided to exploit it for political gain. He allegedly advised the Wisconsinite to "keep talking and if one case doesn't work out . . . proceed with another," and helped to underwrite the cruel attacks upon his former friend and classmate at Yale, Dean Acheson. It was Taft who, in 1952, after McCarthy's repeated failures to find a single Communist in the State Department, told assembled reporters: "I did and do approve of McCarthy's accomplishments in rooting Communists and subversives out of Government."[10] For this particular conservative, at least, McCarthy's unscrupulous methods were viewed as the most effective means to a proper end—the eradication of New Deal-Fair Deal "socialism" from the American political scene.

To many other conservatives, however, McCarthy was essentially a moral figure who refused to compromise with evil. In attacking the traditional devils of conservatism—Godless communism, alien social legislation, intellectual reformers, and radical bureaucrats—he was trying to awaken a frustrated and confused citizenry to the evils of "a particular set of ideas and values which past generations of Americans explored and emphatically rejected."[11] To criticize McCarthy, therefore, was (in the words of William F. Buckley and L. Brent Bozell) "to oppose the decline of Communism at home." It was that simple. As one prominent conservative editor lamented at the senator's passing, "at the heart of what McCarthy said and did was the very essence of Western civilization . . . McCarthy saw the gargoyles of the anti-Christ staring and sneering at him from everywhere and, innocent, he reached out to crush him . . . and it killed him."[12]

9. State Representative Albert Canwell of Washington, quoted in the American Civil Liberties Union pamphlet, *In the Shadow of Fear*, 1949, p. 18. For other conservative tracts linking the New Deal with communism or subversion, see, John Flynn, *The Roosevelt Myth* (New York: Devin-Adair, 1948); Martin Dies, *The Trojan Horse in America* (New York: Dodd, Mead, 1940); Whittaker Chambers, *Witness* (New York: Random House, 1952).

10. William White, *The Taft Story* (New York: Harper, 1954), p. 87. See also, Patterson, *Mr. Republican*, pp. 445–49.

11. William Buckley and L. Brent Bozell, *McCarthy and His Enemies* (Chicago: Regnery, 1954), p. 334.

12. William Schlamm, "Across McCarthy's Grave," *National Review* 3 (May 18, 1957), pp. 469–70. See also, the eulogy by Congressman Wint Smith, quoted in Rogin, *The Intellectuals and McCarthy*, p. 228. For further

II

Since most of the available evidence indicates that organized labor viewed McCarthyism as a dangerous assault upon the New and Fair Deals, one is tempted to hypothesize that a substantial percentage of the business community supported the senator for the very reasons labor found him so abhorrent. By 1950, it will be remembered, McCarthy's conservative voting record in Congress, his dedicated work for certain financial lobbies, and his important role in the defeat of Wisconsin progressivism had already endeared him to many influential industrialists. Indeed, it seemed highly probable that as the leader of a movement aimed primarily at the removal of assorted New Deal subversives from positions of power the senator was "the perfect instrument for the realization of the social aims of those who were to benefit from his attacks." [13]

This provocative theory was first offered by Charles J.V. Murphy after a survey of "McCarthy and the Businessman" for a national magazine in 1954.[14] He concluded that among a large number of successful corporate executives, McCarthyism and anti-New Dealism were synonymous. "Among businessmen who approve of McCarthy's war on subversion," wrote Murphy, "there is a satisfaction, subconscious perhaps but very strong, over his incidental licks at all the longhairs, eggheads, professors, and the bright young men of the 1930's and 1940's. Only one named Alger Hiss. But the others in the NLRB, REA, TVA, etc., etc., were scarcely less dangerous."[15] Many of these individuals were bitter over the treatment they had received from government agencies and clearly envisioned McCarthyism as a lethal weapon with which to strike back at their tormentors. Longen Warren, president of Safeway Stores, claimed that "having taken my full share of blows from the NLRB crowd and other New Deal longhairs," he welcomed "the McCarthy brickbats."[16] Others, like Clinton Murchison, the oil magnate, saw in the Wisconsinite a means to destroy all liberal opposition. Murchison declared emphatically that he was for "anybody who'll root out the people who are trying to ruin the American system." His catalogue included, along with card-carrying Communists, the ADA, the CIO, and "eggheads and long-

---

information on McCarthy as the savior of conservatives, see, Willmoore Kendall, *The Conservation Affirmation* (Chicago: Regnery, 1963), pp. 50–76; "The End of McCarthy," *National Review* 3 (May 18, 1957): 462.

13. Latham, *The Communist Controversy in Washington*, p. 423.
14. Charles J.V. Murphy, "McCarthy and the Businessman," *Fortune* 49 (April 1954): 180.
15. Ibid.
16. Ibid., p. 192.

hairs in their infinite variety."[17] Although these businessmen expressed personal preferences as to which specific groups of individuals should be singled out for special censure, one dominant theme pervaded their thinking: McCarthyism, above all, was viewed as a sure way "to keep the albatross hung about the neck of the New and Fair Deals."[18]

Yet, what would have happened, one may logically ask, had Senator McCarthy kept up his anti-Communist crusade while suddenly becoming more liberal on domestic economic policy? What, for example, if he had called for a more liberal revision of the Taft-Hartley Act, or for more public works, or for cheaper money? Among McCarthy supporters interviewed by Murphy, the answer was both obvious and unanimous: they would have unloaded him immediately.[19] His value to them, it seemed, lay not so much in his watchdog technique against communism, but rather in the antiliberal, antireform climate that his crusade had fostered.

To some degree, McCarthy's relationship with the Republican party substantiated Murphy's hypothesis. When the GOP swept the national elections in 1952, thereby terminating twenty years of New and Fair Dealism, the senator's popularity among his business supporters decreased noticeably. With a more friendly, probusiness Administration now in control, it was hoped that McCarthy, having done what was necessary to discredit the previous Administration, would terminate his investigations. As Earl Latham has written:

> The frustrations of twenty years had been eased. Although it seemed desirable and even necessary for more aggressive and less liberal Republicans, when they were on the sidewalks looking in, to throw rocks at the house they hoped to occupy, they were now inside and they hoped to keep their property intact. But McCarthy was inside also, and although he was no longer throwing rocks, he was breaking up the furniture.[20]

Most businessmen interviewed were concerned over McCarthy's continued blasts at his Republican colleagues. Charles Percy, president of Bell and Howell, was clearly dismayed over the Wisconsinite's attempt "to embarrass a friendly administration," while G.S. Crane, president of Cutler-Hammer, expressed disappointment in the senator's actions because he had hoped "when Eisenhower was elected, McCarthy would calm down." Perhaps the feelings of many execu-

17. Ibid.
18. Ibid., p. 180.
19. Ibid.
20. Latham, *The Communist Controversy in Washington*, p. 400.

tives were summed up by R.A. Weaver, president of the Bellinger Corporation, when he stated, "McCarthy has served his purpose, it's too bad he can't seem to taper off."[21]

As McCarthy's investigations broadened throughout 1953 and 1954 to include the Voice of America, the Overseas Library program, and the United States Army, traditional Republican businessmen clearly perceived the senator as a liability. In a secret poll taken at New York City's exclusive Links Club in June, 1953, three-quarters of those who voted expressed disapproval of McCarthy and predicted that his influence would decline in the near future. F.P. Hefflefinger, chairman of the Republican National Finance Committee, informed Senator Karl Mundt (Republican, South Dakota) that the Wisconsinite's vendetta against the army was at least partially responsible

21. Quoted in Murphy, "McCarthy and the Businessman," pp. 182, 184, 190. More recently, social scientists studying support for McCarthy have concluded that corporate executives were among the least likely to be attracted by the senator's crusade. This, they believe, was because of their instinct for self-preservation. As one wrote: "In the scapegoat portrait in which McCarthy thrives, the professional man is a prime target. For him, as well as for the man in a large corporation, the upsurge of a mass movement represents an implicit threat." Immanuel Wallerstein, "McCarthyism and the Conservatives," M.A. thesis, Columbia University, 1954, p. 34. See also, Trow, "Right-Wing Radicalism and Political Intolerance," pp. 275–80; Richard Hofstadter, "The Pseudo-Conservative Revolt," in Bell, *The New American Right*, pp. 43–46. They believe, like Wallerstein, that the executive's commitment to the existing hierarchy made him hostile to anyone, like McCarthy, who attacked it.

This particular hypothesis, which assumes that McCarthyism was both a mass movement and one dedicated to the destruction of the existing status hierarchy, has come under heavy attack. (See, Rogin, *The Intellectuals and McCarthy*, pp. 1–31, 218–60). It is true, however, that most public opinion polls did show business executives (especially those in large corporations) to be very anti-McCarthy. (See, Lipset and Raab, *The Politics of Unreason*, pp. 234–35). And the most prestigious business publications, including the *Wall Street Journal* and *Business Week* were also highly critical of the senator. (See, *Wall Street Journal*, October 9, 1952; September 3, 1953; *Business Week*, April 8, 1950, p. 16; February 16, 1952, p. 196). Social scientists admit that the high levels of education of corporate executives were also a factor. As Lipset and Raab wrote in 1970 (p. 227): "The relationship between . . . education and support for McCarthy is consistent with what is known about the effect of education on political attitudes in general: higher education often makes for greater tolerance, greater regard for due process, and increased tolerance of ambiguity." Another factor, which some historians have considered, is that as early as the mid-1930s, many corporate executives had come to see that the New Deal was not out to destroy capitalism but rather to try to revitalize it with massive federal assistance. Therefore, much of the social and economic legislation of the New Deal was not greatly opposed by sections of the big business community. See especially, Ellis Hawley, *The New Deal and the Problem of Monopoly* (Princeton: Princeton University Press, 1966), pp. 3–130, 472–95.

for a drop in contributions from the nation's business community. Harry Bullis, chairman of the board of General Foods, reported to President Eisenhower that at financial meetings he had recently attended in New York, Washington, and Toledo, he could find no one who was not "utterly disgusted" with McCarthy's behavior. Businessmen, he concluded, were united in their contempt for the senator, although some "do not have the courage to express their views publicly."[22]

McCarthy's continued attacks upon alleged subversion in the new Republican Administration seemed to have the sympathy of only the most radical right-wing business elements. Certainly his most powerful allies were the numerous Texas oil millionaires, who had made huge sums of money in the previous fifteen years and who now felt secure enough to exert their personal and economic influence upon the national political scene. To their thinking, the two greatest problems facing America were the emergence of the International Communist Conspiracy and the deterioration of the free enterprise system, and it seemed to them that Senator Joseph McCarthy was the politician most acutely aware of these dangerous developments.

When Martin Dies, the creator of the House Committee on Un-American Activities, claimed in 1954 that "Texas businessmen had radically changed their outlook on the importance of the issue of subversion," he was, more than likely, referring to the Texas oilmen who had adopted Joe McCarthy as their "third senator."[23] The four wealthiest Texans, oilmen H.L. Hunt, Clint Murchison, Sid Richardson, and Hugh Roy Cullen, took it upon themselves to finance McCarthy's anti-Communist crusade. Murchison admitted spending more than $50,000 for the senator's campaigns, and for several others the figure was probably higher. The eccentric Hunt, while helping to bankroll McCarthy, also found enough spare cash to begin a newsletter and a series of radio stations dedicated to the preservation of his own "American ideals," which were anticommunism, free enterprise, racial segregation, and Christian fundamentalism. McCarthy was often a featured guest on Hunt's radio hookup, and the Texan distributed copies of the senator's two most significant journalistic endeavors—*McCarthyism: The Fight for America and America's*

22. The Links Club Poll is found in White House Central File, Box 723, June 4, 1953, Dwight D. Eisenhower Papers, Eisenhower Library, Abilene, Kan.; the Bullis correspondence is in the Official File, 99-R, May 9, 1953; May 4, 1954; Hefflefinger's letter to Mundt is in the General File 171, Box 1272, May 5, 1954, Dwight D. Eisenhower Presidential Library.

23. Charles J. V. Murphy, "McCarthy and Texas Business," *Fortune* 49 (May 1954): 100.

Retreat From Victory: The Story of General George C. Marshall—to interested listeners. Hugh Roy Cullen, as the single largest contributor to the Wisconsinite's senatorial reelection campaign in 1952, sponsored a fund-raising dinner during which McCarthy, the host's candidate for "greatest man in America," was presented with a shiny new Cadillac. The senator also spent a considerable amount of time at the homes of these oil tycoons and often lunched with them at Dallas's exclusive Petroleum Club.[24]

As expected, many of McCarthy's critics suggested that this harmonious relationship was not based exclusively upon the issue of Communist subversion. Indeed, Edwin C. Bayley, writing in the *Milwaukee Journal*, wondered aloud why the senator from a midwestern dairy state would take such an active interest in the passage of the Kerr-Thomas Gas Bill (which exempted producers of natural gas from regulation by the Federal Power Commission) and the Tidelands Oil Bill (which provided for continued state, rather than federal, operation of submerged oil lands on the continental shelf) while lobbying so vociferously for the defeat of a series of amendments aimed at reducing the 27.5 per cent oil depletion allowance.[25] In any event, McCarthy was able to count on the moral and financial support of these influential Texans until the very day on which he was censured by the United States Senate. While commenting on the shrewd manner by which the Wisconsinite exploited the hysterical anti-New Deal, anti-Communist apprehensions of these oilmen, newspaper editor Houston Harte noted sourly: "The word Communist, at least in Texas usage, has come to mean practically anybody the rest of us don't like—a regrettable perversion of the old-fashioned son-of-a-bitch."[26]

*   *   *

While students of the McCarthy period have been somewhat uncertain about the level of the senator's support among major business leaders and executives, they are convinced of his tremendous popu-

24. "McCarthy, Hunt and Facts-Forum," *The Reporter* 10 (February 16, 1954): 19–27. *New York Times*, October 22, 1953. Another large campaign contribution came from H.B. Keck, president of Superior Oil Company. Keck also put the company's plane at McCarthy's disposal. See, Michael O'Brien, "Senator Joseph R. McCarthy and Wisconsin, 1946–1957," Ph.D. dissertation, University of Wisconsin, 1971, pp. 275–76.
25. *Milwaukee Journal*, March 15, 1953.
26. Quoted in Murphy, "McCarthy and Texas Business," p. 214.

larity among smaller businessmen, merchants, and manufacturers.[27] While the small businessman often expressed a frantic fear of communism, he was far more distressed by his bitter alienation from what Talcott Parsons has called "the bureaucratic organization of the productive processes."[28] He was painfully aware that the combined growth of large corporations, massive industrial unions, and a highly centralized federal bureaucracy had rendered him impotent as an effective social or political force in modern America, and his resentment increased as he realized he could neither control nor accept these "disturbing complexities" that altered his daily life. The small businessman was therefore forced to strike out blindly at the symbols of this impersonal new society—the college-educated bureaucrat, the powerful and politically effective labor leader, and even the successful industrialist who had sacrificed the true principles of free enterprise to compete successfully in the market place. As R.H. Shaw, assistant chairman of the Conference of American Small Business Organizations, noted: "Big business too often goes along with big labor, with big government, with fascist and co-operative tendencies in the government—with the NRA first and then the OPA and WPB industry committees—anything for harmony and convenience and job safety for management, regardless of what happens to the other fellow."[29]

As an outlet for this hostility, the small businessman seemed to identify with politicians who attacked the institutions that were destroying old-style living patterns, and Joseph McCarthy was just such a politician. He often stood alone, challenging the largest and most powerful organizations—the State Department, the army, and, at times, a few of the nation's great journalistic and industrial concerns. In a certain sense, McCarthy was the hero of the little man as he attacked the well-dressed, well-educated, self-assured managers of modern society. And what's more, he usually cut them down to size by exposing their "subversive" tendencies as well as their human frailties.

This theoretical correlation between the small businessman's alienation from modern society and his alleged support for McCarthy

27. Martin Trow, "Small Business, Political Intolerance and Support for McCarthy," *American Journal of Sociology* 64 (November 1958): 270–81. Rogin, *The Intellectuals and McCarthy*, pp. 218–60; Lipset and Raab, *The Politics of Unreason*, pp. 166–219.
28. Talcott Parsons, "McCarthyism and American Social Tensions," *Yale Review* 44 (December 1954): 228.
29. Quoted in John Bunzell, "The Ideology of American Small Business," *Political Science Quarterly* 70 (March 1955): 100. See also, Kurt Mayer, "Small Business as a Social Institution," *Social Research* 14 (September 1947): 332–49.

was studied at some length by Martin Trow in Bennington, Vermont.[30] After hundreds of interviews, he broke down his sample into four basic categories: first, those who expressed sympathies for large, powerful labor unions but feared large enterprises (New Deal liberals); second, those who favored big business but were antilabor (traditional right-wing conservatives); third, those who accepted both big unions and big business (moderates); and fourth, those who feared both big unions and big business (nineteenth-century liberals). His survey revealed that among the first three groupings there was scarcely any difference in the percentage of McCarthy supporters. But the fourth group had a distinctly higher percentage, the vast majority of whom were small businessmen. Trow concluded:

> Findings showed that small businessmen in our society tend to develop a generalized hostility toward a complex of symbols and processes bound up with industrial capitalism, the steady growth and concentration of government, labor organizations and business enterprises, the correlative trend toward greater rationalization of production and distribution, and the men, institutions and ideas that symbolize these secular trends in our modern society. These trends and symbols were, we believe, McCarthy's most persuasive targets. Quite apart from the questions of Communists in government, and blunders or worse in foreign policy, the congruence between McCarthy's attacks and the small businessman's hostility to the dominant characteristics and tendencies of modern society account, we believe, for much of the disproportionate support McCarthy gained from small businessmen.[31]

30. Trow, "Small Business, Political Intolerance, and Support for McCarthy," pp. 270–81.

31. Ibid., p. 277. As expected, the organizations and periodicals that represented small businessmen and merchants took a more sympathetic approach towards McCarthy. The Chamber of Commerce of the United States rarely mentioned McCarthy by name but consistently supported investigations into domestic subversion. In fact, it condemned liberals for smearing Red-hunters like McCarthy. "The inconsistencies and negativeness of many 'liberal' attacks on anti-Communists could normally be overlooked," wrote the chamber in its pamphlet, *Communism: Where Do We Stand Today?*: "But today such attacks give comfort to the Reds at a time when they have few defenders. Moreover, they might frighten off many who wish to oppose Communism but fear to be tagged as opponents of liberty. Hence it is well to label muddled liberals correctly. They must be considered as completely negative in the face of conspiracy, subversion and treason." See also, Peter Irons, "American Business and the Origins of McCarthyism," in Griffith and Theoharis, *The Specter*, pp. 72–90. The National Association of Manufacturers went a step further. "When a man, who by his own lights is a patriotic American, has reason to believe that certain public servants have affected the nation's interests adversely because of their own ideological slant, but does not have the kind of evidence which will stand up in court, what is he to do?" asked the

Certainly these hypotheses are open to debate and to more thorough research. Yet they do provide some evidence that a substantial percentage of the business community viewed McCarthyism as something more than strictly a political issue. In some instances, it was synonymous with anti-New Dealism; in others, it was viewed as a necessary assault upon the well-entrenched establishment. In all cases, however, the businessman, like his union counterpart, realized that the issues at stake were far more important than a simple determination of the number of Communists in government.

III

At the outset of his anti-Communist crusade, Senator McCarthy acted as if he might center a great deal of attention upon the labor movement. In September, 1950, he raised the then explosive issue of subversion in the defense plants by noting that several officials of the United Electrical Workers had filed false non-Communist affidavits with the National Labor Relations Board. The senator claimed that the time was ripe for government action. "If the Communist party masquerading as a labor union, cannot be tolerated in the family of the CIO," he stated, "why should it be tolerated in the plants of General Electric, Sylvania, Westinghouse, or RCA? . . . American industry is being forced to produce vital war materials under the complete domination of Communists." McCarthy then dropped his traditional investigatory threat by warning that "if 200,000 union members could willingly support Communist leaders it is time to take another look at the alleged 'solid Americanism' of the rank-and-file."[32]

Yet aside from a few peripheral thrusts at certain labor unions, the senator did not take another look until late in 1953. In November of that year, he began a series of investigations into the subversive influences in defense plants in New York and Massachusetts.[33] At these hearings, McCarthy invariably produced two types of witnesses: the thoroughly cooperative FBI undercover agent and the recalcitrant subversive. In Boston, for example, the FBI man, William H. Teto,

NAM News. "This question contains the essence of what has come to be called 'McCarthyism'—a term which may go down in history as one of honor and high courage despite the strenuous efforts which are being made to make it sound like something bad" (*NAM News*, September 8, 1951).

32. *New York Times*, September 29, 1950.

33. U.S., Congress, Senate, Permanent Subcommittee on Investigations of the Senate Committee on Government Operations, *Hearings on Subversion and Espionage in Defense Establishments*, 83d Cong., 1st sess., 1953–1954.

answered McCarthy's last thirty questions with a simple "yes, sir." Actually the senator made quite certain that the witness's replies were kept to the bare minimum, for the questions he posed dealt more with personal judgment than with actual fact. Teto repeatedly gave his affirmation to probes like, "Do you feel that up to this moment there are no secrets from the Communist party in the GE plants," and "Do you consider it an extremely dangerous situation, a great threat to national security, to have men who are Communists as of this moment working in the GE plants?"[34]

The second type of witness proved far more uncooperative, although McCarthy did his best to enliven the proceedings. Those who used their constitutional guarantees against self-incrimination were called "Fifth Amendment Communists," and the few who persisted in their refusals were informed that only in a democracy could their traitorous attitudes be protected. On one occasion, when a witness refused to state whether or not he was a Communist but volunteered to answer other questions pertaining to his past, McCarthy turned him down for fear he would "make a long speech and use this hearing as a transmission belt for other Communists."[35] At times, the senator's accusations were answered with stinging rebuttals. One witness, who had been called a Communist but was refused the right to confront his accuser, told McMarthy:

> I believe that I am entitled to the same judicial process which has been demanded and received by you . . . Senator . . . at other hearings. . . . I demand that I be given due notice of the nature of these proceedings, as well as the specific nature of the charges against me, in the form of a bill of particulars . . . that I be advised of the testimony against me which has already been taken by this committee, and that I be granted the right to confront and cross-examine my accuser. . . . It seems to me that all I am asking for is for the same rights that you, yourself, demanded and I cannot see how you can deny me these rights.[36]

McCarthy continued his hearings the next year in the Albany area, a stronghold of the United Electrical Workers of America. Many union members came to the proceedings at their own expense to heckle the senator. According to one source: "The workers jammed the hearing room and hundreds more milled through the corridors and outside the building. . . . They booed and jeered McCarthy . . . and shouted approval of the seven subpoenaed GE workers. . . . Workers in the corridors held aloft for photographers an outsized

34. Ibid., p. 334.
35. Ibid., p. 553.
36. Ibid., p. 519.

valentine inscribed: 'GE Loves McCarthy.' "[37] After two days of constant turmoil, McCarthy adjourned the hearings, claiming that valuable evidence had been compiled about espionage in the defense plants.

The senator's charges of Communist infiltration in the defense industry reached their climax at the well-publicized army-McCarthy hearings. Here, he stated that his recent investigations had uncovered a minimum of 130 known Communists in critical defense establishments in Syracuse, Dunkirk, Rome, and Buffalo, New York; and Boston, Pittsfield, Quincy, Lynn, and Fitchburg, Massachusetts. Yet, when Senator Stuart Symington asked him to turn over the names to the Department of Justice, McCarthy turned a deaf ear, saying that he "did not feel too deeply in need of advice of the Senator from Missouri at this time on the question of exposing Communists."[38] By this late date, however, neither McCarthy's sarcasm nor his threats were enough to silence those who demanded proof of his charges. In June, 1954, Assistant Secretary of Defense Fred Seaton asked for the list in a public letter to the senator. When McCarthy replied that he would turn over the names only if certain conditions were met—including a promise by the assistant secretary to keep the names secret—Seaton told him that the Defense Department would take whatever action it deemed appropriate "without consulting you."[39] Not only did McCarthy refuse to submit the list but, having been placed in a position where he had to produce some real evidence or back down entirely, the senator dropped the subject. Never again did he mention the issue of Communists in labor unions or defense plants.

37. Harry Ring, as quoted in Art Preis, *Labor's Giant Step: Twenty Years of the CIO* (New York: Pioneer Publishers, 1964), p. 498. The sign "GE Loves McCarthy" was probably a reference to the fact that by 1953 the company was advocating the discharge of any employee who refused to answer questions concerning his Communist affiliations before congressional committees. See, David Oshinsky, "Labor's Cold War: The CIO and the Communists," in Griffith and Theoharis, *The Specter*, p. 141.

38. *New York Times*, June 4, 1954. At the army-McCarthy hearings, the senator's charges about Communists in the defense industries initiated a heated exchange between Joseph Welch, counsel for the army, and Roy Cohn, McCarthy's staff assistant. Welch so embarrassed Cohn about releasing the names of these alleged Communists "before sundown" so Americans could "rest safely," that McCarthy counterattacked by accusing Welch of having a former National Lawyers Guild member, Fred Fisher, in his law firm of Hale and Dorr and of trying to foist Fisher upon the army's legal staff. Welch's famous rebuttal ("Senator McCarthy . . . little did I dream you could be so reckless and so cruel") was considered to be the most effective piece of oratory in the entire hearings. See, especially, Griffith, *The Politics of Fear*, pp. 257–59.

39. *New York Times*, June 5, 1954.

Some of McCarthy's allies, however, used the tensions and anxieties brought about by the Korean conflict to initiate a movement for the enactment of stricter anti-Communist legislation in the labor field. In an attempt to rally public support to their side, they contended that the nation's defense effort was in danger of being sabotaged by leftist labor leaders whose true loyalties lay not with their own country, but rather with the North Korean and Chinese aggressors. Although CIO President Philip Murray did his best to allay these fears by stating, quite correctly, that "there has been no evidence of a single such stoppage despite a year and a half of war and an even longer period of cold war," some politicians were convinced nonetheless that drastic steps were in order.[40]

In the midst of this pressure to enact stricter legislation, Senator Hubert Humphrey of Minnesota, chairman of the labor-management subcommittee of the Committee on Labor and Public Welfare, began a series of hearings "to investigate Communist influences in the labor unions."[41] Humphrey, a strong labor supporter, seemed well aware of the antiunion sentiments of many of those pressing for tighter controls. "One of the real problems we have had," he said, "is that too many unions have been called Communist-dominated when there was no Communist domination."[42] Yet Humphrey also believed that proposed legislation in this area was an alternative that merited serious consideration. Especially pertinent, he noted, was the formulation of a new amendment to strengthen the non-Communist affidavit provisions of the Taft-Hartley Act. "My own feelings," stated Humphrey in his most inoffensive legalistic jargon, "are that this is of sufficient importance so that an amendment to the Taft-Hartley Act could conceivably be appropriate."[43]

Labor leaders did not agree with the senator. Their position was that Communist influence in the labor movement was an internal problem requiring no governmental interference; rather, it was for each union to decide for itself the political course it would pursue. Calling any legislation "both unnecessary and unwise," Philip Murray told the subcommittee that "if the Government undertakes to determine what unions can represent workers in this country, it will have embarked upon the long trail towards government control of

40. U.S., Congress, Senate, Committee on Labor and Public Welfare, *Hearings on Communist Domination of Unions and National Security*, 82d Cong., 2d sess., 1952, p. 280.
41. Ibid.
42. "Interview With Senator Hubert H. Humphrey of Minnesota," *U.S. News and World Report* 36 (December 28, 1951): 21.
43. Ibid., p. 26.

unions."[44] Murray's AFL counterpart, William Green, was in total agreement, asserting that "it would be extremely difficult to prove that a member of a labor union is a Communist," and for the government to attempt to do so would be disastrous.[45] These unionists, while staunchly anti-Communist, were resisting any governmental attempt aimed at regulating the internal affairs of individual unions.

Although the Humphrey subcommittee made no recommendations, other legislators pressed for more decisive action in this area. Within a period of weeks, three of McCarthy's most loyal allies—senators Pat McCarran of Nevada, John Marshall Butler of Maryland, and Herman Welker of Idaho—formed a subcommittee of the Committee of the Judiciary known as the "Task Force Investigating Communist Domination of Certain Labor Organizations."[46] The first union to be called before the subcommittee was the International Union of Mine, Mill and Smelter Workers. While informing these union officials that by following the Communist line "labor will lose everything it has gained by the free enterprise system of the United States," Senator McCarran warned them, as McCarthy had earlier, that the exercise of their constitutional rights against self-incrimination would be severely limited. "If a man comes here and he is asked, 'are you a horse thief' and he is not a horse thief, all he has to say is 'no I am not,' " stated the senator. "If he comes here and he is asked 'are you a Communist' and he is not a Communist, all he has to say is 'no I am not.' But when he resists and resorts to the Fifth Amendment and says 'It might incriminate me if I answer,' his attitude and his conduct must be judged by his answer."[47]

Early in the investigations, McCarran told the labor officials that their appearance before his committee was only the beginning of an exhaustive search into all labor unions, not simply the ones suspected of subversive activities. "Boys, don't get excited," he told them after they balked at being singled out for questioning, "they're all going to be before me before this is over." However, because the unionists refused either to testify about their political activities or to give in to McCarran's aggressive tactics, the hearings quickly degenerated into

44. *Hearings on Communist Domination of Unions and National Security*, p. 280.
45. Eggleston, "Labor and Civil Liberties," p. 647.
46. The "Task Force" was formed in what seemed to have been an effort to ensure that the problem of subversion in any field of labor activity would be handled by the Red-hunters of the Internal Security subcommittee rather than by the more prolabor members of the Committee on Labor and Public Welfare.
47. U.S., Congress, Task Force Investigating Communist Domination of Certain Labor Organizations, *Hearings on Communist Influence Among Officials of Unions in Vital Defense Industries*, 82d Cong., 2d sess., 1952, p. 5.

a shouting match between the participants. One labor reporter at the scene wrote that far from being objective, the hearing seemed little more than a "fraudulent cover for an attack on all liberals, progressives, New Dealers, and effective labor leaders and unions."[48] Indeed, the publicity surrounding the investigation was so adverse that the task force soon discontinued its activities.

While McCarran was holding his hearings, other conservatives moved quickly to establish a second legislative front. In the spring of 1953, Senator Butler proposed the first of several bills to regulate alleged subversive activities within the labor movement. His proposal to amend the Internal Security (McCarran) Act of 1950 stated, in part:

> If a labor organization is substantially controlled or dominated by an individual or individuals (whether officers of such organizations or not) who are or ever have been members of the Communist Party or any other Communist action organizations as described in sections 3 and 4 of said Internal Security Act of 1950, as amended, or who have in any manner contributed to or furthered the activities of such organizations . . . the Subversive Activities Control Board shall investigate such charge and if it has reason to believe that the allegations . . . are meritorious, it shall cause to be issued on such labor organization a complaint stating the charges together with a notice of hearing before the Board . . . three copies of such complaint and notice of hearing together with an immediate suspension order providing that such labor organization shall be ineligible to act as exclusive bargaining agent . . . by virtue of the Labor-Management Relations Act of 1947, as amended.[49]

Not surprisingly, the wording of the Butler bill was specific only in relation to the restrictions placed on Communist-dominated labor unions. Any labor organization suspected of subversive activities was to be stripped of all privileges before the National Labor Relations Board and placed on trial before the Subversive Activities Control Board. Almost all other sections of the bill were so vague that their interpretation became the paramount concern. When, for example, was a union "substantially directed" by Communists, or when was it "contributing to [or] furthering" the activities of a subversive organization? CIO General Counsel Thomas Harris warned that "the proposed bill could very easily condemn any organization because its policies happen to coincide with those of the Communist Party. . . . Thus," he continued, "support by a labor organization of objectives also supported by Communists—such as abolition of the poll tax,

48. Eggleston, "Labor and Civil Liberties," p. 647.
49. *S. 1606*, 83rd Cong., 1st sess., (1953).

enactment of adequate housing proposals, and the protection of civil rights—could, under the standards of the proposed bill, furnish the basis for the conclusion that the organization is a Communist front."[50] In a similar vein, labor columnist Bernard Nossiter noted that the definition of the bill was "broad enough to cover any organization left of the Women's Christian Temperance Union."[51] These provisions were viewed by liberals as a blatant attempt to rid the labor movement of its more aggressive leadership by putting union leaders in such a position that a strong stand on any controversial social, economic, or political issue could easily be interpreted as subversive.[52]

Even more damaging to labor unions was the fact that the Butler bill did not stipulate exactly who was entitled to bring these charges of Communist domination before the Subversive Activities Control Board. Since the board had the right to suspend privileges extended to any labor organization by the National Labor Relations Board when a complaint was first filed and not when final judgment was rendered, an employer, a rival union, or dissidents within the union could severely weaken or possibly wrest control from the existing leadership by fabricating a complaint. Many observers, including Senator Humphrey, were aware of the dangers inherent in such a provision; Humphrey had stated several months before that "as chairman of the subcommittee ... I heard an employer representative brand the Textile Workers as a Communist union because the union attempted to do some organizing."[53] Under the provisions of the Butler bill, a union such as the one mentioned by the senator would have forfeited, at least temporarily, the rights to represent and bargain for its membership.

The section of the Butler bill that gave labor the greatest concern, however, was the one that afforded the Subversive Activities Control Board the right to investigate Communist influence in unions; in the past, this task had been performed primarily by the National Labor Relations Board. Yet, in recent years, the NLRB had come under intense fire from conservative legislators for, among other things, its failure to decertify certain pro-Communist unions and for its policy of accepting at face value the validity of all non-Communist affidavits filed by labor leaders.[54] Senator Butler, in a candid appraisal of the

50. *CIO News*, March 17, 1953.
51. Bernard Nossiter, "The Butler Bill," *The Nation* 179 (September 4, 1954), p. 193.
52. Ibid. See also, *The United Mine Workers' Journal*, August 15, 1953.
53. "Interview With Senator Hubert Humphrey," p. 21.
54. See, "Taft-Hartley Flaws Cheer Communists," *Business Week* 967 (March 13, 1948): 102; "Republican Effort to Change NLRB," *U.S. News*

situation, claimed that it was inconsistent for "a group of New Deal cryptosocialists on the Labor Board" to determine who was subversive and who was not. The Subversive Activities Control Board, he added, was in a better position to "carry out the philosophy of the new Administration and assist in reversing the socialist trend in government for the past twenty years."[55]

Senator Wayne Morse, a liberal Oregon Republican, took exception to this new proposal, and a heated debate with Butler ensued.

Morse. I would much prefer a proposal, which I have urged for years, namely that the National Labor Relations Board be assigned by Congress with the obligation to exercise complete jurisdiction over the infiltration of Communists into . . . labor unions.

Butler. Does not the Senator from Oregon feel that the more appropriate body to conduct such a hearing would be the Subversive Activities Control Board?

Morse. No. I am aware of the Senator's bill, but I do not think it provided for the most appropriate body to handle the problem because in my opinion, it is a mistake to split jurisdiction over a common subject matter, and I believe the NLRB should have complete jurisdiction over labor issues.

Butler. Does it not involve a matter of internal security?

Morse. Certainly it does, but it does not follow automatically that the NLRB is not the best qualified to determine whether a particular union is Communist-dominated. It seems to me that its knowledge of and familiarity with labor problems places it in an advantageous position to determine at the outset whether it is dealing with a union which is Communist-dominated or has Communists in it.

---

and World Report 24 (May 7, 1948): 51; "The Man Who's Hired to See Red," *Nation's Business* 39 (January 1951): 29–30.

55. U.S., Congress, *Congressional Record*, 83d Cong., 1st sess., 1953, 99, pt. 5:6513. While Senator Butler and other conservatives believed the NLRB to be a haven for "cryptosocialists," labor leaders were as firmly convinced that the SACB was made up, in part, of several notorious antilabor politicians. The chairman of the five-member board was T.J. Herbert, ex-governor of Ohio, a man who as chief executive of the buckeye state had enraged large segments of the labor movement by mobilizing the National Guard to break up a strike at the Univis plant in Dayton. Herbert claimed that he had "never been a labor champion," but then again, he recalled, neither had he been "a labor baiter" (*Business Week*, November 6, 1954, p. 59). Second in command was ex-Senator Harry Cain of Washington, a conservative, antilabor legislator who since his defeat in the 1952 elections, the *CIO News* claimed, "was busily shopping around for any kind of government job in Washington" (*CIO News*, November 9, 1954).

Butler. I agree with the senator's observation that the Board has a peculiar knowledge of matters dealing with labor, but it has no knowledge of matters dealing with internal security. This is strictly a matter of internal security.[56]

Aside from the Butler bill, several other pieces of legislation were proposed by conservative legislators to curb "Communist influence" within the labor movement, but they were, with minor variations, almost carbon copies of S. 1606. Senator Barry Goldwater, for example, offered a bill that paralleled the Butler proposal on all but three major points. First, while it too relied on the Subversive Activities Control Board to determine which organizations were Communist-dominated, only the attorney general of the United States could actually prefer a charge before the board. Second, if a union were found by the board to be in violation of the Internal Security Act of 1950, it was given a thirty-day period to rectify the situation; if, in the opinion of the board, there had been a satisfactory change in union policy, no penalty would be levied. Third, in the case of a union official suspected of Communist activities, the board had the power to suspend his constitutional guarantee against self-incrimination in return for the promise of personal immunity from federal prosecution. This last proposal was set forth, no doubt, to encourage union leaders to expose not only their own subversive activities but those of their colleagues as well.[57]

Although the Butler and Goldwater bills were both defeated, the belief that unions could not be fully trusted pervaded the thoughts of many legislators. In the summer of 1954, Congress made this painfully clear to the labor movement by passing unanimously the Communist Control Act. While designed ostensibly to outlaw the Communist party in America, the act combined the major sections of S. 1606 and S. 2650 to read that "the Subversive Activities Con-

56. *S. 2650*, 83d Cong., 2d sess. (1954).
57. *Public Law No. 637*, 83d Cong., 2d sess. (1954). See also, Oshinsky, "Labor's Cold War," pp. 135–47; F.S. O'Brien, "The Communist-Dominated Unions in the United States Since 1950," *Labor History* 9 (Spring 1968): 184–209. Ironically, the Communist Control Act was supported by Senate liberals who, in the midst of Washington's anti-Communist hysteria, felt that something rational and concrete had to be done in dealing with the issue of domestic subversion. As Senator Humphrey stated: "I'm tired of reading headlines about being soft on Communism. . . . I want to come to grips with the Communist issue. I want the Senators to stand up and to answer whether they are for the Communist party or against it." Senate conservatives were only too happy to oblige Humphrey, and in the process they slipped most of the provisions of the Butler bill (which the liberals had earlier complained was unconstitutional and antiunion) into the Communist Control Act.

trol Board, on petition from the Attorney-General . . . shall determine whether a labor organization . . . is substantially directed, dominated, or controlled by an individual or individuals who are working with the world Communist movement or who have been within the past three years." If, to the board's thinking, a union fell into this category, it would be "deprived of all legal standing before the National Labor Relations Board," which meant, in practical terms, that the organization in question would be forced to defend itself against constant membership raids from rival, anti-Communist unions and from harassment by hostile employers.[58]

The Communist Control Act was most damaging to those ultraleft unions that had been suspended by the CIO some five years before. During the past half decade, the legal standing these organizations enjoyed before the NLRB was the only thing that kept them from complete extinction. Now, suddenly, without the ability to get their names on a representation ballot, or to bring a complaint against an employer or a rival union, or in any way protect their vital interests, these unions were in an impossible position. The hopelessness and frustration engendered by this situation was clearly exemplified by the reactions of those union leaders directly involved. Albert Fitzgerald, president of the United Electrical Workers, bluntly told his membership that "by putting into practice the basic principles of McCarthyism" Congress had brought the union to the brink of destruction.[59] Even more pathetic was the farewell speech of Ben Gold, president of the International Brotherhood of Fur and Leather Workers (and, according to the House Committee on Un-American Activities, a member of the Communist party) in which he told the annual convention that he was resigning because, in his own words, "I do not want the demagogues to interpret my activities against this and other Fascist . . . laws as a pretext for intensifying their attacks upon our union."[60] Other suspected Communist labor leaders expressed similar beliefs with the full knowledge that their denials

58. *New York Times*, September 30, 1954.
59. Ibid., October 3, 1954.
60. To a large extent, the unions expelled by the CIO in 1949 and 1950 were on the verge of extinction before passage of the Communist Control Act. Some had been raided by other AFL and CIO affiliates; several others were situated in sick and dying industries. However, a few unions—most notably the United Electrical Workers and the Mine, Mill and Smelter Workers—held on tenaciously (for reasons of leadership, popularity, or solid control over collective bargaining procedures) and managed to survive the CIO expulsions and the Communist Control Act. See, O'Brien, "The Communist-Dominated Unions in the United States Since 1950," pp. 184–209; Philip Taft, "Communism in the Trade Unions," *Monthly Labor Review* 77 (February 1954): 134–42.

and denunciations could not hope to forestall the dismal fate that awaited them. They were at least partially correct in their assumptions.

For the majority of anti-Communist labor leaders, however, the Communist Control Act was viewed in a more rational perspective: as the inevitable culmination of a feverish postwar era that had changed labor's former image of radicalism to one of grudging respectability. Having successfully purged Communist influence from their own organizations in recent years, these men were not about to jeopardize this respectability by defending the political rights of their former left-wing adversaries. Therefore, most labor leaders and labor journals, rather than attacking the Communist Control Act as a dangerous assault upon a vital civil liberty, were content to fall back upon the well-worn, almost conservative argument that the government had no right to interfere with the internal affairs of a labor organization. When the CIO national convention of 1954 passed a resolution condemning loyalty oaths and secret informers, it touched only lightly on the Communist Control Act. "The Communist Control Act, providing for the branding and busting of 'Communist-infiltrated unions,'" the resolution stated, "continues a dangerous first step toward state control of all trade unions. . . . American trade unions will remain a bulwark of democracy only so long as they remain independent of state licensing systems."[61] As an integral part of the American system, the labor movement of the mid-1950s now viewed political radicalism, once so vital to the growth of a progressive trade union philosophy, as something of an embarrassment.

IV

It was one of the great political ironies of the 1950s that at the very time Congress enacted far-reaching anti-Communist legislation, it also condemned the man most responsible for it. For, as the Senate was voting into law the Communist Control Act of 1954 in one part of the Capitol building, it was in the process of censuring Joseph McCarthy for conduct unbecoming a United States senator in another. In the four years leading to his condemnation, however, years

61. *Proceedings of the Thirteenth Convention of the Congress of Industrial Organizations*, 1954, p. 413. Further evidence of labor's rigorous anti-Communist mentality during the 1950s is seen by the rash of provisions barring Communists from holding positions of leadership (and, in some cases, membership in the union itself). See, William Paschell and Rose Theodore, "Anti-Communist Provisions in the Union Constitutions," *Monthly Labor Review* 77 (October 1954): 1097–99.

in which he became a fearless patriotic crusader to many Americans and a slanderous character assassin to many others, the senator had left an indelible mark upon the nation's conscience.

When Joseph McCarthy began his attacks upon the State Department in February, 1950, he did more than simply "expose" the alleged Communist activities of some of its employees. While his accusations seemed to have ripped the lid off a Pandora's box of conspiracy and subversion, they also accelerated the drive for an intensive revaluation of the role of government in American society. The labor union field was of particular interest. Many Americans believed that the federal government had exhibited a deliberate pro-labor, antibusiness philosophy designed to inhibit the growth of free enterprise. In order to reverse this dangerous trend, several powerful political figures (including senators McCarran, Butler, Welker, Goldwater, and Jenner) felt the need to combat not only the aggressive economic and political drives of labor organizations but also to destroy the prestige and influence of those government agencies that encouraged them. Following the lead set by Senator McCarthy in his new position as chairman of the Permanent Subcommittee of the Senate Committee on Government Operations, these politicians created a power base within the Senate Committee of the Judiciary in the hope of forcing the federal government to establish a more favorable balance between organized labor and the business community. While some of the more rabid McCarthy supporters were undoubtedly out to ruin the labor movement, it seems more logical to assume that the goal of most conservative anti-New Dealers was one of control, not destruction. They wanted a national administration in Washington that would curb the abuses of militant trade unionism, Communist or otherwise, rather than encourage them. They looked to McCarthy because as the major political figure of that era he had become a symbol of defiance—a politician who refused to kowtow to New and Fair Dealers and their "abusive socialist doctrines."

As a result of this maneuvering, there were several changes in government policy. First, the problem of communism in the labor movement, normally handled by the "cryptosocialists" on the National Labor Relations Board, was placed primarily under the jurisdiction of the Subversive Activities Control Board. Second, a subcommittee of the Senate Committee of the Judiciary known as the "Task Force Investigating Communist Domination of Certain Labor Organizations" was formed to hold hearings on the same subject, thereby usurping power from the more sympathetic Committee on Labor and Public Welfare. Third, for the first time in years a group of legislators introduced and had passed a strongly worded antisubversion law for labor unions.

As a historical footnote, it must be mentioned that these efforts to get the government to intervene in cases of alleged union subversion had little practical effect. The Subversive Activities Control Board proved itself to be of little consequence in dealing with this problem, and its overall ineffectiveness, both past and present, has recently led to increased legislative sentiment for its permanent dismemberment. Similarly, the "Task Force" never came close to fulfilling Senator McCarran's promise to investigate all labor unions, and disbanded shortly after the threat was made. Only the Communist Control Act proved significant in dealing with the problem of alleged subversion in the labor movement, but its provisions were directed almost exclusively at those ultraleft organizations that, by 1954, were already close to extinction.

While the dogmas of McCarthyism had, at least, a profound short-term effect upon the government's attitude towards the problem of subversion in the labor movement, they were also responsible for an intensive reappraisal among labor leaders of some of their own social and political positions. On the issue of communism, or for that matter militant left-wing activism of any form, these leaders took something of a swing to the right throughout the Cold War era. Yet, in most cases, they retained the perception to differentiate between liberal anticommunism and the reactionary doctrines of McCarthyism. Their sober mood of introspection could not help but identify the senator and his allies with the political party that spawned them, and McCarthyism and antiprogressivism were clearly synonymous with Republicanism in the labor mind. This association was at least partially responsible for the rejection of political neutrality by the American Federation of Labor (which, it will be remembered, joined with the Congress of Industrial Organizations in supporting the national Democratic ticket in 1952). Labor leaders realized that the McCarthyites were not only standing up against communism but also against repeal of the Taft-Hartley Act, against a higher federal minimum wage, against public housing, against a stronger civil rights law, or for that matter against any progressive, legislative program. McCarthyism was a distinct danger to the labor movement because it represented, at least partially, an antilabor resurgence by a large segment of the American population. Labor leaders, fearful of growing sentiment against their organizations, could identify with the words of the mythical Orestes: "A terrible thing is the mob, when it has villains to lead it."

Bibliography

A. Interviews by the Author

David Dubinsky, president, International Ladies Garment Workers' Union.

George Haberman, former president, Wisconsin State Federation of Labor.

George Hall, secretary-treasurer, Wisconsin State AFL-CIO.

Charles Hymans, former Executive Board member, Wisconsin State Federation of Labor.

Joseph Keenan, president, International Brotherhood of Electrical Workers.

Miles McMillin, editor, *Madison Capital-Times*.

Loren Norman, editor, *Racine Labor*.

George Poreden, editor, *Kenosha Labor*.

B. Labor Newspapers

The Advance, 1950–1954.
AFL Building and Construction Trades Bulletin, 1946–1954.
AFL News-Reporter, 1950–1954.
The American Federationist, 1945–1954.
The American Photo-Engraver, 1950–1954.
The American Pressman, 1950–1954.
The Boilermakers' Journal, 1950–1954.
The Brewery Worker, 1950–1954.
The Butcher Workman, 1950–1954.
The Carpenter, 1946–1954.
CIO News, 1945–1954.
The Electrical Workers' Journal, 1950–1954.
The Hat Worker, 1950–1954.
International Molders' and Foundry Workers' Journal, 1950–1954.
The International Oil Worker, 1950–1954.
The International Teamster, 1946–1954.
Justice, 1950–1954.

Kenosha Labor, 1945–1954.
Labor, 1946–1954.
The League Reporter, 1950–1954.
The Machinist, 1950–1954.
Madison Union Labor News, 1945–1954.
The Metal Polisher, Buffer and Plater, 1950–1954.
Milwaukee AFL Labor Press, 1945–1954.
The Packinghouse Worker, 1950–1954.
The Pilot, 1950–1954.
Political Action of the Week, 1950–1954.
The Public Employee, 1950–1954.
Racine Labor, 1946–1954.
Steel Labor, 1950–1954.
Textile Labor, 1950–1954.
The United Automobile Worker, 1946–1954.
The United Mine Workers' Journal, 1946–1954.
The United Rubber Worker, 1950–1954.
Voice, 1950–1954.
Wisconsin CIO News, 1945–1954.

C. General Newspapers

Appleton Post-Crescent, 1946, 1952.
Daily Worker, 1946.
Green Bay Press-Gazette, 1946, 1952.
Janesville Daily Gazette, 1946, 1952.
LaCrosse Tribune, 1946.
Madison Capital-Times, 1945–1954.
Milwaukee Journal, 1945–1954.
Milwaukee Sentinel, 1946.
NAM News, 1950–1954.
New York Times, 1945–1954.
Oshkosh Daily Northwestern, 1946.
Sauk-Prairie Star, 1954.
Sheboygan Press, 1946.
Superior Evening Telegram, 1946.
Wall Street Journal, 1950–1954.
Washington Post, 1945–1954.
Waukesha Daily Freeman, 1946.
Wisconsin Democrat, 1951–1952.
Wisconsin State Journal, 1946, 1952.

D. Manuscript Collections

Catholic University of America

Philip Murray Papers

Dartmouth College, Manuscripts Division

Charles Tobey Papers

Dwight D. Eisenhower Presidential Library, Official File, Central File

Dwight D. Eisenhower Papers

Library of Congress

Jack Kroll Papers

Wisconsin State Historical Society

AFL-CIO Papers
Thomas Amlie Papers
Dane County Industrial Union Council Papers
Roy Empey Papers
Milwaukee County Industrial Union Council Papers
Papers of the Brotherhood of Railway and Steamship Clerks, Marinette, Wis.
Papers of the Eau Claire Building and Construction Trades Council
Papers of the United Automobile Workers, Local 95, Janesville, Wis.
Wisconsin State Industrial Union Council Papers

E. Unpublished Manuscripts

Adler, Les. "The Red Image: American Attitudes Toward Communism in the Cold War." Ph.D. dissertation, University of California, Berkeley, 1970.
Cloak, Ted and Cloak, Jane. "Joe Must Go: The Story of Dane County in the 1954 Recall Against McCarthy." Wisconsin State Historical Society, n.d.
Crosby, Donald. "The Angry Catholics: Catholic Opinion of Senator Joseph R. McCarthy, 1950–1957." Ph.D. dissertation, Brandeis University, 1973.
Dalstrom, H.A. "Kenneth S. Wherry." Ph.D. dissertation, University of Nebraska, 1965.

Emspak, Frank. "The Break-Up of the Congress of Industrial Organizations, 1945–1950." Ph.D. dissertation, University of Wisconsin, 1972.

Foster, James. "The Union Politic: The CIO Political Action Committee." Ph.D. dissertation, Cornell University, 1972.

Haney, Richard. "A History of the Democratic Party in Wisconsin Since World War II." Ph.D. dissertation, University of Wisconsin, 1970.

Irons, Peter. "America's Cold War Crusade: Domestic Politics and Foreign Policy, 1942–1948." Ph.D. dissertation, Boston University, 1973.

Johnson, Ronald. "The Communist Issue in Missouri, 1946–1956." Ph.D. dissertation, University of Missouri, 1973.

Kommers, Donald. "Organized Labor's Political Spending and the Catlin Act." M.A. thesis, University of Wisconsin, 1957.

Knudson, Donald. "The Extent of Unionism in Wisconsin." M.A. thesis, University of Wisconsin, 1964.

Krieseberg, Martin. "Public Opinion in Soviet-American Relations." Ph.D. dissertation, Harvard University, 1947.

Lichtenstein, Nelson. "Industrial Unionism Under the No-strike Pledge: A Study of the CIO During the Second World War." Ph.D. dissertation, University of California, Berkeley, 1974.

McAuliffe, Mary. "The Red Scare and the Crisis in American Liberalism, 1947–1954." Ph.D. dissertation, University of Maryland, 1972.

Meyer, Karl. "The Politics of Loyalty, from LaFollette to McCarthy in Wisconsin, 1918–1952." Ph.D. dissertation, Princeton University, 1956.

O'Brien, Michael. "Senator Joseph McCarthy and Wisconsin: 1946–1957." Ph.D. dissertation, University of Wisconsin, 1971.

Ozanne, Robert. "The Effects of Communist Leadership on American Trade Unions." Ph.D. dissertation, University of Wisconsin, 1954.

Paul, Justus. "The Political Career of Senator Hugh Butler." Ph.D. dissertation, University of Nebraska, 1966.

Riker, William. "The CIO in Politics, 1936–1946." Ph.D. dissertation, Harvard University, 1948.

Schwartz, Donald. "The 1941 Strike at Allis-Chalmers." M.A. thesis, University of Wisconsin, 1943.

Steinke, John. "The Rise of McCarthyism." M.A. thesis, University of Wisconsin, 1960.

Trow, Martin. "Right-Wing Radicalism and Political Intolerance: A Study of Support for McCarthy in a Small New England Town." Ph.D. dissertation, Columbia University, 1957.

Wallerstein, Emanuel. "McCarthyism and the Conservatives." M.A. thesis, Columbia University, 1954.

F. Convention Proceedings

AFL-CIO Archives, Washington, D.C.

Proceedings of the American Federation of Labor, 1946–1954.
Proceedings of the California State Federation of Labor, 1953–1954.
Proceedings of the Congress of Industrial Organizations, 1939–1954.
Proceedings of the Connecticut State Federation of Labor, 1953–1954.
Proceedings of the International Association of Machinists, 1950–1954.
Proceedings of the International Ladies Garment Workers' Union, 1946–1954.
Proceedings of the International Union of Brewery Workers, 1950–1954.
Proceedings of the Massachusetts State Federation of Labor, 1950–1954.
Proceedings of the Michigan CIO Council, 1950–1954.
Proceedings of the Minnesota State Federation of Labor, 1950–1954.
Proceedings of the Ohio CIO Council, 1950–1954.
Proceedings of the Oregon State Federation of Labor, 1950–1954.
Proceedings of the United Brotherhood of Carpenters, 1946–1954.
Proceedings of the United Hatters and Millinery Workers' Union, 1950–1954.
Proceedings of the United Steelworkers of America, 1950–1954.
Proceedings of the Wisconsin State Federation of Labor, 1946–1954.

Firestone Library, Princeton, N.J.

Proceedings of the Amalgamated Clothing Workers, 1946–1952.
Proceedings of the Fur and Leather Workers, 1946–1954.
Proceedings of the Illinois State Industrial Union Council, 1950–1955.
Proceedings of the Textile Workers of America, 1946–1954.
Proceedings of the United Automobile Workers of America, 1940–1954.

Harvard School of Business Administration, Cambridge, Mass.

Proceedings of the Building and Construction Trades Department, 1947.

G. Published Documents

Biennial Report of the Milwaukee Board of Election Commissioners, 1947–1953. Wisconsin State Historical Society.
Political Contributions to Wisconsin Candidates (filed with the Secretary of State of Wisconsin), 1946–1952. Wisconsin State Historical Society.
U.S. Bureau of the Census. *Seventeenth Census of the United States: 1950.*

Characteristics of the Population, Part 49, Wisconsin. Washington, D.C., 1952.

———. *Seventeenth Census of the United States: 1950. Milwaukee Area Census Tracts.* Washington, D.C., 1952.

U.S. Congress. Senate, Committee on Banking and Currency, *Hearings on the Defense Housing Act.* 82d Cong., 1st sess., 1952.

———. *A Study of the Reconstruction Finance Corporation*, 82d Cong., 1st sess., 1950.

U.S. Congress. House, Subcommittee of the House Committee on Education and Labor. *Hearings Into Communist Infiltration in the Fur Industry.* 80th Cong., 2d sess., 1948.

———. Senate, Subcommittee of the Committee on Foreign Relations. *A Resolution to Investigate Whether There Are Employees in the State Department Disloyal to the United States.* 91st Cong., 2d sess., 1950.

———. Permanent Subcommittee on Investigations of the Committee on Government Operations. *Hearings on Subversion and Espionage in Defense Establishments.* 83d Cong., 1st sess., 1953–1954.

———. Subcommittee of the Committee on the Judiciary, *Hearings on Communist Domination of Union Officials in Vital Defense Establishments.* 82d Cong., 2d sess., 1952.

———. *Subversive Influences in the Educational Processes.* 82d Cong., 1st sess., 1962.

———. *Subversive Influence in the United Electrical Radio and Machine Workers of America.* 82d Cong., 1st sess., 1952.

———. *Subversive Control of the United Public Workers of America.* 82d Cong., 1st sess., Washington, D.C.: Government Printing Office, 1952.

———. Subcommittee of the Committee on Labor and Public Welfare. *Hearings on Communist Domination of Unions and National Security.* 82d Cong., 2d sess., 1952.

———. Subcommittee of the Committee on Rules and Administration. *Hearings on the Maryland Senatorial Race of 1950.* 82d Cong., 2d sess., 1952.

———. *Hearings to Determine Whether Expulsion Proceedings Should be Instituted Against Senator Joseph R. McCarthy.* 82d Cong., 1st sess., 1952.

H. Books

Acheson, Dean. *Present At the Creation: My Years in the State Department.* New York: Norton, 1969.

Alinsky, Saul. *John L. Lewis: An Unauthorized Biography.* New York: Vintage Books, 1949.

Anderson, Jack, and May, Ronald. *McCarthy: The Man, the Senator, the 'Ism.'* Boston: Beacon Press, 1952.

Auerbach, Jerold. *Labor and Liberty: The LaFollette Subcommittee and the New Deal.* Indianapolis: Bobbs-Merrill, 1966.

Bell, Daniel, ed. *The Radical Right: The New American Right.* Garden City, N.Y.: Doubleday, 1964.

Berelson, Bernard, ed. *Voting: A Study of Opinion Formation in a Presidential Campaign.* Chicago: University of Chicago Press, 1954.

Bernstein, Irving. *Turbulent Years: A History of the American Worker 1933–1941.* Boston: Houghton Mifflin, 1969.

Buckley, William, and Bozell, L. Brent. *McCarthy and His Enemies.* Chicago: Henry Regnery, 1954.

Chambers, Whittaker. *Witness.* New York: Random House, 1952.

Cook, Fred. *The Nightmare Decade.* New York: Random House, 1971.

Danish, Max. *The World of David Dubinsky.* Cleveland: World Publishing Co., 1957.

Davies, Richard. *Housing Reform During the Truman Administration.* Columbia: University of Missouri Press, 1966.

DeCaux, Len. *Labor Radical: From the Wobblies to CIO.* Boston: Beacon Press, 1970.

Derber, Milton, and Young, Edwin. *Labor and the New Deal.* Madison: University of Wisconsin Press, 1957.

Dies, Martin. *The Trojan Horse in America.* New York: Dodd, Mead, 1940.

Doan, Edward. *The LaFollettes and the Wisconsin Idea.* New York: Rinehart, 1947.

Donovan, Robert. *Eisenhower: The Inside Story.* New York: Harper and Row, 1956.

Epstein, Leon. *Politics in Wisconsin.* Madison: University of Wisconsin Press, 1958.

Fink, Gary. *Labor's Search for Political Order: The Political Behavior of the Missouri Labor Movement.* Columbia, University of Missouri Press, 1973.

Flynn, John. *The Roosevelt Myth.* New York: Devin-Adair, 1948.

Freeland, Richard. *The Truman Doctrine and the Origins of McCarthyism.* New York: Random House, 1972.

Galenson, Walter. *The CIO Challenge to the AFL.* Cambridge: Harvard University Press, 1960.

Gavett, Thomas. *The Development of the Labor Movement in Milwaukee.* Madison: University of Wisconsin Press, 1965.

Goldman, Eric. *The Crucial Decade*. New York: Alfred A. Knopf, 1956.

———. *Rendezvous With Destiny*. New York: Alfred A. Knopf, 1952.

Gore, Leroy. *Joe Must Go*. New York: Messner, 1954.

Greenstone, J. David. *Labor in American Politics*. New York: Alfred A. Knopf, 1969.

Griffith, Robert. *The Politics of Fear: Joseph R. McCarthy and the Senate*. Lexington: The University Press of Kentucky, 1970.

———, and Theoharis, Athan. *The Specter: Original Essays on American Anti-Communism and the Origins of McCarthyism*. New York: Franklin-Watts, 1974.

Hardman, J.B.S., ed. *The House of Labor*. New York: Prentice-Hall, 1951.

Harnsberger, Caroline. *A Man of Courage: Robert A. Taft*. New York: Wilcox and Follett, 1952.

Hawley, Ellis. *The New Deal and the Problem of Monopoly*. Princeton: Princeton University Press, 1966.

Haynes, Frederick. *Third Party Movements Since the Civil War*. Iowa City: State Historical Society of Iowa Press, 1916.

Hicks, John. *Republican Ascendancy, 1921–1933*. New York: Harper and Row, 1960.

Hook, Sidney. *Common Sense and the Fifth Amendment*. New York: Criterion Books, 1957.

Horowitz, Morris. *The Structure and Government of the Carpenters' Union*. New York: Wiley, 1962.

Howe, Irving, and Coser, Lewis. *The American Communist Party*. Boston: Beacon Press, 1957.

———, and Widick, B.J. *The UAW and Walter Reuther*. New York: Random House, 1949.

Jacobs, Paul. *The State of the Unions*. New York: Atheneum, 1956.

Johnson, Roger. *Robert M. LaFollette, Jr. and the Decline of the Progressive Party in Wisconsin*. Madison: Wisconsin State Historical Society Press, 1964.

Josephson, Matthew. *Sidney Hillman: Statesman of American Labor*. Garden City: Doubleday, 1952.

Kampelman, Max. *The Communist Party versus the CIO: A Study in Power Politics*. New York: Praeger, 1957.

Karson, Marc. *American Labor Unions and Politics, 1900–1919*. Carbondale: Southern Illinois University Press, 1958.

Kendall, Willmoore. *The Conservative Affirmation*. Chicago: Henry Regnery, 1963.

Kornhauser, Arthur; Sheppard, Harold; and Mayer, Albert, eds. *When Labor Votes: A Study of Auto Workers*. New York: University Books, 1956.

LaFollette, Belle, and LaFollette, Fola. *Robert M. LaFollette.* 2 vols. New York: Hafner Publishing Co., 1953.

Latham, Earl. *The Communist Controversy in Washington: From the New Deal to McCarthy.* Cambridge: Harvard University Press, 1966.

Lee, R. Alton. *Truman and Taft-Hartley.* Lexington: University Press of Kentucky, 1966.

Leuchtenburg, William. *Franklin D. Roosevelt and the New Deal, 1932–1940.* New York: Harper and Row, 1963.

Lipset, Seymour, and Raab, Earl. *The Politics of Unreason.* New York: Harper and Row, 1970.

Lorwin, Lewis. *The American Federation of Labor.* Washington: Brookings Institution, 1933.

Lubell, Samuel. *The Future of American Politics.* New York: Harper and Row, 1952.

McCarthy, Joseph. *McCarthyism: The Fight for America.* New York: Devin-Adair, 1952.

Markowitz, Norman. *The Rise and Fall of the People's Century: Henry A. Wallace and American Liberalism.* New York: Free Press, 1973.

Mortimer, Wyndham. *Organize: My Life as a Union Man.* Boston: Beacon Press, 1972.

Nye, Russel. *Midwestern Progressive Politics, 1870–1958.* East Lansing: Michigan State University Press, 1959.

Parmet, Herbert. *Eisenhower and the American Crusades.* New York: Macmillan, 1972.

Patterson, James. *Mr. Republican: A Biography of Robert A. Taft.* Boston: Houghton Mifflin, 1972.

Perlman, Mark. *The Machinists: A New Study in American Trade Unionism.* Cambridge: Harvard University Press, 1961.

Phillips, Kevin. *The Emerging Republican Majority.* New Rochelle: Arlington House, 1968.

Preis, Art. *Labor's Giant Step: Twenty Years of the CIO.* New York: Pioneer Publishers, 1964.

Raddock, Maxwell. *Portrait of an American Labor Leader: William Hutcheson.* New York: American Institute of Social Science, 1955.

Radosh, Ronald. *American Labor and United States Foreign Policy.* New York: Random House, 1969.

Rice, Stuart. *Farmers and Workers in American Politics.* New York: Columbia University Press, 1924.

Rogin, Michael. *The Intellectuals and McCarthy: The Radical Specter.* Cambridge: M.I.T. Press, 1967.

Romer, Sam. *The International Brotherhood of Teamsters.* New York: Wiley, 1962.

Rorty, James and Dechter, Moshe. *McCarthy and the Communists.* Boston: Beacon Press, 1954.

Ross, Irwin. *The Lonliest Campaign.* New York: New American Library, 1968.

Rovere, Richard. *Senator Joe McCarthy.* Cleveland: World Publishing Co., 1960.

Saposs, David. *Communism in American Unions.* New York: McGraw-Hill, 1959.

Sherwood, Robert. *Roosevelt and Hopkins: An Intimate History.* New York: Harper and Row, 1950.

Stouffer, Samuel. *Communism, Conformity and Civil Liberties.* Garden City: Doubleday, 1955.

Straight, Michael. *Trial by Television.* Boston: Beacon Press, 1954.

Still, Bayrd. *Milwaukee: The History of a City.* Madison: Wisconsin State Historical Society Press, 1948.

Taft, Philip. *Organized Labor in American History.* New York: Harper and Row, 1964.

———. *The AF of L from the Death of Gompers to the Merger.* New York: Octagon Books, 1959.

Theoharis, Athan. *Seeds of Repression: Harry S. Truman and the Origins of McCarthyism.* Chicago: Quadrangle, 1971.

Uphoff, Walter. *Kohler on Strike.* Boston: Beacon Press, 1966.

White, William. *The Taft Story: Biography of Robert A. Taft.* New York: Harper and Row, 1954.

Wisconsin Citizens' Committee on McCarthy's Record. *The McCarthy Record.* Madison, 1952.

Young, Donald, ed. *Adventure in Politics: The Memoirs of Philip La-Follette.* New York: Holt, Rinehart and Winston, 1970.

I. Pamphlets

American Civil Liberties Union. *In the Shadow of Fear.* New York, 1949.

Bean, Louis. *Influences in the 1954 Mid-Term Elections.* New York, 1954.

Chamber of Commerce of the United States. *Communist Infiltration in the United States.* New York, 1946.

———. *Communism: Where Do We Stand Today?.* 1952.

CIO-PAC. *Speakers' Book of Facts.* Washington, 1948.

Greenhill, H. Gaylon. *Labor Money in Wisconsin Politics.* Madison, Wisconsin, 1964.

Heard, Alexander. *Money in Politics.* Chapel Hill, N.C., n.d.

National Association of Manufacturers. *Freedom From Victory: A Program Adopted by the War and Reconversion Committee of American Industry.* New York, 1944.

Spivak, John. *The "Save the Country" Racket.* New York: Specter, 1948.

Workers' Defense League. *Labor, Defense and Democracy.* New York, 1941.

J. Articles

"The AFL and Politics." *Newsweek* 40 (September 29, 1952): 32–33.

"Author, Author." *Time* 55 (June 26, 1950): 16.

Bernstein, Irving. "John L. Lewis and the Voting Behavior of the CIO." *Public Opinion Quarterly* 5 (June 1941): 233–49.

Braunthal, Alfred. "American Labor in Politics." *Social Research* 12 (February 1945): 1–21.

Bunzel, John. "The General Ideology of American Small Business." *Political Science Quarterly* 70 March 1955): 87–102.

"Defense Worry: Damage Four Key Unions Could Do." *U.S. News and World Report* 31 (September 7, 1951): 62–64.

Dubinsky, David. "Instead of the McCarthy Method." *New York Times Sunday Magazine* (July 26, 1953): 9ff.

Eggleston, Arthur. "Labor and Civil Liberties." *The Nation* 174 (June 28, 1952): 647–50.

Fitch, John. "The New Congress and the Unions." *Survey-Graphic* 36 (April 1947): 231–34.

Frank, John. "The Team Against McCarthy." *The New Republic* 126 (March 10, 1952): 16–17.

Fuller, Helen. "Labor and Politics." *The New Republic* 110 (January 24, 1944): 111–13.

Gallup, George. "How Labor Votes." *The Annals of the American Academy of Political and Social Science* 274 (March 1951): 123–24.

Glantz, Oscar. "Protestant and Catholic Voting Behavior in a Metropolitan Area." *Public Opinion Quarterly* 23 (Spring 1959): 73–82.

Green, James. "Working Class Militancy in the Depression." *Radical America* 6 (November–December 1972): 1–30.

Greer, Scott. "Catholic Voters and the Democratic Party." *Public Opinion Quarterly* 25 (Winter 1961): 611–25.

"Interview With Senator Hubert H. Humphrey of Minnesota." *U.S. News and World Report* 31 (December 28, 1951): 20–26.

Kristol, Irving. "Civil Liberties—1952: A Study in Confusion." *Commentary* 13 (March 1952): 228–36.

LaFollette, Eleanor. "A Room of Our Own." *Progressive* 10 (August 26, 1946): 8.

Leeds, Morton. "The AFL in the 1948 Election." *Social Research* 17 (June 1950): 207–18.

"Leftist Unions: Defense Risk?" *U.S. News and World Report* 31 (December 14, 1951): 62–66.

Lens, Sidney. "Labor and the Election." *Yale Review* 41 (June 1952): 567–78.

Lonergan, Edna. "Anatomy of PAC." *The Freeman* 1 (November 1950): 137–40.

Lubell, Samuel. "Post-Mortem: Who Elected Roosevelt." *Saturday Evening Post* 213 (January 25, 1941): 9–11, 91–96.

Matthews, J.B. "Reds in Our Churches." *American Mercury* (July 1953): 3–13.

Mayer, Kurt. "Small Business as a Social Institution." *Social Research* 14 (September 1947): 332–49.

Mayer, Milton. "The People Lose." *Progressive* 10 (August 26, 1946): 1.

"The McCarthy Controversy." *Time* 58 (October 22, 1951): 21–24.

"McCarthy, Hunt, and Facts-Forum." *The Reporter* 10 (February 16, 1954): 19–27.

Murphy, Charles. "McCarthy and the Businessman." *Fortune* 49 (April 1954): 156–58, 180–94.

———. "Texas Business and McCarthy." *Fortune* 49 (May 1954): 100–1, 208–16.

"New Executioner for Red-Led Unions." *Business Week* 1314 (November 6, 1954): 59–62.

Nossiter, Bernard. "The Butler Bill." *The Nation* 179 (September 4, 1954): 192–93.

O'Brien, F.S. "The Communist-Dominated Unions in the United States Since 1950." *Labor History* 9 (Spring 1968): 184–209.

Overacker, Louise. "Labor's Political Contributions." *Political Science Quarterly* 54 (March 1939): 56–68.

Parsons, Talcott. "McCarthyism and American Social Tensions." *Yale Review* 44 (December 1954): 226–45.

Paschell, William, and Theodore, Rose. "Anti-Communist Provisions in the Union Constitutions." *Monthly Labor Review* 77 (October 1954): 1097–1000.

Polsby, Nelson. "Towards an Explanation of McCarthyism." *Political Studies* 8 (October 1960): 250–71.

Prickett, James. "Communism and Factionalism in the United Automobile Workers, 1939–1947." *Science and Society* 32 (Summer–Fall 1968): 257–77.

———. "Some Aspects of the Communist Controversy in the CIO." *Science and Society* 33 (Summer–Fall 1969): 299–321.

"Republican Efforts to Change the NLRB." *U.S. News and World Report* 24 (May 7, 1948): 51–53.

Rogin, Michael. "Voluntarism: The Political Function of an Anti-Political Doctrine." *The Industrial and Labor Relations Review* 15 (July 1962): 521–35.

"The Roots and Prospects of McCarthyism." *Monthly Review* 5 (January 1954): 417–34.

Rovere, Richard. "The Most Gifted and Successful Demagogue This Country Has Ever Known." *New York Times Sunday Magazine* (April 30, 1967): 23, 115–20.

Rubin, Morris. "The First Column." *Progressive* 10 (August 26, 1946): 1.

Saposs, David. "Voluntarism in the American Labor Movement." *Monthly Labor Review* 77 (September 1954): 967–71.

Schlamm, William. "Across McCarthy's Grave." *National Review* 3 (May 18, 1957): 462–63.

Seidman, Joel. "Labor Policy of the Communist Party During World War II." *Industrial and Labor Relations Review* 3 (October 1950): 55–59.

———. "Organized Labor in Political Campaigns." *Public Opinion Quarterly* 3 (October 1939): 646–54.

Seligman, Daniel. "The U.E.: The Biggest Communist Union." *American Mercury* 69 (July 1949): 35–45.

"Should Labor Organizations Be Subject to the General Techniques of the 1950 Internal Security Act." *Congressional Digest* 33 (May 1954).

"Stalinists Still Seeking Control of Labor in Strategic Industries." *Saturday Evening Post* 223 (February 24, 1951): 12.

Taft, Philip. "Communism in the Trade Unions." *Monthly Labor Review* 77 (February 1954): 139–41.

"Taft-Hartley Flaws Cheer Communists." *Business Week* 967 (March 13, 1948): 102–8.

"The Scare Campaign." *The New Republic* 115 (October 21, 1946): 503–4.

"The Man Who's Hired to See Red." *Nation's Business* 49 (January 1951): 29–30.

Thelen, David and Thelen, Esther. "Joe Must Go: The Movement to Recall Senator Joseph McCarthy." *The Wisconsin Magazine of History* 49 (Spring 1966): 185–209.

Trow, Martin. "Small Business, Political Intolerance, and Support for McCarthy." *The American Journal of Sociology* 64 (November 1958): 270–81.

Windmuller, John. "The Foreign Policy Conflict in American Labor." *Political Science Quarterly* 82 (June 1967): 205–34.

"Wisconsin Testifies Against McCarthy." *The Nation* 175 (August 30, 1952): 164–70.

"Work Stoppages Caused by Labor-Management Disputes in 1945." *Monthly Labor Review* 62 (April 1946): 718–35.

Index

C

Cain Housing Amendment, 84
California State Industrial Union Council, 108
Capehart, Homer, 66, 103
Carey, James, 94
Carpenter, The, 113; on book burnings, 126
Carter, Bradford, 73
Case, J. I., 11, 34
Case bill, described, 40–41
Catholics, 152, 154; in Wisconsin Labor force, 11; as blue-collar voters, 140
Chamber of Commerce of the United States, 88, 163
Chippewa Valley, 158
Christiansen, Ernest, 159
Christoffel, Harold, 24, 30
CIO News, 40, 99; ignores LaFollette's candidacy, 34; criticizes McCarthy, 103
CIO-PAC, 53, 54, 117, 143; analyzes McCarthy's domestic voting record, 82–86; relationship with Democratic party, 101; attacks McCarthy, 102–4; supplies anti-McCarthy material, 105; financial contributions in 1952 elections, 145; and Communists, 163. *See also* Congress of Industrial Organizations
Clausen, Fred, 43, 44, 47
Cleveland, Ohio, 90
Cleveland Chamber of Commerce, 67
Closed shop, 65
Cold War, 88, 184; as factor in McCarthy-McMurray senatorial election, 52–58. *See also* Communism; Soviet Union; Joseph Stalin
Coleman, Thomas, 19, 41, 51, 59, 60, 66; anti-LaFollette position, 9–10; supports McCarthy's candidacy, 37
Columbus, Ohio, 75
Committee on Political Education, 141
Communism, 106, 164; deplored by *Building and Construction Trades Bulletin,* 125; condemned by AFL, 130. *See also* American Federation of Labor; Congress of Industrial Organizations; United Automobile Workers (Local 248); Wisconsin State Industrial Union Council
Communist Control Act, effects on left-wing unions, 180–82
Communist party, 111, 172, 174, 179; in electronics industry, 173–74
Communist party of Wisconsin, 24, 54

Conference of American Small Business Organizations, 170
Congressional Reorganization Act, 38
Congress of Industrial Organizations, 27, 31, 113, 157, 165, 182, 184; attitude toward LaFollette, 33–34; and Communist influence, 89–100; relationship with Democratic party, 100–102; officially condemns McCarthy, 107; and McCarthyism, 108–10. *See also* CIO-PAC; Wisconsin State Industrial Union Council
Cooper, William, 17
Cowan, Nathan: sends LaFollette letter of support, 27; and LaFollette's labor record, 34
Crane, G. S., 166
Cullen, Hugh Roy, 168
Cutler-Hammer Corporation, 166

D

Daily Worker, 54–55
Dallas, Tex., 169
Dane County, 17, 158. *See also* Madison, Wis.
DeCaux, Len, 90
Democratic Organizing Committee of Wisconsin, 135
Democratic party, 113; strength among Wisconsin's blue-collar workers, 12; and CIO, 97, 100–102; and AFL, 113–17; calls for Taft-Hartley repeal, 120; as barometer of anti-McCarthyism, 153. *See also* CIO-PAC; Democratic party of Wisconsin; Fair Deal; New Deal
Democratic party of Wisconsin, 47, 135; and New Deal resurgence, 5; desires LaFollette's membership, 10–14. *See also* Democratic party; Wisconsin State Industrial Union Council
Dennis, Eugene, 24
Dies, Martin, 125, 168
Dirksen, Everett, 103
Doyle, James, 147; and McCarthy's election victory, 137
Dubinsky, David, 115, 130; opposes McCarthy, 121; on AFL's reluctance to condemn McCarthy, 133–34
Dulles, John Foster, 126
duPont, Lammot, 54
Dunkirk, N. Y., 174

E

Eastern Establishment, 141
Eastern Europe, 56, 112, 141